A Recipe For Bliss

A Recipe For Bliss

Kriya Yoga For a New Millennium

by

Carl Schmidt

NEW FALCON PUBLICATIONS
TEMPE, ARIZONA, U.S.A.

International Standard Book Number: 1-56184-159-5
Library of Congress Catalog Card Number: 2001086355

First Edition 2001

Cover by Carl Schmidt

The paper used in this publication meets the minimum requirements of the American National Standard for Permanence of Paper for Printed Library Materials Z39.48-1984

Address all inquiries to:
NEW FALCON PUBLICATIONS
1739 East Broadway Road #1-277
Tempe, AZ 85282 U.S.A.
(or)
320 East Charleston Blvd. • # 204-286
Las Vegas, NV 89104 U.S.A.

website: http://www.newfalcon.com
email: info@newfalcon.com

TABLE OF CONTENTS

THE AUTHOR

In certain segments of society there is a custom of holding a "Coming Out Party." An announcement is made that a young lady is no longer just a girl… She has become a woman. The personality is now worthy of notice.

In a somewhat more sophisticated way, groups have formed in the West seeking to emphasize and promote rites of passage. From bar mitzvahs to Robert Bly's, *Iron John*, an assumption is made that the formation of a well-established personality…a mature identity…has profound and lasting significance.

In one sense I cannot disagree with this premise. The struggle of the young to cast off limitations is persistent. Every parent who nurtures his own children aspires for each one to emerge secure, happy and free.

Now…lets fast-forward a bit…not very far. Lets imagine the passage of a mere one hundred years of earth time. Where is the debutante now?

The personality is not the end of the story. In fact, the personality is the greatest hurdle. Every thing that is born must die. In a state of shock, the youthful Siddhartha stares into eternity. How can he possibly cope with his own eventual demise?

Until we discover **who we are**, we will always be somewhat neurotic. Our apparent "situation" will force us to make a series of temporary adjustments. We are like the little Dutch boy with his finger in the dike, trying to stem the tide of the inevitable oceanic conclusion.

There is a simple and straightforward passage from the diaries of Lahiri Mahasaya that reads, "At the moment of *samadhi*…place, time, name and form are all absent. Then all merge harmoniously together. All these that are within the limits of name and form cannot be permanent... Drown yourself in the quest for soul-essence and through the medium of *samadhi* settle in that tranquil state. Then you will note that the name and shape of the world no longer remains. By calming the petty feeling of pride, you can realize the indivisible still entity as your own form."[1]

So it is that I am somewhat reluctant to offer a personal description of myself. My eagerness is to share the Holy Sound, Om...and the path to the Oceanic Consciousness. This is the soul purpose for assembling these writings. Yet the reader will almost surely wonder, "Who is the one who suggests all of this?" We are reluctant to trust those who remain anonymous.

So, I will make a somewhat awkward concession. I will travel backward through time and space, into the vague realm of personality, trusting that this may provide some indication of my own orientation.

One evening when I was five years old, my father sat at my bedside and posed a question to me, before I might drift into sleep. He asked, "Can you figure out how many seconds are in one year?"

Despite the clock on the wall, time appeared to me to be a vast continuum...and a year seemed like an eternity. So I could not even begin to imagine how the total number of seconds could be determined.

My father then got some paper and a pencil, made a few calculations and demonstrated that there are 31,536,000 seconds in one year.

I was stunned.

Mathematics is a game, invented by the mind. It is a mirror of the mind itself. The Whole is eternally here. Trying to grasp all of it, we examine the parts. Mathematics lies somewhere between reality and imagination. At the age of five, mathematics seemed more like pure magic to me.

---

[1] *Purana Purusha: Yogiraj Sri Shama Churn Lahiree*, Ashoke Kumar Chatterjee, p. 162.

A seed of fascination was planted in my mind that evening. Sixteen years later I was a Woodrow Wilson Fellow in graduate school at Brown University, studying rational numbers, advanced algebra and set theory. The simple game, initiated at a fertile moment in time, reached a high degree of abstraction for me in 1967 and 1968. This abstraction became utterly absurd in the face of the Vietnam War.

The prospect of being drafted into the army loomed for me, as it did for all young American men. I could not imagine participating in the killing of other individuals involved in their own private struggle for self-rule. Not once did I imagine that I would be in personal danger. I could only see that I would not allow myself to help rain violence upon innocent people. I had appealed to my draft board as a conscientious objector, but this deferment was denied without comment. I faced an ever-shrinking list of options.

Yogi Berra offers this sage advice, "When you come to a fork in the road... Take it." So, in September 1968 I found myself in a small coastal town on the Philippine Island of Mindanao, teaching physics and mathematics in college with the U.S. Peace Corps.

I loved the idea of the Peace Corps from the moment it was initiated by the young and charismatic President Kennedy. I shared his optimism. For years as a teenager I had held the plan to become a Catholic priest. I imagined it to be the most righteous path available. As I progressed through university, my idealism became more secular.

Aspirations are tested and honed by the physical world. My buoyant enthusiasm slowly ebbed during my stay in the Philippines. I began to recognize that my impact upon this barrio community would not amount to much. Gradually I realized that I was not going to be a mover and a shaker, but more of a curiosity. For two years I was a goldfish in a fishbowl...constantly on view each morning as I stepped outside of my home. I was an instant celebrity for the simple reason that I was different.

Two books held particular fascination for me at that time...*Siddhartha* and *Steppenwolf*, both by Herman Hesse. Siddhartha spoke softly to my soul, inviting me to awaken to a new wonder. Steppenwolf spoke to my mind and reinforced my dilemma. I was living a dual, separated life... There was a definite inside and a definite outside. I loved the one, but not the other.

I enjoyed solitude. I enjoyed listening to John Coltrane, Jimi Hendrix and Ravi Shankar. I was inspired by their sensitivity, insight and creativity. No one in my community shared my interests. Many of them enjoyed the simple pleasure of evoking a response from me as I walked to work each morning. I heard the expression, "Hey, Joe," literally dozens of times every day. On the surface it was quite friendly. Underneath it seemed meaningless, and sometimes even taunting. Everywhere was idle chatter, leading nowhere. I imagined that I was trapped. When I responded, I felt like a parrot on a leash. When I didn't respond, I was rude. I faced this dilemma over and over each day.

During my second year there I grew more and more introverted. This tropical island "paradise" became my cage. My house was my only sanctuary. I began counting the days till my release.

I managed to survive this two-year mental ordeal, and landed in Tokyo in June of 1970. I intended to spend a couple of weeks in Japan, before returning to America. Five years later I would fly "home" and realize it was no longer there.

In large measure the Japanese submerge their egos within some larger entity, or superego. At that time this was normally their company of employment. On the surface a kind of mass hypnosis seemed to be in effect. "Gambatte" was the resounding mantra, roughly meaning, "Carry on! Keep at it!" I was amused to observe large groups of employees exercising together in the morning, before beginning their work. Teamwork was the key... All for one and one for all.

The Japanese seemed totally occupied by their work. They did not dote upon the personality, neither their own nor that of others. This afforded me great personal freedom. I no longer felt trapped by my environment. I began to notice that I was free to make a critical choice regarding my individuality. I could remain singular and isolated, or I could allow my personality to evanesce...to observe things as they are, without imagining any relationship to myself.

This second choice proved to be more interesting and more comfortable. In slow, often imperceptible increments, there began the dissolution of the awareness of any distinction between the inside and the outside. This dissolving process, however, was not automatic. The personality is etched in the stone of assumptions and habits. It will not be erased without an effort. I studied the Zen essays of Suzuki Daisetz and the Haiku translations and commentaries of R.H. Blyth. These afforded me a vision into a world without ego. I let these writings enter deep into my experience.

One cool summer evening an English friend and I were enjoying the quiet of a small park in the middle of Tokyo...two hippies, hanging out at the edge of nowhere. A lovely young Japanese woman drifted fearlessly toward us. She (Futaba) was perky and independent...perhaps a bit envious of our free and easy lifestyle. For me, she lit up the evening. After a rambling conversation, she hopped on my motorcycle and came home with us. She and I were inseparable for the next four years.

In the fall of that year Futaba and I found a small Zen temple, an hour and a half northwest of Tokyo, in the quiet country town of Agano. We made this our home. The building had been vacant for some time. It had one large room with dozens of small windows opening to a panoramic view of mountains all around.

The walls of our home were thin. The single pained windows and sliding glass doors were loosely fitting and often rattled in the wind. Two dangling light bulbs lit up the entire place. A small adjoining room with a dirt floor became the kitchen. We drew our water from a nearby well. Futaba and I experienced the slow onset of winter as it closed in. We had only a small kerosene heater to keep us warm.

I began practicing meditation. Bodhidharma, who brought Buddhism to China, became my mentor. He sat facing a wall for nine years. Gradually I was able to do that for six hours at a time. This was my practice for approximately a year. I waited. I looked. But all I could see was the habit and the traces of my own mind.

There was a large bronze bell hanging just outside on the porch. I loved to strike it with a wooden mallet, and then listen deeply as its resounding tone gradually faded below the background sounds of the evening breeze and the little stream flowing through the canyon below.

A full change of the seasons visited us there. Nature and time were mirrored almost perfectly through Haiku.

> A branch shorn of leaves,
> A crow perching on it –
> This autumn eve.[1]

> A weathered skeleton
> In windy fields of memory,
> Piercing like a knife.[2]

> The dawn of day;
> On the tip of the barley leaf
> The frost of spring.[3]

---

[1] Haiku by Basho, from *Essays in Zen Buddhism, Third Series*, by D.T. Suzuki, p. 358.

[2] Haiku by Basho, http://www.geocities.com/Tokyo/Island/5022/basho.html

[3] Haiku by Onitsura, from *Haiku, Volume 2, Spring*, by R.H. Blyth, p. 70.

The silence;
The voice of the cicadas
Penetrates the rocks.[1]

When entered deeply, these poems articulate time in a timeless way. They expose nature directly, leaving the personality behind.

The community of friends I found in Japan was an international assortment of young seekers. It was a fertile environment. The past was irrelevant. Each one there had left it behind to find a new mode of experience. The atmosphere held little expectation...just the opportunity to open wider.

In the fall of 1971, Futaba and I began making plans to visit India. Specifically we wanted to meet Charan Singh, a living Master according to a trusted friend. The trip would also be a respite from another cold winter.

In November we sailed to Hong Kong on a freighter with a short stopover in Taiwan. Taipei was incredibly crowded and chaotic. The downtown streets were full of bicycles, carts, cars, and people, each one trying to create a private lane through a maze of motion. By contrast, the national museum was quiet and still, full of beautiful antiquities...paintings, calligraphies, and sculptures...that had been gathered up by the nationalists fleeing the advance of communism. The sensitivity, intricacy and craftsmanship of these artworks were breathtaking.

We sailed on to Hong Kong, and then flew to Calcutta.

The moment that I heard the distinctive sweet and easy tone of voice coming from the people of India, I knew I had come home for the first time in my life. It was a total relief to be among people whose response to life seemed like my own. There was humor in small things. Wide eyes watched the parade of events as if everything on view

---

[1] Haiku by Basho, from *Haiku, Volume 3, Summer—Autumn,* by R.H. Blyth, p. 229.

were a movie. The British had taught them to fill out forms in quadruplicate, but they seemed to know it is only a game. They travel a path of little or no resistance. Jesus once said, "Until you become like a child, you cannot enter the kingdom of heaven." In some respects India is what he meant.

I loved Rishikesh, a small community nestled in the foothills of the Himalayas, where the Ganges begins to assert herself. We met with Swami Rama, a somewhat stern fellow, who just the day before had kicked out all but one of his Western devotees for their lack of discipline. He invited Futaba and me for tea, but was still irritated by the upheaval in his ashram. He maintained a commanding presence, but the Indian servant who brought the tea seemed more attuned to the moment.

We visited the ashram of Maharishi Mahesh Yogi, now world famous...and gone...after hanging out with The Beatles and Johnny Carson.

Sadhus were everywhere...eyes blazing...staring into the infinite void, willing to receive a handout if one were available.

I absorbed as much of India as I could in three months. Thirty years later I feel its Radiance. I hear its Sound. I can still taste the *chai*.

Futaba and I returned to Japan in late February 1972. We had no money and no home. We could no longer live out in the country without an income. So we settled into Tokyo and looked for work.

For the next three years I made jewelry and traveled the length of Japan possibly a dozen times on motorcycle, selling my wares on the streets from city to town. In the evenings I would find an empty Shinto shrine or Buddhist temple, unpack my bedroll and spend the night. I imagined myself to be like Basho, my favorite of the Haiku poets...a seeker of **real moments**, wandering like a breeze, looking through time into eternity. The poems and the meditation were wiping the slate clean.

In 1974 Futaba and I separated amicably. I remained in Japan one more year. In the spring I made one last cross-country selling trip before returning to the U.S. to begin a new life. The money proved to be a useful though temporary cushion, for when I landed, I discovered that I was still on foreign soil. I had become empty...and America was so full of itself.

I first met Holly in 1975 in Boulder, Colorado. I was attracted to her carefree and somewhat fiery independent nature. We moved to Sedona, Arizona in June of 1976 to remain involved with a new age spiritual group that was relocating there. I was never completely comfortable with the hierarchy of this group, or the "channeling," but I tagged along to see what might come from it.

I enjoyed writing and playing music for our meditations. I practiced long hours to bring my voice and guitar into a sound that was appropriate for the sensitivity of these meetings. I endeavored to be in tune with the Spirit in a natural way...to sing like a child, nurtured with imagination and understanding.

The group consciousness grew as more and more people began to show up. There were actors and other musicians who joined in. We mixed media and gave performances in our small budding community. For a time it was very inspirational. At times we managed to evoke a deep sense of wonder. Hearts and minds were, for the moment, in tune. There was no distinction between inside and outside. There was just a vibrant Harmony giving birth to form.

When ego began to encapsulate the expression, I decided to move on to something new.

* * *

The second half of my life has been a family affair.

Children change everything.

A popular bumper sticker reads, "Insanity is hereditary. You get it from your kids." Well...yes...you can go insane, if you choose to. But there are better options. With their memories wiped clean at birth, children mirror everything. We can see ourselves clearly in them...or not. It is our choice. It depends on how we look. What we do with our children and for our children is a perfect *sadhana*. It is not necessary to don saffron robes, assume vows of celibacy and abandon the world to experience the Life of the Spirit. It is always near at hand. And it is nowhere manifested any better than in our own children.

In the spring of 1978, after our first child was conceived, Holly and I moved back to Sedona to prepare for a real "coming out party." We were flat broke, yet wide open to possibilities. We started a crystal business, moved into a tiny home and began nesting.

It is my opinion that the family is the most effective laboratory for spiritual awakening available on this earth, though it is not usually recognized as such. The design of family is remarkably effective. It initiates a profound sense of responsibility, and it makes a continual demand upon each individual to chisel away the habits of ego.

Yogiraj[1] states that, "...by donning saffron robes, people can distinguish a person as an ascetic, and this impedes *sadhana*. By donning ordinary attire, recognition is absent and *sadhana* can be well practiced."[2] He encouraged his devotees not to change their outer form. The *samnyasins* (renunciates) should stay in their ashrams, and householders should stay at home. The significant Action is the **inner practice**.

Usually when the outer form undergoes dramatic change, the inner stillness and silence are disturbed. Change is inevitable and continuous to some degree, but change is not the significant issue. Outer change is how the Infinite Undivided Being demonstrates itself in time and space. **There is no real change.**

In my own time of family, I have managed to enjoy a number of creative adventures. Holly and I designed and built a comfortable solar home by ourselves. Our small crystal business has supported us adequately through the

---

[1] *Yogiraj* is the affectionate name for Lahiri Mahasaya.
[2] *Purana Purusha: Yogiraj Sri Shama Churn Lahiree*, Ashoke Kumar Chatterjee, p. 107.

years, and recently has grown dramatically through the Internet. I recorded two musical albums in the mid 80's, an effort to preserve the sounds and feelings of a decade gone by. I also helped manage the baseball and softball programs in our community for a number of years. I continue to be an avid tennis player.

I designed and currently maintain a Kriya Yoga website[1] to help illuminate the path of Kriya, and to demonstrate its immediate and timeless effects. Kriya is often imagined to be an esoteric and isolated practice. Historically it was "revived" by Babaji, the ageless saint, said to be dwelling in the remote regions of the Himalayas. Yet for Kriya Yoga to impact this world, it has to take form and practice within **you**. It is not meant to hide in esoteric and cult-like enclaves. It is not separate from "normal life." Its purpose is to bring out the Light from within your self, by drawing you into the place that has no inside and no outside. Awareness finds itself in the center of the Whole Being, without the urge to distinguish things.

Zen emptied me out, and Kriya filled me up...to overflowing. These two paths are totally compatible. Zen emphasizes how to begin. Kriya describes how to finish.

I will close by including some pictures of family. Within every human being is a unique and resonant Heart, beating with purpose...to express some part of God, as we proceed along the way that becomes His Whole Being.

My warmest blessings to each one of you.

---

[1] http://www.ThehOMeFoundation.com

Holly and Carl enjoying an
outdoor concert in Sedona, Arizona

Rudy Schmidt's memorial service at Arlington National
Cemetery. From left, Steve (Rudy's brother) and the seven
sons: Carl, Richard, Chris, David, Michael, Paul & Robert

INTRODUCTION

Once there was a tremendous young philosopher who spoke eloquently about the nature of life. Many people were amazed by the depth of his understanding and the warmth of his feeling. But there were those who did not trust him. They even reproached him for his boldness. They could not believe that anyone so young as he could be so wise. They questioned and belittled his authority. He responded to them by saying, "Before Abraham was, I Am!"

Wisdom illustrates the truth...the precise Reality of the present moment. The greatest wisdom is the clearest expression of this truth. In a natural way it allows and causes others to experience it as well.

A genuine philosopher must learn how to **stop**. If he never stops, he is carried on by the noise and the activity of this life and does not attain the perspective needed to unveil the deepest understanding. He feels the activity and hears the noise, but he has no reference point for the Whole Truth. That reference point is complete Stillness... Silence... Transparency. When we are silent and still, we begin to perceive our Self. Meditation is the art of becoming utterly Transparent.

Amid the noise of this life, we may **think**, "I am." We may contemplate and imagine our true nature. However, in the Transparency before and after this noise... **I Am**. Our Essence is Consciousness.

We are unborn and formless. Our true nature is everlasting consciousness, not form. We may appear to be a solitary, physical being, mysteriously extracted from Spirit, separate and vulnerable...but we are not what we "appear" to be. We are visiting a world of form to make a discovery. We have come here to uncover a mystery that has plagued our consciousness for a time that curiously predates our present memory. We are here for a reason... to find out exactly **who we are**...and to experience bliss.

This world of our visitation can seem peculiar in many ways. First and foremost, it appears dense. The ground floor seems quite solid. Then again, upon three quarters of its surface is a clear, slippery liquid. And we are immersed in a delicate, almost weightless vapor. From the soles of our feet, upward, we are wrapped in an environment of air. Yet there seems little we can do about the prison of our cells. There is an undeniable, sustained density in our appearance.

If there is one "thing" that binds us to a world of density and form, more than any other, it is our **attitude**. Whether we realize it or not, the nature and extent of our bondage results from our own choices, conscious or unconscious, individual and collective. Most of these choices are predicated upon a misconception. We think we are this body and we think we are **separate**.

The basic assumptions and choices we make play a definite role in the discovery of our Self. If we persist in believing that the material and separate aspects of our experience are the "real thing," our prison will seem essentially material and, in a deep way, we shall feel alone and fundamentally helpless. We will hardly notice that this appearance is assumed. However, if we make no limiting assumptions at all and look intently and continuously into the life that is given, a delightful wonder begins to unfold. Gradually, or quite suddenly, our seemingly mundane environment becomes extraordinary. The physical appearance begins to evanesce. In its place emerges the Primordial Resonant Heart, filling the form with an ecstatic, etheric substance. This vibratory substance is **Bliss**.

Meditation is the single most clearly defined "activity" of this life, whose design and purpose is to unite our experience with the exact Essence of our Self. The plan is to get to the Heart of substance...to feel it, hear it and see it as it is, underneath the appearance. Meditation is the essential ingredient in this *Recipe for Bliss*.

The Divine Life is the only life that yields permanent satisfaction. Every other life is destined to pass away. This physical life will pass away. Every specific physical condition will undergo ceaseless change and eventual dissolution. That to which we might cling today, will vanish tomorrow. There is no permanent physical support anywhere. There can never be such a support. There are only temporary havens.

The Divine Life, however, has a permanent quality. It is the one quality that separates it from all other lives. While there is an infinite variety of possible expressions of the Divine Life, there are a few clearly discernible manifestations that form the essence of this life. Take a moment and look at the graphic on the cover of this text. The pyramid represents the evolving divine experience. Within it are seven manifestations that form a path that gradually converges upon the experience of the **Primordial Inner Light of our Self**.

These qualities are found within. They are available. Search for them. Do not settle for anything less. Do not stop until you find them. Do not rest until they are permanently yours. There is plenty of time to rest, once this conscious transformation is complete.

At definite points along our conscious journey, we recognize that we need help. Some know this early on. The more willful often discover this later, after a long and painful attempt to forge through life, independent of the Whole. A misdirected urge to dominate our environment twists the willful consciousness into an egoic pretzel. All the ends join in a continuous loop, but the quality of separation is maintained.

As we search for the Primordial Inner Light, we may find it partially evolved within ourselves, but we can find it completely manifested through a Master Soul. To achieve this Resonance directly on our own, usually requires a very long and lonely journey...perhaps a million years or more. This, of course, depends upon our starting point...the present condition of our vibrant consciousness. With the help of a highly conscious Soul, our movement along the path is hastened. We accelerate through contact. In **no time**, Bliss is there. His Resonance awakens our own.

How will we recognize such a Soul? When we look at someone, we will usually see the elementary parts of an ordinary human being. The appendages are in place. Some feelings show. Some preferences are there. Some tendencies are expressed. However, as we look deeper...much deeper...a Master Soul will reveal a **path** that extends from where we stand at this very moment, to a luminous experience of our Self. A path like this is always available.

In a curious way, the Master experiences the Divine Presence in every single "other" being. Having **become the entire Path** himself, each "separate" experiencing entity is known to be a part of the Whole Being God Is. There is no problem in any part.

From one perspective this path has two basic parts. One part is the practice of special attention techniques that guide and accelerate the Soul toward divine experience. The other part is the actual vibrational qualities of the Primordial Spirit.

It is a profound truth that what we ask for is what we shall eventually receive. The one we look for is the one we meet. Finding the Master is exactly like that. The one we are seeking is the one we shall find. Yet it is certain that we shall be challenged along the way. We must learn to persevere. To find the greatest Soul requires the greatest search, the greatest perseverance, and perpetual courage. Do not assume it shall be easy. If you do, you will certainly become discouraged.

How shall we begin?

One way is to look non aggressively, but very deeply, into each resonating being in your sphere of life. Keep on looking with kindness and patience. Be receptive. You are searching for some **One** who is absolutely waiting for **you**...at this moment! Perhaps he or she resides in a physical body...perhaps not. Look beyond any rudimentary features. Look for that One, with those exquisite qualities, who sympathetically **causes** them to resonate within yourself. It is this **Resonance** that identifies the Master and illuminates the path.

He can be recognized only from within. That is where the resonance takes place. That is where the path is. That is where the bliss is. Do not be fooled in this regard. The Master does not own the bliss privately. He experiences it as all parts of himself...and he recognizes it as your Self! He cannot see you separate from God, for the simple reason that **there is no separation in Reality**.

To help edit these writings, I used the grammar tool of the popular word processing software, *Microsoft Word*. Over and over it placed a notice on the screen that read, "The main clause may contain a verb in passive voice." At first I paid little attention to this. I simply thought it curious that this tool contained this "safeguard" on its agenda. But it kept appearing like a little dog that grabs hold of your pant leg and won't let go.

Suddenly a light went on. Most popular writing reflects the customary state of our mind...namely, it is active rather than passive. Our mind and our senses seek experience outside of our self. We are persistently and perpetually searching for something beyond our own physical form.

A Recipe for Bliss largely employs the passive voice. This reflects an open **meditative state of perception** that watches the outer energetic substance dance about us and then within us. Our perception focuses upon an interiorized Center...and remains there. This meditative state is inviting. It is receptive. Its "voice" is not a speaking voice, but rather a listening voice.

As you read these chapters, you will surely experience a turning inward of the voice. Your attention may gradually assimilate this pattern of quiet introspection, because the thoughts expressed here issue from that condition. This kind of listening is the foundation of the Divine Life.

We discover and acquire many things through osmosis. We absorb feelings and patterns that are not always directly stated or clearly recognized. Our environment impacts our conscious way of perceiving. In the 1960's, Marshall McLuhan coined the phrase, "The medium is the message." The medium of these writings is **Meditation**... an interiorized and directed focus of conscious attention.

Through meditation, we absorb the path to God. This path opens wide as we begin to hear a definite and consistent Inner Sound. We cannot help but feel awe in its presence. It appears to be everywhere, yet it slips in behind our conscious mind and is just barely perceived at first. As it fills the inner space, intuition flowers like a lotus, slowly rising from a garden of earth and water, into the etheric landscape. We gradually merge with its Essence.

The cow has long been revered in India as divine. Why? She endlessly chews and chews the simple grass. She then slowly passes this cud through four stomachs to extract all the nutrients that it contains. Through a divine blueprint, this patient digestion and assimilation of simple grasses produces a tremendously massive, yet calm mother. An inner design and fire convert grass and water into the proteins and other nutrients that form flesh and blood. All the while, the cow appears content.

If we become like that cow, we can gaze into our surroundings and chew on the Essence that is here. And then, we chew on it some more. We digest it... We assimilate it... We **Meditate!** Gradually something new and wonderful begins to happen inside.

A title for this book came to me in the early stages of the writing. It was to be *The Path to God*. It seemed appropriate. The path of every spiritual seeker is aimed toward God. Actually, a path leading to God is there for everyone...for those who are seeking and for those who have not yet realized that this is what they are doing. Some of us are meandering... Others are getting on with it directly.

But I became concerned that this title sounds presumptuous and exclusive. Each Soul is unique, therefore isn't it reasonable to assume that there is a unique path for each one us? There must be! There is! If there were only one path, why would God create so many "different" souls to experience it. One single Soul would be enough.

Then, one day, I met a young man on the campus of the University of Arizona in Tucson. He had a smile on his face, a book under his arm and a coupon in his hand. He did not have that smug look of one who thinks he has "The Answer." Rather, he radiated a calm, sweet contentment. As I looked deeply into him, I felt his resonance...his grace. Clearly he had discovered a **way to live**.

Gently he showed me the book, *The Bhagavad Gita*,[1] and asked if I had seen it. I responded that I had first begun reading it almost thirty years before, while traveling in India. As we briefly discussed this book, his eyes lit up. We could both feel the warmth of this inner dialogue. He then handed me a coupon for a local Indian restaurant and invited me to come there for dinner. After a short visit, he drifted off to meet others.

I had eaten there a few times before. Its ambiance was sweet, just like the countenance of this young man. I closed my eyes and began to smell the curries and taste the tea.

The next morning in meditation, a new title for this book presented itself... *A Recipe for Bliss*. It drifted in on the memory of the dishes I had imagined the day before.

We are searching for God. We are trying to get ever closer and closer. We are moving along a path. But how do we know where we are? What does it feel like as we begin to merge consciously with our Essence? What is the **feeling**?

Paramhansa[2] Yogananda calls it, "Ever New Bliss!" This is the feeling! It is so real and so satisfying that we can even taste its sweetness.

---

[1] The *Bhagavad Gita* is a tremendous dialogue. It is a dialogue between Lord Krishna and his foremost disciple, Arjuna. It is also a dialogue between the higher and lower self of a single Soul. This dialogue proceeds on many levels. It contains an unfolding description of the Path that leads this lower self into its own Higher Dimension.

[2] The word *Paramhansa*, a religious title signifying one who is master of himself, and literally meaning "supreme swan," today is commonly written *Paramahansa* (having five *a*'s, rather than four). The author leaves any arguments regarding the correct

After fifty years of trial and error, searching, imagining and decades of meditation, Bliss began to glide slowly into my own experience, on the wings of Sound. A Current of this wondrous Vibration gradually began to awaken and then fill inside. The Flow first played hide and seek with me. It was elusive. But, as I became committed to experience it, **above everything else**, it gradually became my partner. Now it has changed me in a fundamental way... from the inside out.

Why did it take fifty years to find its way to me? I brought some stubborn traits to the dance. These held me back. And...I developed a few more along the way. I began meditating thirty years ago, but I didn't maintain an adequate discipline. A complacency can set in when we feel a zone of comfort that is acceptable in the moment. The Design of this life, however, will not let us remain complacent indefinitely. Eventually we will become sufficiently disturbed. This forces us to get on with the Reality search. **But the Dance is always here!** Its Radiance and Resonance can dissolve fifty years of confusion and turmoil in the time between our last out-breath and our next in-breath.

The Current of Bliss is ever growing...ever expanding... ever new. It stretches farther than the eye can see...beyond what the ear can hear...into realms more wondrous and subtle than my consciousness can feel in this moment. It is a soft, enveloping, omnipresent Harmony. I am not able to swallow it whole, so I taste its sweetness, piece by piece.

In a very simple way, these writings are a recipe for a feast. If you will, please join me in the kitchen. Everyone is welcome. There is no worry that there will be too many cooks. The more, the merrier. A banquet is being prepared. Yet, be forewarned. The preparation will definitely take some time. It is not fast food!

---

spelling to Sanskrit scholars, but chooses the use of *Paramhansa* for these writings, for this is the way Yogananda, himself, signed his spiritual name.

But this I know as certain…If it is not already the case, one day to come, Bliss will saturate all of your cells and fill your Heart. A Sound shall fill you and assert with Vibrant Certainty…

⁊ Am ᔆhat!

When we become excited by a new outlook…some focus that awakens or deeply inspires us…we may try to digest the whole thing at once. Like a profound book that carries deep, multi-layered, transcendent messages, this new outlook should be "read" over and over again to uncover its depth. It is almost always better to focus upon one nuance at a time, rather than skimming lightly over the whole thing. Enter in deeply. Breathe in the Essence. Take your time.

Skimming over life is what most of us do, most of the time. We may feel we lack the guidance or the courage to dive deeply into the Real Essence of ourselves. Surrounding us, there is a material appearance that often seems unworthy of our deep attention. It can gradually put us to sleep. We may begin to assume that everything is like that…that everything and everyone is unworthy of our deepest attention. This is not so!

We have been born to discover who we are, and to experience Bliss. To achieve this, we need to develop spiritual discrimination. We must learn how to avoid being mesmerized by the ocean of superficial information…to avoid becoming jaded by the seemingly endless stream of inconsequential "news." We must learn to keep our attention firmly focused upon the Formless Reality. Behind this desert of data is a Well of Wisdom. Its waters shall quench any thirst.

From here begins the Path. Listen quietly for the Harmony. Discover a knowing that is like no other. Follow your Heart to its Center, and…

ᛒliss will enter!

THE WAY IN

Imagine a vast endless space of vibrant, ceaseless light energy of dazzling beauty, dancing with exquisite enthusiasm in all directions and within all that appears "real" or physical, sustaining the very life and consciousness we call our self and every single other self and thing that exists. Going deeper than the actual force and vitality of this Cosmic Light, imagine an Intelligence that joyously and lovingly commands this vibrant Reality with infinite precision, forming each and every thing as creation and imbuing it all with its own Conscious Essence. Going deeper still, imagine a Central Presence that dwells beyond time, form, vibration and thought, that, without effort of any kind, exists in Eternal Stillness...a calm, watchful, all-seeing Eye within this cosmic feast of light and mind.

Allow this vast evolving perspective to become an inspiration to move on creatively and a means to temper and cool the ego, which easily overreacts to events and its own visions and opinions. In this way a calm, joyous Center begins to make its presence known. This helps to leave us undisturbed by the passing dream, which, for now, we shall call the grand, but temporary illusion.

To arrive at a point that might inspire, that might in some significant way make available a wider and more clear vision of this Reality and Essence, we begin within the prison of illusion itself, wherein, almost without exception, we all appear to be placed, and approach the Eternal Presence through events as they seem to happen and careful, sometimes scientific observations of things as they seem to be. A deep need exists to find the path to that Presence. And a deeper longing insists that we begin to take some definite steps along that path, eventually to enjoy a sudden leap into the arms of Spirit. For now we begin by being truthful and understanding that an effort will be required to remove ourselves from prison.

There is ample information already existing in the spiritual literature of our time to form a variety of blueprints for the true seeker of God, Self-realization, Enlightenment or Divine Union. A problem, however, lies in the enormous quantity of dis-information available. The spiritual marketplace is brimming with "glamour." We can be lured outside of our real inner path by wondrous or mysterious claims, which have no basis in fact, or are useless to us in the present moment. The pursuit of the imaginary can be a huge waste of time and opportunity.

How do we learn to discriminate sufficiently to avoid these centrifugal forces?... Forces that draw us outward from ourselves. It can be a slow, painful process, taking countless lives, repeated archetypically over and over, until there is a dawning of Reality within the conscious Center of the Soul Life. A knowing emerges that gradually...or on occasion quite suddenly...clarifies the entire Essence of our Being.

What is this path?

It is not the lure of physical, alien, space beings. It is not the egoic, material power that comes from wealth and status. It is not the proficiency of a dueling, intellectual mind. It is not even the respite one gains from a "job well done." There is an endless list of things imagined, believed, achieved or grasped that it is not. Many of these impediments are now lodged as habits within ourselves and need to be removed, to allow that primordial Light to shine undiminished. Let this process of cleaning house be the first step upon the path. We thereby begin The Way In.

The preparing, pouring and drinking of tea is a highly refined art form in the East. To master this art normally requires an experienced teacher, extensive practice and precise inner realization. It is difficult for a Westerner to appreciate this. After all, it is only tea. What could be more simple? However, with pure attention, every movement of this ceremony demonstrates one's exact attunement with the natural rhythm of the inner life in the present moment. It is a performance in microcosm of the divine dance...*Lila*. Nan-in (1868–1912) was one such Japanese tea master.

A famous professor had heard of Nan-in, who lived far away. He decided to make the journey to experience his preparation. This professor imagined he could add to his own academic authority the quality of Spirit that belonged to Nan-in. When he arrived at the master's home, he requested that he be served the master's tea. After some reluctance, Nan-in eventually allowed him in. The two sat down, and Nan-in began to prepare the tea. Every part of the preparation was performed to perfection...the table cleared...two cups set out...the boiling of the water...the delicate and precise strokes of the wicker brush, blending the green, aromatic, powdered tea within the steaming pot...the poignant, almost timeless moments watching and smelling the tea as it steeped and matured. At the right moment, Nan-in began filling the professor's cup. The professor was delighted and charmed by the whole scene to this point. His cup was filling with the perfect tea. All seemed well. But when the cup was full, Nan-in continued pouring. The tea overflowed the sides of the cup and spilled onto the table. He kept on pouring. Bewildered and unsettled, the professor shouted out, "It is full! It cannot hold any more tea!"

Nan-in looked directly into him and said quite simply, "It is the same with you. How can I fill you, until you first empty your own cup!"

To become empty is to prepare for The Way In. We must empty our cup of opinions and assumptions. We must empty ourselves of our peculiar delusions. We must empty ourselves of false hope and specific expectations. We must empty ourselves of our own incessant, self-created pattern of habitual activity and inclination. We must empty ourselves of tension. We must stop the perpetual inner dialogue. We must become completely empty, in order that we may begin to "see" ourselves fill with the Light of Primordial Spiritual Intelligence.

After this "filling" reaches a critical stage, something strange and indescribable happens. The individual's recognition to this point is: "I" am improving myself. "I" am becoming something new. "I" am changing. "I" am filling with Light. But then an experience dawns that completely destroys the experience of "becoming" anything. Suddenly there is nothing to become. Suddenly it is known "I AM THAT." The separation created by the outgoing urge utterly dissolves in the Light of Self-Realization.

The Way In is not an exercise of mental gymnastics. This is not some form of self-hypnosis. It is not wishful thinking. It is not a contented state of mind that arises artificially to satisfy an irrepressible need. **It is Known.**

We are the one primordial, vibratory, Spiritual Being, facing a peculiar dilemma. From birth we have forgotten who we are. The process of remembering is part of a larger process of knowing our entire Self. We are merging with Spirit and discovering a Knowledge, accessing an understanding that we did not have in our unseparated, unmanifested and unconscious formlessness. We are the prodigal Son, returning with the wisdom we lacked as a purely vibratory spirit without Self-awareness. Each of us is capable of this journey. The eventual return of each Son is, in fact, assured. The consummate Intelligence, Love and Will of the Cosmic Design inexorably drives and guides each of us Home. What we experience in the meantime, however, depends on us.

A gemstone of perfect shape and quality forms in time through the focus of Spirit (or vibration) imbued with both Force (or will) and Cosmic Intelligence (or design). Its perfection is obvious to almost anyone. Yet it has no apparent way of knowing itself. It simply is itself perfectly. The Intelligence that designed this gemstone, the Force that continuously manifests and sustains this Intelligence, and the Quality that is the living principle, giving this process its fragrance, is this Home from which we emerged and toward which we are bound. This Home is not a place, but a **Way of Experiencing**. It is not a result. It is the Way we process…the Way we proceed.

In human form we have a unique opportunity to return to this original state of Being with Self-Knowledge. The truth, force and fragrance of Being is so vast that it takes an entire universe to completely express it. It is omnipresent. Each and every particle is interconnected by Spirit. Each particle "lives" what appears to be a separate life by resonating with the Whole.

Our limited mind cannot grasp this Whole Thing. In fact, our grasping nature is a very significant handicap we have acquired. It is the very act of limiting ourselves. As we seek to discover truth and relevance, we are unconsciously seeking our whole Being. That Being is eternal and changeless, despite our persistent grasping and our temporary ignorance. We know some of the parts, but we ignore the Whole.

When we have emptied our cup completely, and we sit and wait in a loving presence, a Sound...a Resonance... enters. It enters in such a subtle way that we are hardly even aware that anything has changed. It seems normal. It seems vaguely familiar. Gradually it becomes glorious.

Life is like a harvest, a process of separating the wheat from the chaff. The wheat represents more than just the nuggets of truth that we seek to satisfy some innate curiosity. It represents our entire conscious way of Being. The chaff represents those habitual idea-forms about ourselves that are un-useful at best and self-destructive at worst.

First, it is impossible actually for anything to be "self-destructive." We cannot destroy anything about our Self. However, we can identify consciously with a false image of our Self and a false perception of the environment in which our Self resides. When this happens, we take ourselves out of joy and health, and cause ourselves anguish and disease. Indeed, we have separated the wheat from the chaff, but chosen the chaff.

It's time to choose the wheat!

We have the mistaken idea that the wheat is a vastly complex part of the plant of life and we must figure it out, or mentally grasp it all, in order to harvest it. It's as if we are farmers, harvesting our grain, but instead of gathering up the part that serves us, we are spending an inordinate amount of our time and energy analyzing each kernel. Ultimately we lose sight of what it is we are doing. We are lost in the details and miss the point.

The "point" is the joyous flow of our life energy, observed at ease by the Consciousness (Soul) that dwells therein.

As brothers and sisters, we differ from each other in one way that appears more significant than it really is. That apparent difference arises because we develop separate and contradicting belief systems. We each use our limited, localized mind to define what is happening to ourselves and to each other, and why it is happening...and we place undue significance upon our resulting opinion. We arrive at a viewpoint that is, at best, only slightly, temporarily and locally true. We thus bring to each moment a forceful distortion of what is happening by clinging to our own analysis of it.

The limited mind acts like a double edged sword. One edge cuts through the primordial soup of our being, trying to discover meaning from our experience. The other edge vents our pain and alienation. In so doing, we unwittingly sever the bonds of the Heart, leaving us feeling separate and lost. We dispose of friendships, marriages and families over differences of opinion or simple misunderstanding. Our imagined separation is not a fact. It is an appearance. We remain apparently divided, in part because we stubbornly insist upon a perfect meeting of divided minds. We put the cart before the horse. **The meeting must first take place within each Heart.**

The Heart is the geometric center of human life. When open, its nature is to love, accept, include and nurture. This is its zone of comfort. It does this naturally. When fully open, each Heart is radiant and all inclusive.

Like the mind of the professor who approached the tea master, what separates us from our Self is a single cupful of our own limited assumptions. We have no trust in the Divine Process, so we load up our life with all kinds of thoughts, things, habits and feelings, to avoid the "emptiness" that we fear. But, until we become empty, we cannot begin to recognize that **the Soul needs no support**...that it is deathless and omniscient. Whatever "we" put into our cup must eventually come out. Our full cup is the one and only Ocean of God.

The Path is the definite inner searching to dis-cover our Self in God. The Master waits to demonstrate this very thing. He is the great Comforter. If we meet Him just once, a profound **bond** is formed. It slowly dissolves the shell of ego...the alien attitude, arising from the primal misunderstanding. We think we are now separate from God. This is why we do not experience Him completely.

Cosmic Devotion, Love, Wisdom, Joy, Vibration (or feeling), Sound and Light become our practice. Our discipline is to allow these finer qualities to saturate our life experience. As we learn to let them in, marvelous unexpected things happen. How we feel is more joyful, because our focus is turned upon joy. We learn how simple it really is to hear the Music of the Spheres...that symphonic Sounding within the dance of Life. Devotion becomes an easy unfolding of the life we live. When we become fully saturated with all these qualities, we become completely intoxicated with the Divine Being.

At this point we begin our journey with the first logical step. Having recognized that we are fundamentally divided against each other and divided against ourselves, we must stand where we are, apparently outside the oneness of our Being, and look with our whole attention inward, searching for Reality...searching for God.

THE PATH TO GOD

Those who are seriously seeking God must find the way to Him. The mind of man has conceived all manner of ideas about this. Despite these ideas, man's unhappiness is testimony that he remains separate from his Father. But I offer to you this insight. He is just nearby. He is issuing a call to all His Children, at all times, that each one might be with Him. The call is as constant and as certain as the very breath that man draws throughout his entire life. In fact, an intimate relationship exists between God and Breath.

God forces nothing upon us. It is always our choice. It has always been our choice. We are free to come or not. We may dwell in a world of the body for its temporary duration, or we may take this body and unite it with Spirit. A way to do this is available. It is not difficult to understand this way, but it requires a definite effort. To transform our experience will absolutely require a substantial effort. If it was to happen without our own effort, it would have already happened. We must strive, but we are capable! This is an absolute fact. Every Saint and every Master is testimony to the possibility. The only reason why the **appearance of separation** is still felt is that the right effort has not yet been made. The effort to achieve this Union is the Path of Yoga.

Where to begin?

Meditation is a conscious metaphor for life. It is the foundation of the Path to God, and it is the Path itself. The Path is the inexorable non-movement into the Witnessing of the Self as God. It is no less than this:

It is the Non-movement from the mundane into 𝒟𝑒𝑣𝑜𝑡𝑖𝑜𝑛.
It is the Non-movement from alienation into 𝔏𝑜𝑣𝑒.
It is the Non-movement from distraction into 𝒲𝑖𝑠𝑑𝑜𝑚.
It is the Non-movement from stress into 𝒥𝑜𝑦.
It is the Non-movement from chaos into 𝐻𝑎𝑟𝑚𝑜𝑛𝑖𝑐 𝒱𝑖𝑏𝑟𝑎𝑡𝑖𝑜𝑛.
It is the Non-movement from noise into 𝐻𝑜𝑙𝑦 𝒮𝑜𝑢𝑛𝑑.
It is the Non-movement from matter into 𝒟𝑖𝑣𝑖𝑛𝑒 𝔏𝑖𝑔ℎ𝑡.

"Yoga" means union. Meditation is that yogic processing that sets out to unite matter and Spirit...man and God.
It is the letting in of the Infinite into a finite dwelling place.
It is also the expanding of a finite awareness into Infinite
Being. The purpose of this is to know our Self and to experience the same Joy God Is. So we shall begin there. "Enjoy
your Self!" This is an essential meditative technique.

Whether or not you have ever practiced meditation, do
not hold the idea that it is difficult or painful. An effort
will be required for sure, but see it as an opportunity to
enjoy yourself...a time-out from the world of suffering and
decay...a time-in with the Essence of God, which, sooner
or later, we discover to be our very Self. So, at this new
beginning...here and now...even if you have never been
"initiated" into a particular technique of meditation, decide that meditation is a tremendous opportunity to enjoy.

There is an expression in the West, "An idle mind is the
devil's workshop." Yet until our mind-body becomes completely idle...until it rests in neutral without an urgency to
seize upon some idea...until it rests quietly and tunes to
the central Note of its Being...it cannot begin to experience
God's playhouse. God's mansion is a Playhouse.

So, at the very beginning and throughout, recognize
meditation as enjoyment, not work. Maintain the attention,
but remove the effort and the struggle from it. Put the
mind in neutral. Let it idle. And let the Voice of God sing!

Walt Whitman wrote, "I hear America singing!" He was
no stranger to the Cosmic Sound. Its Song played everywhere he listened. This was no accidental metaphor. The
robust self-realization he experienced and expressed came

quite naturally from his enjoyment of his whole Being...
God's Whole Being.

Music and meditation form an interesting parallel.
Schools of music with formal instruction begin with their
primary focus upon theory and technique. These form the
foundation. Scales, arpeggios and chord progressions are
studied and practiced over and over, so that the fingers (or
the voice) can become fully acquainted with, and focused
upon, the movement of notes and the underlying harmonic
field. After that, there is more practice, practice, practice.
The demand of the work will weed out all but the very
dedicated. If a real devotion does not take hold, the practice will fall by the wayside. Meditation is much the same.

A student of music must discipline himself early on
with the understanding that in order for the Inner Music to
flow through him, he must become proficient with many
very specific, technical movements. He must trust from the
outset that only after mastering the prescribed techniques,
will he be able to feel his way naturally through music. In
the process he will find that music is a wedding of three
things...what he knows, what he feels and what he wills.
Meditation is much the same.

There is a tremendous number of different musical
instruments that one can play, and an equally large number of different musical styles. When we combine these
two options with our own unique, individual, human, creative qualities, we are left with a virtually infinite variety
of possible musical variations. Meditation is much the
same.

At some point, if he is so blessed, after a tremendous
effort over a long period of time, and particularly after
studying with a master, the student of music experiences
something magical. After years of methodical, linear effort,
a new dimension appears. A Sound emerges. From the
ashes of a fire that has burned for an eternity, real Music
happens. He uncovers a secret. He finds the union of
melody and harmony expressed naturally through his own
personality. He becomes an assistant in a vast world of
creative potential. He brings forth a vibrational quality that

can be an inspiration to others, because it honestly represents some inner Truth. The underlying Reality is felt, or intuited, through a heartfelt connection in the outer expression. The Inner becomes Known. Here music and meditation are identical.

As we enter an area of deeper and deeper meditation, we begin to enjoy our self more and more. This subtle change comes over us... God manifests within us, and slowly we begin to recognize His Essence. Little by little, we begin to **merge with Him**.

Paramhansa Yogananda describes seven distinct manifestations of God in man. These are: Cosmic Light, Cosmic Sound, Cosmic Feeling (or Vibration), Cosmic Joy, Cosmic Wisdom, Cosmic Love and Cosmic Devotion (or Worship). These manifestations are the natural, inherent qualities of God that find their way into our experience as we allow them. Meditation is essentially the practice of letting these manifestations into ourselves.

Consider exactly what they mean to you. They form an interlaced Path of Divine Experience.

Specific, highly effective techniques of meditation, called *Kriyas*, are revealed by the Master. They are shown over time, promoting a state of Grace. These are the greatest gifts that the Master can give. They initiate the Way In. They are a living map of the Path to God. They are always simple. This is part of their beauty. They are also very potent.

Techniques of this kind are revealed to those upon the inward Path. They issue forth from a Conscious Presence that has turned utterly inward and has discovered a way to travel upon that Path. These are the techniques of Sat Gurus...Realized Masters. They are unique in form, when compared to the "information" of the outer world. They are revealed to anyone who has begun to walk earnestly upon the Inner Way. They are the answer to deep prayers. They clarify the manner of search.

The outer aspect of this work is the creation of perfected relationships with genuine seekers. The inner aspect of this work is the revealing of Life as it is and the conscious Union of matter with Spirit through Yoga.

These techniques are available to anyone who has a genuine desire to know God and a deep appreciation for the evolving delicacy along the Inner Path. The deepest teachings are for the seeker only. They are not designed to be discussed and analyzed in casual human terms. They are private. They are for you alone, if you can for a while bear a kind of lonesome knowing. It would be impossible to fully understand and appreciate these techniques without an exquisite blending of devotion and wisdom... without actually walking the walk...without meeting your Self.

A technique is one answer to the question, "What am I to do?" There is ultimately no "doing," but this simple answer does not adequately satisfy the inquiring mind of a man, **apparently** separate from God. He still feels his separation, whether it is real or not. The "doing" is a process of consciously merging the so-called lower self with the so-called Higher Reality in order to **know**. The fact that this Reality is **not yet completely known** is absolutely certain. Hence it is absolutely necessary to make an effort and travel along a Path to the Knowing. A Master stands visible along that Path at every point of unique need. At all other times he stands invisible, leading us along with a whisper. Our apparent aloneness is the gentle ache of an urge, patiently leading us to a wondrous Union.

Do not be seduced by the assumption that this will be done for us. It requires that we do the Work. It demands nothing less than our total attention, which, we discover, is something we have not yet gathered together. The pieces of our attention have led us around in circles. When we have come around enough to recognize that we have been there before, we are then ready to begin to recognize a number of important things: Our attention has been partial. Our awareness has been incomplete. The conclusions we have drawn have been somewhat irrelevant. The direction we have been going got us somewhere, but not exactly to the Here and Now.

All of this can change. It is up to us to seek, and it is up to God to reveal. As we begin to seek in the right direction, **all of this changes**!

The ultimate objective is for the Conscious Attention to be drawn through the Star within the Eye, into the Presence…the Omnipresence…of God.

Each technique forms the foundation for the next. They begin within the duality of our experience as it is right now. In the beginning we focus in such a way to secure the first level…

Stillness within Vibration.

Then we move into the second to secure…

Silence within the Holy Sound, Om.

Then we move into the third to secure…

Transparency within the Divine Light.

ASANA

We are moving toward **ecstasy**...the wondrous experience of the Whole Being God Is. This ecstasy is incomparable to all forms of temporal human joy. We can expedite this passage by merging with the infinite and endless Holy Sound, Om. This we can all experience through meditation. But we must begin where we are NOW. Regardless of what we may imagine and despite our somewhat incomplete understanding and our less than total joy...we begin HERE.

The purpose of meditation is to merge with this Whole Being God Is. If we are to experience His Omnipresence, the presence of a body that distracts or limits this experience is a problem. To complicate matters, there are three "bodies," or sheaths, that clothe the Soul. Each one makes its own set of demands upon our attention. We dwell in a physical body, an astral or emotional body and a mental body. These three bodies are interlaced energetically, but they remain somewhat distinct and separate, owing to their relative densities, the environments in which they take form and the way we experience them.

Asana is the Sanskrit term for the position or posture that we assume in meditation. When asana is discussed, usually only the position of the physical body is being considered. But a deeper recognition is that each body must assume some "position." Thus there are three distinct asanas. These are the ways we position ourselves in the three worlds of form...the physical, the emotional and the mental.

We seek a posture that allows the body to remain in a long, continuous meditation. We dwell in a physical body.

23

It should sit in a way that allows us to forget about it. We dwell in an emotional body. It should assume a position that allows us to forget about it. We dwell in a mental body. It should assume a position that allows us to forget about it as well. To "forget" about a body means that we lose any limiting sense associated with it. We must do what is necessary to drop our association or attachment to it. Simply put, we leave it, or at least we leave it alone. If we are to meet God, we must drop our bodies entirely.

The three asanas that we practice are those positions of our three bodies that allow us to maintain a continuous, steady focus without distraction. The asanas as they are described here form a basic outline. In the end each one finds the exact subtle positioning that permits him to meditate with **ease**. The environment that we are seeking by means of asana is:

STILLNESS – SILENCE – TRANSPARENCY

To describe the asana of our physical form will require a very delicate discussion of the nature of the human body itself. Many teachers and gurus have been reluctant to say much about this. It is a difficult subject. It is taboo.

The physical asana is designed to help lead us to this exquisite experience of ceaseless ecstasy, which is absolutely and eternally available to each of us. While essentially incomparable to physical pleasure, this ecstasy has a unique and mysterious relationship to sexual function and experience. The physical union of the male and the female is, in fact, the essential, creative metaphor for the deeper Spiritual Union within our Self.

The human sexual orgasm is an intensely joyous experience, isolated in a very brief moment of time. We have a keen appreciation that this experience is fleeting. In fact, it is known deep within our subconscious that orgasm resembles and imitates death itself...a "death" that mysteriously gives rise to the birth of a "new" human being.

Within the infinite and endless temple of the Holy Sound, Om, however, is birth...not death. This birth is the awakening into the ecstasy of Life Eternal...Everlasting Life. That which is to die is a persistent deception, the false conception of what appears to be our separate self.

All children...all babies...are born into this world completely pure, natural and without shame of any kind. Whether it is cold or warm, the newborn is wrapped in clothes. He is mostly hidden. We remain mostly hidden throughout our lives. Being hidden is so common, that when someone shows himself completely, there is always an awkwardness. We are very uncomfortable about our form.

Do not mistake my meaning here. I am not suggesting that we should suddenly take off our clothes indiscriminately as a gesture of our innate freedom. But when we look into the attitudes we have assumed, we must recognize that in a very deep way we are uncomfortable with our form.

But God created this form. It is His Design. How shall we understand it? How shall we use it? What is the mystery revealed?

Let us begin by understanding one crucial point regarding meditation. At the outset, we should recognize where we are going. Regardless of where we begin to place our meditative focus, eventually we will find that our conscious awareness gravitates toward a Center that radiates a definite harmonious Vibration of Sound and Light within the **medulla oblongata**, somewhat in the back of the head, where the brain joins the spinal column. Once the asanas are established, special techniques of *Pranayama*, *Mantra*, and **Inner Focus** balance the physical body and dematerialize our self-perception. Our conscious attention enters this Center, and then begins naturally to look forward and somewhat upward to the point between the eyebrows, where we shall begin to observe a **visual projection** of the essential inner Being upon the "Third Eye." Our awareness of our Self expands beyond the boundaries of our physical body into limitless space...yet the **Center** remains steady, luminous and conscious.

The "lower" chakras resonate in response to the opening of the Spiritual Path. The Heart opens and then radiates an exquisite Sound, issuing tremendous intelligence, magnetic power and loving warmth. All the chakras come alive with vibrancy. They all respond. The *Kundalini* awakens naturally according to its design.

Swami Prajnananda, a master in the lineage of Babaji Maharaj, Sri Yukteswar and Paramhansa Hariharananda, relates the various chakras in a beautiful allegory:

When Jesus was born, there were three animals and two humans present for the birth. There was an ass, a cow and a sheep. The two humans, of course, were Mary and Joseph. The baby was placed in a manger. Three wise men saw a star in the eastern sky, which led them to the sight of the birth. They arrived bearing gifts of gold, frankincense and myrrh.

This is the simple story we know so well about the birth of Jesus. Each element of this story has a symbolic meaning that relates to the design of the human body and the path available to the Soul to recognize his own birth as the Son of God. The three animals relate to our three lower chakras, which are saturated with the physical essences of earth (1st chakra, the coccygeal center at the base of the spine), water (2nd chakra, the sacral center, animating the organs of sex) and fire (3rd chakra, the lumbar center, producing the directed heat of digestion and assimilation). It is our "animal" nature that binds us to the earthly plane and focuses our attention upon physical things.

Mary (the female aspect) and Joseph (the male aspect) relate to the human essences of air (4th chakra, the dorsal center of the heart) and ether, the medium of consciousness (5th chakra, the cervical center, which activates the voice of human intelligence).

The wise men...the awakening Consciousness of the Soul...observe a star in the East, which symbolically represents the point between the eyebrows where a definite Star of Light is seen within a dark blue, opalescent Sphere. They come bearing gifts, devotional offerings of the earthly plane's purist essences. The treasures of the earth are offered up when they arrive at the place of birth (Bethlehem, or the Middle East), which lies within the Medullary Center (6th chakra).

To complete the allegory, the manger, where the Son of God is placed, is the inverted bowl of the top half of the human head. This is the place where the Son is born. This is the specific location where the Spiritual awakening takes place. Within this microcosm of the human body, the Father resides in the crown (7th chakra, the Thousand Petaled Lotus).

The Spiritual Man is conceived entirely within his singular human form. He is born within the Medullary Center. He then matures by consciously expanding and then merging with the one sweet Consciousness of Spirit. The yoga of the Holy Sound, Om, is a divinely inspired and precise Path of practice to assist us in this realization process.

Every man and every woman are spiritually identical! The Spiritual Being is absolutely the same. Furthermore, within every man and every woman born into this physical world there are two contrasting aspects...two qualities... the male and the female. Usually those born as males experience and exhibit a dominance of male attributes. Similarly, most females experience and exhibit predominantly female attributes. Some are near the balance point and some even swing somewhat to the other side. The point here is not to judge any of this. The point is to understand that we all are essentially **both** male and female.

There are many adjectives to describe the qualities and nuances of the masculine and the feminine natures. The masculine qualities are described as virile, potent, assertive, dominant, robust, etc. The feminine qualities include being fair, gentle, sensitive, tender, receptive, etc. These synonyms do not form a value judgment. They are meant to demonstrate two contrasting and balancing attributes, found to some degree in every human being and in all manner of dualistic life forms.

What does all this have to do with asana?

An insight of tremendous importance is available to us by looking deeply, without shame, at the form of making love...sexual union...and making the remarkable intuitive discovery of how this intimates the asana of the physical body. We recognize the genesis of form itself...the division of One into two. **The physical asana is the outward metaphorical expression of the reabsorption of the two into the primordial One Whole Being God Is.**

I had practiced meditation over a period of thirty years before I discovered, quite suddenly, the essence of what I am sharing with you. Please open your minds and hearts to this sweet inspiration.

What are the "male" and "female" parts of ourselves? The male aspect of our body consists of the spine and head, augmented by the specific muscular tissues that support them in an upright position. The female aspect is everything else...the flesh, the bones, the water, the blood...everything else...with **one, very significant addition**. We include in our feminine aspect the entire, manifested universe...our Divine Mother. Our body does not end at the surface of our skin. **It is infinite!** Look closely at this Whole Body. Do you see how this is it?

Once we see this, the ideal physical asana becomes clear. The spine and head are held firm, straight and still. The rest of the Infinite Body is released. It becomes soft, relaxed and still. **The inner, erect, male part of our self is completely surrounded by the outer receptive and nurturing, female part of our self.** Take a while to feel this. It has profound significance in the practice of yoga.

If it sounds as though this asana resembles "making love" within ourselves, it cannot be denied. It is unfortunate that we may feel awkward and embarrassed when discussing the physical activity that results in our incarnation. Physical man is conceived and then born, in part, by a physical action that is mysterious to him. Not knowing that it is an allegory of the Spiritual Conception and Spiritual Birth...not having understood the significance of the often stated proverb, "As above, so below"...unwittingly, he ridicules the very way God has created his form.

The love of a man and a woman is the metaphor of the Divine Love radiating throughout the Whole Being God Is. Our individual physical life is the metaphor for the Non-Separateness of God Himself. **The physical asana is the loving union of the male and female parts of our Self.**

This description may be enough for you to recognize how to "sit." In fact, as this union matures, a graceful, energetic spontaneity will begin to animate the body at all times. The asana has a dynamic quality as well as a stationary one. If you understand this asana, you will not need to give extensive consideration to the specifics of how you place your legs…how you place your hands…how you align your torso and head, etc. You will know this intuitively. However, a description of these particulars will follow for anyone who feels any uncertainty or confusion about the sitting position. When you find the perfect asana that works for you, review the first part of this chapter to ensure that you understand the full meaning of **Asana**.

The positioning of the physical body is the simplest of the three asanas to describe, but to maintain a still, relaxed, alert, physical position for a long time, lets say an hour or so, is not easy at first. A restless person may find it almost impossible to sit still for even one minute.

For those who are physically capable, the classical cross-legged lotus or half lotus positions are ideal. With some practice the legs become quite comfortable and deeply relaxed. The heels of the feet rest gently against the two thighs where they join.

Sit upon a pillow or two so that you do not need to strain forward to maintain balance. The back needs to be straight and the muscles need to be relaxed. With a little practice you will feel this balanced position. Make sure you are not leaning or straining forward. A desire is there to experience something special, which will manifest itself as a tension to move forward. Relax. Be patient. **Enjoy this moment**, even if this moment is not as special as you would like it to be. Almost all moments are like this in the beginning.

We cannot hurry the blossom of a flower. We must wait for the elements of earth, water, fire (sun), air and design to bring forth the blossom at a natural pace. The gardener labors to bring these elements together, but the Spirit will manifest its Flower in the time of its own Design.

Some teachers recommend a special position(s) for the hands. This is called *mudra*. Dozens of mudras are described in Eastern yogas. The positioning of the hands and fingers is intended to do two things. It permits the flow of subtle electrical energy (*ki, chi* or *prana*) along certain meridians of the body to be stimulated and unimpeded. The intent is to increase vitality and alertness.

This positioning of the hands also serves as a metaphor of form. The hands emulate certain spiritual qualities... devotion, compassion, the ceaseless flow of Spirit, omnipresence...

Try this one mudra: Make a ring by lightly joining the tips of the thumb and forefinger of each hand and allow the other three fingers to extend outward, not touching each other. Now, let the hands rest upon the thighs, where they join the body, with the palms facing upward. The circle made with the thumb and forefinger represents and stimulates a circular flow of the endless Spirit. The upward turned palm and extended fingers represent and stimulate the female quality of patient receptivity. Softly hold the hands in this position for a long time, until you begin to sense a subtle understanding of the relation of form and attitude. If you intuit this understanding, you will know the purpose of mudras.

Some people will have a natural inclination to hold their hands in some particular way. Others will do so because they have been taught a particular mudra. I suggest that you do what you want. Don't make a big deal about it. Remember, the purpose of the position you assume is to be able to completely get beyond or "forget" the limitation of the physical body. This is most easily achieved by assuming a steady and graceful asana. How you refine the details is up to you, but don't lose sight of the forest for the trees.

Meditation is not what you do with your hands…it's what you do with your Consciousness.

As you sit on the floor, it is advised that you place a blanket of natural fiber (preferably wool) on the floor or ground. This will help to isolate you from certain etheric currents that are part of the earth's energy field.

Some may choose to meditate while sitting in a chair. I cannot recommend this position, however. There are significant currents to be generated within the spine that are best initiated through the cross-legged positions. But, for those who begin meditating later in life, and for those who are physically incapable of the classic positions, this will have to do. Place your feet on the blanket. Do not allow your back to rest upon the back of the chair. Place the hands gently on the thighs. The spine must remain straight and firm, and the rest of the body should be soft and relaxed.

Most physical alignment problems are the direct result of attitudes we develop as habits, expressing themselves in the spine and shoulders. If our environment is nurturing early on in life, we have feelings of optimism and great expectations. We hold our spine straight, our chest out, our abdomen in and our head up. As we walk, we lead with our heart, and our limbs flow with ease and confidence…a deep joy is felt.

Then, with certain "failures," or perhaps some hurtful criticisms by others, we may slowly develop spinal habits that reflect disappointment, fear, anger or disillusionment. These psychological and physiological responses gradually shape our body.

Once we recognize this disabling process, we are in the position to reverse these effects. With a profound sense of understanding and rededication to that enthusiastic life expression, we realign ourselves to that original joyous condition. Initially this will require a continuous effort. Gradually our body re-forms straight and pain free.

One simple technique that can reverse years of apathy is to simply **lead with your heart!** …As you walk, draw your shoulder blades back as far as is comfortably possible.

Draw the abdomen in and gently, but firmly, throw the
chest out. Let the arms swing freely. Lead with your heart.
Do not fear for any kind of resistance from the outer
world. Be prepared to meet any obstacle or criticism with
kind, intelligent reflection. Do not allow the reactions of
the outer world to translate as a loss in any way. There can
never be such a loss in Reality. So do not accept any as
your own.

Once you have contacted the Holy Sound, Om, you will
notice that this posturing amplifies the Sound. It expands
its vibratory sphere.

Translate this new "shape" into your meditation. Keep
the shoulders back (as if you were drawing the shoulder
blades in back as close together as possible), chest out and
the abdomen in. Lay your hands upon your thighs where
they join. Hold the palms upward...receptive to the universal Cosmic Vibrations.

This is the shape of a spiritual amplifier. It is exactly the
same principle employed in the design of a radio and its
speakers, except that the body is now attuned to God.

Maintain this asana in a state of ease.

As you watch your physical body sitting, a variety of
physical sensations will occur. There will be electrical
impulses, involuntary tightness or movements, vibrations,
shakti, muscular contractions, etc. Regardless of what
happens to the physical body, the single most important
feature to remember is that **you are not a physical body**. In
fact, you do not even "have" a physical body. It's not
something you have. It is just **there**. It is really just a transient drop of God's ever changing...ever new, physical
Body.

What position do we assume for our emotional body?

The *Bhagavad Gita* gives a long description of the three
gunas. These are the manifesting qualities of nature. The
three gunas are *tamas, rajas* and *sattva*. When tamas prevails, man is filled with sloth and ignorance. When rajas
prevails, man is filled with activity, restlessness and desire.
When sattva prevails, man is filled with harmony and
wisdom. When "lighted" (both as in the light that is seen

and the weightlessness that is felt) sattva saturates the emotional body. Joyousness is there. The emotions are calm. There is a feeling of intelligent optimism, resulting directly from the growing understanding of what is known about the Spirit. This optimism is cool rather than hot. There is not an anxious "looking ahead," but rather a calm viewing of the present...the Presence. This **Calm Joy** is the asana of the emotional body.

The mental body is normally the most difficult body to "forget." We are so attached to our minds, that even if we recognize both our physical body and our emotional body as transient, we often involuntarily think that what we are is "what we think." We feel utterly identified or supported by our ideas. But this is not true. We are independent of any idea in Reality. Our ideas are simply transient qualities of mind that appear as a way to understand and use our experience of ourselves.

To be sattvic, our minds must become clear, open, receptive, non clinging, awake, and "empty." The Zen masters call it Mu (or "No Mind"). When seeking the mental asana, Mu is the last frontier. It is the gate of the Divine Entry. Mind becomes formless. This formless Asana is:

STILLNESS – SILENCE – TRANSPARENCY

The Sage does not hold on to a particular set of proverbs and force one or more to apply in situations as they arise. Rather, he remains endlessly clear in order to access ideas that are completely appropriate and useful in each situation. He is perfectly spontaneous and relevant. He waits in a complete clarity to see just what is required, and then responds effortlessly in the precise manner that reveals itself to him in that moment. His foundation is the wisdom of God, but he claims no single aspect of it as his own. It is simply There. He has learned how and when to access it. In so doing he must learn how **not to think**, because that is the essence of his wisdom. His "thinking" is merely a response to a need that arises. He eliminates his own needs and thus attains Mu. He knows how to access wisdom for situations that arise, but he has no need, and thus does not waste his effort and his energy accumulating and storing ideas.

When an idea arises upon this still lake, it has a singular potency. It echoes in great clarity. It stands alone without attaching itself to the sage himself. It is just there. This is the essential Asana of the mental body. The mind is forgotten. It is left alone. If a thought arises, it has no place to permanently reside and soon it returns effortlessly to nature whence it came.

In order for an automobile to operate properly, it must be well lubricated in many places. Oils and greases line its moving parts to reduce friction. This allows ease of movement. It also protects each part against excessive wear and extends the life of the vehicle. We must properly lubricate the moving parts of all three of our own bodies. We must reduce the friction that is there.

Physically: We must properly feed, exercise and rest our bodies. We must remove the tensions that build up. Eventually, if we become alert and fully awake, we avoid tension before it begins. We replace the habit of tension with beauty, grace and function. We recognize the Design and align with it. We allow it to generate our individual, personal expression.

Emotionally: We must enjoy ourselves. We must experience joy as our essential emotional quality. It is there for each one. All we have do is go with it. The more we know about our true nature...our Essence...the more reason we have to be joyous. It is the natural result of understanding our Self and merging with God.

Mentally: We must allow clearer, more subtle and larger thoughts to appear, without attaching ourselves to them. "Larger" means more inclusive...holding a greater, more complete truth. Eventually our small individual mind merges with the clear and faultless Mind of Spirit.

Having said all this about asana...having broken down the Whole into the localized three bodies and considered the minute workings and adjustments there, we must not lose sight of a basic simplicity. We must remember that these three bodies have a DESIGN. A natural intelligence is there to operate them appropriately, if we permit it. We can simply allow it to function as God wills it.

A wonderful Zen proverb says, "When hungry eat. When tired sleep." It means this: Once you get the **feel** of your Whole Heavenly Form, you can completely forget the individual parts. But, if a particular part is hanging you up, find a way to lubricate it. Eliminate the tension. Eliminate the resistance. Bring it back into its natural state…

STILLNESS – SILENCE – TRANSPARENCY

LISTENING

God speaks to everyone. Our deep need is to LISTEN! This is the foundation of the Spiritual Life. Arjuna listens to Krishna. The disciple listens to the Master. The Master listens to God. This act of listening is the condition of Being for which man is searching. It is his rest...it is his peace.

But what shall we hear?

There is a beautiful, harmonious, continuously vibrant, soothing Sound that can be heard by every human being. To hear this Sound we must enter a deep state of listening in complete openness. The heart and mind become like a flute...open and resonant. They contain no thing. They become the Sound itself. The devotee listens patiently for That which continuously gives rise to this material existence, but is not material itself. He listens for the Holy Spirit.

The most elegant and simple yogic technique is listening to Om, this Holy Cosmic Sound. Merging with Om is the technique spoken of by an endless stream of Gurus, from Patanjali to Yogananda, from Krishna to Christ. To hear this Sound, we must be very quiet. To feel this Sound vibrating within us and all around us, we must become very still. Om is not the end...it is the very beginning. "In the beginning **is** the Word."

This "Word" is known by different names in various parts of our world. The Hindus call it *Om* (or *Aum*[1]).

---

[1] The word *Om* is often written *Aum*, because it contains the sounds A (ah), U (oo) and M (mmm...) in one continuous, vibratory sound. A description of the significance of these three sound

Christians and Jews call it *Amen*. Muslims call it *Amin*. Tibetan Buddhists call it *Hum*. Those who meditate sincerely with deep attention and stillness will begin to hear this Sound. Its impact will be felt in a very definite way. Its importance will be clear. It is not a "word" that we can speak as such. We can only approximate its Sound. Its Sound is continuous, without beginning or end. Its Vibration causes the deepest level of healing.

Throughout the Bible there are numerous references to the "Word." Isaiah 30:21 reads, "And thine ears shall hear a word **behind** thee, saying, This is the way, walk ye in it..." The Holy Sound, Om, is normally first heard within the medulla oblongata. The Sound appears to be coming from "behind," because our focus is normally forward looking in the frontal part of our brain, in the area between the eyebrows.

The Gospel According to John opens, "In the beginning was the Word. And the Word was with God. And the Word was God." This Holy Word preexists language. It preexists man himself. As our minds become utterly quiet, we hear the more subtle sounds of the inner environment. Om is the most subtle of these sounds, and yet it permeates every material thing. Om fills all space. Its Vibrancy is the Force that sustains the entire manifested world.

AUM

Standing on the shore
　　I hear the Ocean's waves and think
I am that wave
　　I breathe in... I breathe out
　　I am that wave
But I am not sure
　　and a wave is a restless thing

qualities and their relationship with the three Hindu Gods, Brahma, Vishnu and Shiva, will follow in the chapter, *Om*.

So I sit

Wave after wave rolls
Then, beneath the sound of the waves
    is a whisper... faint
    almost a phantom

A U M

I ask, "God, is that You?"
I hear no reply

But I tire of the daily
    coming and going
So I sit

The day is full and the Ocean is high
    wave upon wave
    each one having three parts as sound
    a beginning, a middle and an end

Each wave a part
    moving... restless

Then the whisper returns

A U M

Again I ask, "God, is that You?"
    and God stirs

"God stirs!" I yell
I'm up and about
    looking for an ear to hear
"God stirs!"
    One says, "Oh?"

One asks, "What is His Name?"
One says, "You are a fool!"

So I retreat once again to the shore
    and the Ocean... and the waves
Again and again
    there is a stirring
The whisper returns
Again I ask, "God, is that You?"
Beneath the waves comes the whole Sound
    not in parts

A U M

faint but undeniable
He speaks!
My ear just barely hears
I follow the Sound of His Voice

Evening comes
    and the waves recede
    still lapping at the shore
    but more quiet
The whole Ocean speaks
    as the waves recede
Steady becomes His Voice
    filling my ears
I ask, "God, will You speak now?"

**I am trying
but... Son
you are in the way!**

"But where shall I go?"
    I wonder aloud

to no reply that I can hear

I return again and again to the shore in evening
  and the waves roll gently
  quieter... more still
  but not retiring
Afraid to cease
Unwilling to call it quits

"The Ocean must have Its waves," I think
  Yet, I am unsure

Again I ask, "God, will You speak now?"

**The Ocean speaks when all is still...
when the last ripple of Life is quiet
and calm settles upon My surface.**

The last wave recedes
All three are in the one Voice
  united and full

An Ocean
  complete without edge
  Single and Whole

Thirteen in a boat
  gale force winds arise
All persons in danger
  yet One without fear
All persons in danger
  yet One without fear
"Master," the twelve ask,
  "Please steady the course.
  Calm the winds.
  It threatens us."

He replies, "You threaten yourselves!
 Fear moves across the screen of your mind.
 Become Still."

And behold, the winds stand still
  and the waves cease
  and the Ocean's Voice fills the Heavens
Doors open for each
 and room after room is there
Each for all... All for each
  One Mansion of Being
  One Being... God

Far had I receded... Extinguished
 no voice left to question, "Is that You?"
Even He is in Love
Even He is Amazed
  Intoxicated with Ecstasy
  Drunk on Who He Is!

Conceptualization is man's attempt to contain that which is Whole from the beginning. We must learn to break this habit. We must penetrate deeper into the Essence of Life. We exist **as** the Whole. It is the only eternal Reality available. All the other temporary realities are forms of confinement or division. Meditation upon Om is the single easiest way to untie this knot of conception. As we listen continuously to this healing Sound, we become absorbed in it. We enter a state of Grace. This dissolves the long standing mental habit of imagining a false, separate identity. Om dissolves ego. We begin to unite consciously with God.

We have all heard the expression, "Put that in your pipe and smoke it." Look closely at this image. Imagine a thinker, smoking his pipe. Watch what is actually happening. Pensively he fills the bowl with tobacco and then firmly tamps it down. Carefully he lights it. As each thought is proposed in his mind, the smoker instinctively and impulsively draws the smoke within himself and considers it...tastes it...is filled by it. When he can contain it no longer, it is exhaled. Every part of this is visible. It's as if each thought itself has physical definition. Yet the smoke eventually dissolves into the All. It merges with it. It becomes part of it.

This smoking-thinking process is the "normal" way man considers things. To begin with, he sees himself as something separate. He draws something "else" into himself. He gives it his attention and exhales the part he can no longer contain. This process goes on and on. This is why smoking is so appealing to the ego of man. It visually expresses his separateness. Instead of merging with the colorless, odorless, pure, non-separate atmosphere, he fills it up entirely with gray definition. No more perfect, dynamic metaphor for his isolation exists. He actually chooses to be isolate.

A much more delicious choice is available. **Be the Whole Thing!** Become it all! This is the Reality as it is.

There is a wonderful expression for a person full of laughter, "She could not contain herself!" In fact...we can't contain our Self. It is impossible. The Self is unbounded. It is All. No container exists large enough. All containers are part of our Whole Being. Nothing can be contained, because there is only One Thing. It is All One Thing. It is God! But for the most part, we do not seem to believe this very deeply. What we need to do is to begin functioning NOW as if this were completely true. Gradually we recognize it as the fundamental Reality, and the struggle of life ceases. It dissolves in the graceful and effortless, omnipresent Holy Sound.

Om has no relativity. It resounds continuously, heard or unheard. Listening to it is a simple technique of inner correction and realignment with God. As we allow Om to do its work upon our consciousness, this sweet Sound becomes our gyroscope for the spiritual adventure.

As Om becomes our steady conscious environment, we develop a level of distrust for any thought or feeling that is experienced when this Holy Sound is not heard. The little selves that have found their way into our conscious patterns of thinking and feeling have selfish ends. Om eliminates this self-centered pattern of experience.

When we eliminate the tendency of listening to our own train of thought, we become free to experience a life more rich in texture than we ever imagined. This "train" of thought...this locomotive...runs along a linear track, takes control of our life and confines it. If we set aside this habit, we open the possibility of hearing the voice of God in each thought. And God has been ready to speak to us throughout every moment of every life. But our own thoughts have been such a drone, we barely hear the first thing. Some have even lost faith in the possibility of ever hearing Him at all.

Every thought and every feeling coming directly from God issues forth from Om. To hear This and to act in harmony with it requires a deep receptivity and willingness. It requires that we sit still and stop emoting. We cut off the habitual stream of our own separate thoughts. We just LISTEN! We listen until we hear and then feel the "Word" of God.

Om then becomes the ultimate truth detector. As thought enters the mind in the presence of this Sound, deep meaning and feeling like none other is experienced. From the Spirit of the Cosmic Sound flows the Truth. Om is the Whole Reality in vibration, and Truth emerges from that which is Real. A deep trust wells up from within and matures wondrously in this environment. As we experience this trust...and wonder...we are released into a world of continuous love and compassion for all Life. This becomes our natural way of relating to it All. We now exist as the whole, sweet Environment of God. How could we love only part?

We are Siddhartha, the Buddha, sharing a description of the Path with anyone who will hear it. We are Lord Krishna playing the Divine Flute in everlasting bliss and ecstasy. We are Jesus giving up a single, physical, life experience so that others may discover how to give up their own suffering. We are the endless and awesome Path, expressing our utter amazement and joy...the essence of Self-discovery. Each one who listens tirelessly into the endless depths of Spirit arrives wholly in this wonderful, sweet Condition.

TRANSCENDENTAL EXPERIENCE

There are myriad accounts of people who have experienced worlds other than the obvious earthly, physical realm. There are descriptions of contacts with beings who come from some unseen dimension to either give us some message or simply observe our planetary behavior. In the spiritual literature of our day we read that people see angels, devas and space beings in UFO's. Some see or hear beings who have supposedly long since passed away from this earth...often well known religious figures like Jesus, Krishna, Buddha and Mohammed, and literally hundreds of lesser known figures such as Enoch, Seth, Thoth, Merlin and the Masters of the White Brotherhood...to name just a few.

Some describe physical meetings with recently departed loved ones. For example, Sri Yukteswar visited Paramhansa Yogananda shortly after his own apparent death in much the same way that Jesus visited his disciples after his burial. My own father-in-law returned from the grave in physical form to discuss his relationship with his spouse, whom he had left behind.

Some visionaries describe their own travel to co-existing worlds of other dimensions, which either may be here, interpenetrating our three dimensional, physical space, or are "nearby," like the planets of our solar system, or somewhat more distant planets, stars or constellations like Pleiades, Orion, Sirius, etc. Some suggest that space and time are illusions of the limited human mind...that everything of all times exists simultaneously here and now.

These accounts may offer specific guidance to the visionary or his colleagues, or general information about other worlds or events that might happen in our own world. However, the first time such an experience occurs to you, the nature of the event itself is always more significant than any information that is delivered. Put simply, the event attests directly to you of the availability of transcendent experience.

The accounts of these experiences by others may help to remove some fear that we have developed concerning the "other side." But as we read these accounts, even if we come to believe a messenger and his message, our formulating a new viewpoint will have minimal impact upon our life until we directly experience such a world ourselves. The medium is the essence of the message...at least in the beginning.

To devise a philosophy, a cosmology or a belief system is very simple. To evolve as a creative expression of love and wisdom is more demanding. To be totally transformed into Divine Experience is completely demanding. And yet, it is completely liberating. It is also totally inevitable and presently available.

We have each become a unique being of experience. We have arrived at this very moment by way of innumerable forces, forms, bodies, feelings, activities and thoughts, which, consciously or unconsciously, we have chosen ourselves. Everywhere there is choice. A virtual smorgasbord of experiential choices lies before us. For the most part, we repeatedly choose only a select few. These have become our habitual pattern, and greatly influence our own self-view. We victimize ourselves unwittingly in a continuous act of limitation. We act as though our destiny is some final resting place, complete with a headstone, briefly describing who we once were...and we don't want to be disturbed.

But the fact remains, we are evolving toward a destiny of sublime radiant Ecstasy. We may first hear only that "still small voice," which hints of things to come, what to do, how to feel or where to be. But through time, as we get out of the way, it amplifies. It speaks to us directly and vibrates in ways that change our perceptions and lift our consciousness. One day in this ever present moment we awaken to a life that resonates with Force and Being. We are that Life! What we now call our body fills with a symphony of harmonic Sound, transforming us from earth bound lumps of clay into beings of bliss and vehicles of love.

Bliss is the primordial, inescapable, attractive Force of the universe and Love is its expression. Bliss is the very Spirit of the "thing" we call God. And we are created precisely in that Image by that Spirit. It is the ultimate energetic "substance." It is the pre-substance...the irreducible stuff of creation.

We shall someday consciously access the *Akashic Record*, which holds a vibrational memory of everything that has ever happened or been thought. This information will not simply satisfy some idle curiosity, but will be used to heal our own life experience and to assist others. We shall recognize through direct perception that each of us is a Body of Light and that we are in no way separate from the Whole Being God Is.

Does this sound too good to be true? Can we discover that this destiny is not just a hope, a belief or a dream, but is absolutely inevitable? If so, where do we begin? We know very little about ourselves. We sense only the slightest fraction of our Being and our environment. At best we have seen only a brief preview, danced just a few steps, sung but a few notes and recognized the tiniest portion of our Divine Life. We are mesmerized by and trapped within the mundane.

Let us begin by looking at some descriptions of individual transcendental experiences. We may then glimpse our larger Being so that a door will open.

Consider the lives of Jesus and Buddha. Feel each of their life experiences. We may admire, idolize, pray to or ask forgiveness from Jesus, but we do not live like him. His understanding is way beyond ours. He is born under a Divine Star. He is recognized as special at birth by wise men. Concerning the first dozen years of his life we know nothing. At twelve years old, he is ministering to the priests of his day. We have all met twelve-year-olds who think they know everything, but never one who does. His life seems beyond our reach. We wonder what he experiences, what he knows, how he performs miracles and who he is.

Apparent contradictions also accompany the historical Jesus. He could raise others from the dead, or at least invoke the will of God to do so. He could even return from the dead himself. Yet, if the reports about his life are true, he too had to face temptation. He had to cry out, "Lord, Lord, why hast Thou forsaken me." It is difficult to deny his divinity, but still he seems both out of reach yet vulnerable.

On the other hand, Buddha is much like us. He may have been born a prince, but he knows what we know. He feels the way we feel. He responds as we would in his place. He is born in ignorance just like us. As a boy he knows nothing about pain and death. He has been sheltered from the harsh realities of human life by parents who wish to spare him all earthly anguish. Then, as a young man, he sees a dead body lying by the side of the road. He does not understand what has happened and insists to be informed about it. (That Voice speaks to him for the first time…a time ripe with possibility.) When he is told that it is the fate of all human beings, including himself, that each must die, his ignorance is made clear to him. He goes into shock. From that point on, a **spiritual quest** takes hold of his consciousness and will not let go. He must discover the Essence and Meaning of this life. He must abandon the life he has been living, because it is now meaningless in the face of eternity. As he sets out, he cannot even know if a meaning exists. He seeks a wider vision and yet does not know if such a vision is available. He cannot even predict if this quest will be of any use or significance at all.

He is drawn with great Force into a new life, whose only direction comes from that Voice of intuition that faintly insists upon what is True and what is Real. A long period of hardship and suffering ensues. There is no real option to do anything else. He cannot hear the pleading of his parents and friends to return to the life of leisure he once had. He hears just the one Voice. He senses his quest will consume and possibly destroy himself in the process, and yet he has no choice but to carry on with it.

Years go by. No lasting, profound evidence or experience has yet transformed his awareness. His life has changed, but for what purpose? His efforts seem futile. Physically, emotionally and psychologically he has completely examined the wall that imprisons himself. He knows no escape and is overwhelmed by his own limitations. Exhausted and discouraged, he sits down under a bodhi tree and gives up.

Then something marvelous happens. Through **Grace** he is transformed. He is Illuminated. The door separating his individual consciousness from that of the Whole is opened. In this one moment his life is changed completely. In this moment the Real Life commences.

This is our own destiny. We may sleep, walk, run or fly along this path, but we will arrive. Our arrival is our true beginning. This path is arduous and completely demanding. In one sense we will never rest again. The quest will become a total effort to evolve into our primordial Being, which is Light itself. The quest will slowly begin to dominate all the smaller desires that now command our attention. It may require a total change of activity. It will definitely require a total change of outlook. We will not be who we were. We will pass through a door, through which we cannot return. We shall become totally honest. We can no longer be, as Bob Dylan describes him, "...the one who tries to hide what he don't know to begin with." This is no longer available. We have no secrets and can no longer pretend to be anything but Who and What we are.

Open... no place to hide
Open... having no thing to hide
Available

Vigilant
and eventually... suddenly
All is Grace!

We then seek to serve, not control...to serve as invisibly as possible, so as to remain anonymous. We "perform random acts of kindness," but more than that...we do it anonymously and with no special sense of self-recognition as well. This way becomes the Way. Life unfolds its wonder. The awesome becomes ordinary, and the ordinary becomes awesome.

How to begin?

The first thing that every human being needs to discover through direct experience is that there is no death in reality. This can only happen when we recognize we are not the physical form, but rather a Spiritual Being transmigrating through domains of physical, astral and mental sensation. We must learn to resonate with the One Conscious Reality in order to shake loose from the appearance of separation. Until that moment comes to any man, life is more like an annoying dilemma than paradise.

The only thing resembling a recipe that will cause a transcendental experience like this to occur is an intense, single-minded desire for it, coupled with a willingness to apply any effort that is required. This desire must be foremost. Jesus says, "Seek ye **first** the kingdom of God." This seeking for the Real must become the fundamental focus. It must be **the number one priority**. If it is second, there is little chance of a deep transformation. There is little chance that we will move into a mystical awareness.

The desire must be like this:

> Bodhidharma, the first Zen patriarch, sat facing a wall for nine years in order to discover his True Nature. When word got out that he had made his entry into the Real World, others naturally wanted to experience the same thing. Many came for his teaching. Most of these, not having adequate inner strength and real desire, were summarily turned away. Hui-k'e, however, was not to

be denied. For an entire night he waited outside, standing in a December snowstorm, just to have a meeting with Bodhidharma. In the morning the snow was up to his knees, and yet he made not a sound. He simply waited.

Finally Bodhidharma took pity on him and asked, "What is your wish?"

Hui-k'e replied, "I am come to receive your invaluable instruction; pray open the gate of mercy and extend your hand of salvation to this poor suffering mortal."

Bodhidharma rebuked him simply, explaining that few men have the will to endure the effort and discipline required to achieve such a goal.

Upon hearing this, Hui-k'e took his sword, cut off his own left arm and presented it to the master. The master simply remarked, **"You are not to seek this Truth through others."**

Hui-k'e persisted, "My soul is not yet pacified. Pray, Master, pacify it."

Bodhidharma then said, "Bring your soul here and I will have it pacified."

Hui-k'e replied, "I have sought it for many years and am still unable to take hold of it."

Bodhidharma struck deeply with his final remark, **"There! Your soul is pacified once for all."**

At this, Hui-k'e became Enlightened.[1]

What are we to make of this?

Two important points are here. First, the effort that is required to merge with the Whole Being God Is must be total. It must be unwavering. It will not be a "piece of cake."

This glimpse of the determination needed may at first seem too much. We may feel we are not prepared for such a commitment...such a struggle. Jesus said, "It is easier for a camel to pass through the eye of a needle than a rich man enter the kingdom of heaven."[2] Only when the complete vacuousness of a purely physical life becomes unbearable, will the spiritual commitment rise up naturally. When we

---

[1] D.T. Suzuki: *Essays in Zen Buddhism* (Second Series), p.42–43.
[2] Matthew 19:24

recognize how dark our current life is, the way to the Light becomes a labor of necessity and the only possible path. That path then becomes simple and direct.

Reality itself becomes the commitment. The glamour of the ego is not something that we must shed, but rather something we no longer care about. We enter here and don't even bother to look back.

And secondly, the Thing that we are after...our very Self...is not something we can grasp. **It is the Whole Thing Itself.** We cannot grip it as we do the things of this physical world. We will not be left holding on to any thing. We shall become the very Thing we are now seeking and which we already are. This path is a continuous letting go of the very activity causing our discomfort. Once this natural state of Being is established, the effort itself dissolves. We discover **I AM THIS.**

We must not, however, put the cart before the horse. We must not deceive ourselves into thinking that since we are to arrive in a place of Being that we already are, there is no effort to be made in the first place. Anyone who experiences pain must do what is necessary to remove this obstacle. We put it there. Thus we must remove it!

Only a deep desire to directly see, hear and know our True Being will sustain our attention across the great physical, emotional and mental chasm of distraction. A deep urgent need drives us to the edge of the ordinary human consciousness of six dimensions...the four physical dimensions of space and time and the two dimensions of emotion and mind. From that edge we leap, or are drawn, into a **new dimension.**

A transcendental experience instantaneously alters our perspective. It is a true beginning. And yet, just because we have a vision, travel outside the physical body, or have a near death experience, does not make us special. We have not really changed. There is a simple, unchanging and blessed Oneness of Being in the world of Spirit. A transcendental experience does not change who we are, it changes **the way we view who we are.** Until this moment, we have relied on other authorities, incomplete logic or vague belief to define what is going on and to prescribe how we should deal with this life. Now the path becomes mysterious. We have tasted an awesome new area of Being, hitherto unknown to us, or perhaps forgotten. We begin here.

We must use this experience to begin a new life. It takes courage to make this change. There will often be a great resistance to our changing by others. When children enter this Dimension, they are almost always encouraged to forget it and return to "normal." For those who submit to this pressure, the memory often fades, and a great avenue is cut off. If you discuss your experience with "normal" people, they may try to disprove the "reality" of your experience, as their egos or limited perspective may find your description a threat to their carefully fabricated order of life. It is usually much better to allow the changes to occur inside and not make too much of them in a public way.

Normally the dynamic of the experience has a greater impact on us than the content of any message. Put simply, the experience is essentially experiential. There may come specific directions for us through vision, voice or impression, but **the vibrational contact itself changes the way we experience**. It inspires awe. It also creates an immediate change in the way we respond to the physical life. In time, with patience and a continuity of inspired effort, this new orientation completely changes our own identification.

This is what happened to me.

MANTRA

Our conscious experience is formed through many different modes of acting, feeling and thinking. We participate as a number of separate selves with an assortment of experiential habits. We are happy when certain conditions are met...sad when other conditions are met...angry when still other conditions are met, and so on. We are any one of several personalities depending on the circumstances.

For a moment let's look again at the union of the male and female parts of our Self. Asana helps us to experience these two as the One Whole Being God Is. We have the feeling of being firm on the inside, and soft and receptive on the outside. But notice what happens when we become angry. We become over-stimulated within, causing the outer female part to become agitated...completely yang or male. The outer softness is lost. The union is thrown out of balance. The luminous, blissful, radiating energy is uselessly expelled. We become depleted almost instantaneously. Dis-ease immediately sets in.

Conversely, when we become sad or disheartened, the inner male part loses its firmness. The will becomes depleted. In this case a different form of dis-ease enters.

Throughout this life we repeatedly allow ourselves to be victimized in ways like this. We become the **reaction** to an endless series of events, which are, in great measure, out of our control anyway.

Ego has the nature of a hunter and an insatiable appetite for activity. When we allow this false separate self to be in charge, we become fully absorbed in the outer world of activity. The reason why most people have no interest in meditation is because they are forced to come face to face with their own restlessness. They do not want the activity to stop. It is their way of putting off the inevitable discovery that **the ego is not in control**.

Furthermore, our memory is incomplete and often uncontrollably selective under varying situations. This discolors our ongoing experience. For example, if we remember to be friendly whenever a particular person enters our life, we develop a friendship with that one individual. Later, if we forget to be friendly with this person, we may lose him as a friend. A different pattern evolves for each encounter and each environmental condition. Our consciousness is generally so fickle that we do not recognize who we Are.

So, how can we unify our experience?

A good idea can help with the distress that sets in, but ultimately good ideas are not enough. Why? The mind is just one part of our Self and not the Whole Thing. The restlessness of the mind goes to the heart of the problem. Between thinking and Being is a vast chasm. Real thinking issues forth naturally from real Being. It is well-timed and appropriate. The reverse is not usually true. A good thought does not always translate into appropriate action or divine experience. We cannot simply think ourselves into bliss. We must feel it in a more direct way. That way is **meditation**.

When we listen to music, unconsciously we make a choice of how to listen. Two completely opposite ways are available. We can concentrate upon the melody and rhythm, and feel ourselves moving with it. When we listen like this, in a subtle way we give up our identity and allow the music to dictate our experience. It carries us along. If the music jumps, we jump with it. If it sways, we sway. If it pounds, we pound with it, and so forth.

The other way of listening to music is to remain completely **still**...centered within the whole sound...absorbed in the harmony and the complete musical environment. We watch the movement of the melody and the rhythm from our own center, which does not move. Without attaching ourselves emotionally or physically to the sound, we simply observe how it dances. We may be emotionally uplifted, but not lost.

These two distinctly different ways of listening to music are the two basic archetypes of all experience. Either we participate or we witness.

Meditation is the process of attentiveness that proceeds from directed participation to Divine Witnessing.

Ordinarily, energy accumulates in each of our Centers. When a sufficient level of energy gathers in any one of them, we have an almost involuntary urge to expel it, or move it to some other place. A restlessness is there, because on a very deep level we are not prepared to hang out with our Self and observe what is happening within. Our attention is glued to the senses. So we initiate an outward movement.

When energy builds up in the head, this movement takes the form of thought. Under many circumstances, thoughts arise simply to extinguish the accumulation of energy there...or at least to direct it outward.

A basic purpose of meditation is to allow this vital energy, or *prana*, to gather in our Centers. When this energy vibrates in harmony, it increases our vitality and raises the vibratory level within our bodies. We begin to glide into higher octaves of experience.

Meditation has three distinct stages:

Concentration – Meditation – Contemplation

We begin with a method of focusing that will help to bring our conscious attention into the Center. This method, or technique, is vital. It steers us through the storms of temporal experience. We may barely recognize it at first, but we are setting out to sail into the tranquil, luminescent Sea of Divine Life.

The Master wants to evoke a change in the way we experience ourselves. He wants to eliminate the endless selves that enter into experience. To do this, a *Mantra* is given to center and harmonize the mind-body experience. We then make the initial effort of **Concentration.**

The Sound of the Mantra, heard with deep concentration, causes our attention to remain focused on the essential Vibration of the whole energetic environment of Being. The primordial nature of this field of Being is **harmonic resonance.** Our Center then begins to vibrate sympathetically in this Sound Field...and our vitality soars. This is the general nature of the energetic experience that we are seeking as we begin to meditate.

Mantra serves to create a singular focus. This helps cut off the mind's endless wandering and calms it down. The Mantra opens the way to the Holy Sound. It is a divinely intelligent vehicle that dissolves discordant vibration into stillness. Slowly we tune in to a new quality...one that resonates with the fundamental Vibration of Spirit itself.

A definite understanding of what Mantra is and how it works will improve its effectiveness.

A Mantra is a sound, word or group of words heard continuously with deep conscious attention, uncovering and amplifying an essential vibration or truth that intentionally awakens and purifies our Self-perception, drawing us into Divine Experience.

Read this last sentence several times, until the meaning of mantra begins to become clear. In it are many, very important indications of the nature of the path.

Notice, for example, a mantra is "heard." In the beginning a mantra is something we "say" either out loud or mentally. But, if the mantra has a deeply true meaning, it eventually becomes something we hear, rather than something we say.

Mantra is that part of the will of God that becomes audible.

The Holy Sound, Om, is the essential Mantra. It is the Sound of the whole manifested universe. It is the complete Sound of Spirit-Matter. However, the Holy Sound, Om, is very subtle at first. Most of us cannot even hear it. Very few are even aware that such a Sound exists.

It is a curious fact that many have actually heard this Sound and still do not know that it exists. Some people who are naturally quiet, perhaps while reading or in deep thought, will hear Om as a background sound, but not give it any special significance. There are also many circumstances which cause us to hear this Cosmic Sound in an involuntary way...illness, a near death experience, a blow to the head or even sudden dizziness. Later we forget about it. We may think that what we heard was just some strange thing, and hardly give it another thought. We go on about our business as if nothing had happened. The memory of such a Sound temporarily settles in the subconscious. We remain oblivious to its Presence and its Power.

All true mantras issue from Spirit...the manifesting power of God. Spirit is the actual Voice of the Mantra. At first, however, the devotee begins to intone the sound in order to make it audible. After a considerable period of time, perhaps weeks, months or even years, gradually there comes a release of effort and Spirit is witnessed as the intoning Sound.

From the beginning, a deep trust in this process evokes the deepest kind of listening. It helps to initiate a state of grace. Spirit purifies our Center, dissolves the edges and unveils its omnipresence. This listening is the absolute essence of the path.

The technique is a kind of "doing." It requires an "activity." Even though the activity is to witness something, in the beginning it is more like a doing than a witnessing. For example, if our technique is to watch the breath, then at first we will undoubtedly feel that our breathing is something **we** are doing.

As we progress with our technique, we do less and less, and observe more and more. This allows us to make a conscious entry into a graceful vibratory condition. Gradually we become familiar and comfortable within it. Grace arises naturally as we eliminate the distracting pattern of **reacting** to the outer world.

In the quiet we discover new insights. We become aware of more creative choices of response. We begin to see the **oncoming** force of mood swings. Until now, these seemed inescapable. But, as we watch carefully and witness with ease, we preempt the emotional disturbance. It never surfaces and loses its control. As this kind of personal success becomes ordinary, we begin to feel more comfortable in a state of inaction.

With practice, the "doing" very definitely progresses into a "dynamic witnessing." Returning to our example, if our technique is to watch the breath, we begin to experience that we are not the one doing the breathing. We are simply witnessing it. This meditative process becomes embedded as a new prototype for our activity. We bring a greater watchfulness and sensitivity to our life. This allows us to disengage from the reactive state of experience.

If the concentration is adequate, something significant begins to occur over time. Slowly the doing process gives way to a continuous watchfulness. We become released from activity as such. That which began as a technique of concentration becomes something that is now happening by itself. This is **Meditation**. We may still have a sense that "we" are there, somewhat separate from what is being experienced, but we feel a new kind of freedom. The Mantra is now something we hear without effort. It is playing like a tape recorded message...and a sweetness is there. It begins to expand. It begins to resonate on its own.

We have all had the experience of hearing a song or verbal phrase, echoing within our minds after having heard it repeatedly elsewhere. This alone is a strong reason to choose our experiences carefully. They will stay with us in memory whether we want them to remain or not.

Now...if the "song" we choose to have echoing in our minds is the **audible will of God**, we become blessed beyond expectation. We have invited Him into our experience. If we persist in this state of invitation, He will enter. He cannot resist. He has been waiting patiently for us to invite Him in.

Our meditations progress. Certain identifications are evolving and others are dissolving. These changes take time. At first we may feel, "I am watching Spirit enter into my individual experience, adding its qualities to my own." We still experience a separateness, but a door is open and something wonderful has entered. A profound trust begins to develop.

We are learning to let go of ourselves. This becomes an essential part of our practice. We get out of the way...and Spirit fills us more and more. As we do this over and over again, it becomes totally natural. We begin to **merge** with the Whole Being God Is. As this happens, we cannot help but see that the only "thing" that stands in our way is our ego.

Ego arises when experience divides into three aspects... witness, action and object. Language supports ego at every turn. We create sentences with a subject and a verb and often an object, such as: "I am going to town." When there is no reference to a place, another individual or thing, we become a little more present... "I am dancing." Yet still there is division...there "I" am "doing" this thing called dancing.

Japanese haiku is a poetic form of language that expresses experience as it is, rather than as something we do or have. There is no "relationship" that is being demonstrated. Things are as they are. Moreover, a great haiku poet will not only present things as they are, but will demonstrate singular enlightened experiences. Matsuo Basho, a poet of seventeenth century Japan, could evoke this kind of listening experience.

The old pond:
A frog jumps in...
The sound of the water.

Here we lose sight of our self...in a place...watching or listening to something. Instead, we only hear the sound. This is the experiential condition of Meditation.

Another of his poems reads:

The temple bell dies away.
The scent of flowers in the evening
Is still tolling the bell.

One could hardly imagine a poem that better describes the feeling experienced as the Holy Sound, Om, enters our hearing and gently eases us into a joyous wonder of this endless Life. A delicate sweetness fills us. Each moment flows effortlessly into the next, until we become a timeless continuity of joyous Experience.

Once we learn to eliminate the endlessly distracting influence of ego, we are prepared to "hear" the Mantra as it **IS**...rather than as something we must sustain through effort. The effort of paying attention proceeds until we recognize and experience that no further effort is necessary. At that point, any effort is counterproductive. This feels very much like making love with ourselves. There is an effortless firmness within, surrounded by a graceful softness.

As we extract the separate ego from our manner of experiencing by direct conscious contact with this Sound, the three forms of identification...witness, action and object...gradually dissolve into one. The so-called physical "reality" becomes the ever changing activity of God experiencing Himself. The emotional world becomes the joyous, unrestricted sensation of God vibrating. The mental experience becomes a freely creating Force of unlimited imagination.

What began as one pointed concentration, and developed into deep meditation, becomes our complete absorption into Spirit...**Contemplation**. Now we are utterly capable of passing through the Eye of the Needle, because we no longer carry the baggage of ego. We are no longer bonded to a web of physical and emotional entanglement. No one dies, because no One was born. We experience our Self as everywhere and every thing. We discover without qualification that, "**I AM THIS!**"

Why did we create this entangled web of conscious attachment to the three bodies in the first place? Because we have a deeply embedded fear, arising from painful experiences, that in order to survive, it is necessary to hang on to something. The tremendously liberating Truth is that no such clinging is necessary. Clinging only supports the continued experience of pain itself. **Consciousness is the unborn Essence of the Whole Being God Is.** We can neither support it nor destroy it as a result of anything we think or do. Consciousness is our very nature.

Divine Consciousness is so totally effective that it persists as an exquisitely graceful, intuitive calling to the outer consciousness, gently reminding it to let go of its self-created dis-ease, so that we might return to Spirit. This calling is **Mantra**.

To hear this we must awaken the intuition and let go of the physical, emotional and mental habits that are clearly fruitless. The Mantra is calling us home. Listening paves the way in. The power of this calling draws us through the appearance of matter into the Consciousness of Spirit.

A sudden, undeniable Vision of the Master, who is just here in the ether, waiting for our visitation, will come as a jolt like no other to shake us from our dreaming.

MALE & FEMALE

Our Divine Father is the complete inner Being...
Unmanifested Himself, yet the Source of all power and all
understanding. He cannot be known directly as we know
the "things" of our universe, but He can be intuited as the
Conscious Force causing forms to manifest in nature.

Our Divine Mother is that nature which accepts and
contains everything and everyone. She is the Whole Manifested Being...the complete Environment. She is the receptive matrix of matter and the nurturing of the consciousness therein.

When we were considering our posture in meditation,
we found the physical Asana to be "the loving union of the
male and female parts of our Self." That form is firm on the
inside and soft on the outside. The inner firmness is
straight and runs along the spine and brain. Everything
else remains flexible, kind and accepting. It is true for men
and it is true for women. It is our Divine Father and
Mother united within our self. This realization carries
tremendous insight into human relations.

The interior, firm quality is not forced. It is not a case of
getting a grip. We do not cause it to happen. It is already
there. With the practice of sitting meditation, we gently get
the feel of a steady magnetic force through the spine. It
feels as if a great interior river is flowing endlessly through
us, yet our conscious center remains still.

Also, when we say the "exterior" is soft and loving, this
is not just some shell of our self. It enfolds all the cells of
our body. It is the complete nurturing, surrounding us and
radiating within our Heart. This love permeates our
extremities and extends far beyond the boundaries of our

skin. In this way we experience the omnipresence...the rapture of a loving connection with all Life.

This soft, gentle, unhurried quality transforms the way we speak to each other. Our tone changes. The edges are rounded. Harmony is there. What we say is filled with genuine kindness, adding a new, important dimension to the meaning of our spoken thoughts.

Softness also becomes a basic quality of our touch. It is there when we place our hand on the shoulder of a friend. It completely saturates our hands when we touch a loving partner.

We actually enter a wondrous biofeedback condition. We begin to radiate the qualities of this design in the things we do and say. We feel the intelligent and powerful current within and the caress of a loving presence throughout our body. This transforms our whole manner. Normally then, the outer world recognizes the design and mirrors it back. Very gradually, perhaps just barely at first, the outer environment becomes conscious of the design.

Generally it proceeds this way: We discover the Spiritual Design. We practice it patiently. We demand of ourselves an abiding consistency, and make the effort required for this to become our experiential reality. We stay with it and perfect it. Gradually this whole quality infuses our surroundings. Because all life is essentially empathetic, it feels what we are feeling. It experiences what we experience, and eventually gives it back to us.

To help experience the full import of this, try this simple exercise: Imagine yourself to be utterly firm, yet relaxed, along the spine. At the same time allow your flesh to be completely soft and loving. Operate for a while with that design, without projecting thought. Just let this feeling be your experience...firm and aligned within...soft, receptive, loving and flexible throughout. Just **feel** it. Allow this to be the complete expression of yourself. As you do this, there will come a gradual intuitive flowering of understanding.

Look at plants, flowers, fruits and trees. Look at their design. A tree has a very firm (and often quite straight) stem. At the appropriate time, when the weather permits, it produces soft, pliable leaves to complete its outer form.

Look at fruits. Deep within lies the seed or seeds...the inner potency. The flesh of the fruit ripens into a sweet, delicious softness. An outer skin is there only to hold the flesh together and protect it from the severity of the sun and weather. It is essentially hard or firm inside and soft outside.

This is the Cosmic Design. We can clearly see the physical mapping of the primal Force, causing nature to take specific form. Except in some extreme environments that require tremendous outer protection from threatening elements, this essential design can be seen everywhere. Among vertebrates, the most evolved of living creatures on this earth, it is the design manifest. As man, it is particularly advanced. The firm inner Current is rising into the womb of Spiritual Conception. The consciousness, now embedded in matter, is returning to Spirit.

When we look deeper than the physical...when we look to see the Cause that produces this design, we see that the source of the firm inner manifestation is **Will**, and the source of the soft outer manifestation is **Love**. When we join these two, we taste a tremendous sweetness. A new independence...a new freedom...arises as we put this form into practice. If this form is maintained, we become unmoved by "disappointing" material events or the negative attitudes of others. We become independent of what others think or say. We can pay attention with ease, but not react. We stay with the form and merge with Spirit.

As the entire outer being becomes soft and accepting, we lose the habit of feeling body identified. We feel as experience, what we know in theory...namely: **We are not this body.** We attune with the Divine Will, and gradually identify with That. It is a conscious identification with an irresistible force, moving within us. Our practice is to merge with this Design. As this union progresses, our consciousness connects with the deep, resonant, omnipresent Holy Sound, Om. Its Current provides the will and its harmony effuses love.

As we assume the perfect Asana, this all happens naturally. The will of our Divine Father becomes our own. The love of our Divine Mother completely enwraps our life. Meditation evolves as a microcosm of this Spiritual Union.

When man turns to aggression to produce results in the outer life, he becomes disconnected from love. He actually chooses not to love, because he is still somewhat ignorant. He doesn't understand what he is doing. In that moment he does not recognize his own form. Outer tension is the hand of the false need to own and to accomplish, through the force of selfishness.

Similarly, when he disconnects from the internal force of will, a variety of problems and diseases are there waiting to become his experience. This inner weakness is the reaction to imagining a loss. But the entire design is a perfectly crafted environment for experience, through which we discover our own spiritual nature. The discovery process is not just a mental recognition, although this is a definite part of the purpose of birth. It is a complete integration of understanding and experience on all levels. This understanding then implements our attention, which connects with the unlimited and endless Current of Life Itself...the Holy Spirit. This design is God's Being Manifest.

A crucial part of this is to direct the attention where this design produces spiritual birth...to the spherical medullary Center, the womb wherein this birth takes place. This primal movement is exquisitely profound. This is the Immaculate Conception! Consciousness enters this womb, and only after the attention has dwelt there **totally undistracted**, does the conception take place. All outer functioning ceases. The whole and continuous conscious attention is gathered and placed solely within the Center. When the consciousness is sufficiently ripe to transit time and space completely, functioning of the three bodies ceases as the yogi-devotee is drawn through the Star of the East, into Samadhi. This highly "unbelievable" outer condition is not the significant part, however. What is significant is the completely new Life conceived, born and viewed within.

A tremendous devotion and inner desire to know one's self completely is absolutely required to perform this concentration. The slightest distraction will hold us back. Without complete trust in God's Design and an utterly one pointed will, we shall fail to pass through, fully conscious. Each night, as we pass into sleep, this passage into Spirit takes place, but the consciousness does not enter there. Our yoga practice is to change this. Instead of "falling" asleep, we rise into a visual and resonant awakening. **The subtle mechanism that guides the Current into the Spiritual Womb and permits this Conception to take place is Conscious Attention.**

It serves no purpose at all just to have an opinion whether this is true or false. It serves no purpose to debate this. Opinion and debate belong in the world of the three bodies, which are destined to pass away...fall asleep... without lasting effect. This conception is the way in! This birth is the way out!

To recognize the design is tremendously important... but to integrate that design in the outward expression of our life is very difficult. It can be quite trying. Let us begin to envision a way to do this, by looking at the relationship of a man and a woman. It is a metaphor for the spiritual union. It is a physical road map, from which we intuit the path to God. As above, so below.

A man and a woman are two heavenly bodies. There exists in each the natural desire to love and be loved by the other. So each man and each woman, from a very early age, begin searching through life, trying to learn how to acquire this love...to make this love part of his or her experience. And because we begin with the presumption that we are the body, we enter a dance of attraction with another body. Eventually for almost everyone this leads to the mystery of love and sex.

There are two ways of "making love."

1. When a man and a woman become sexually aroused, a "birth" takes place...a conception...a feeling they both share. This arousal takes on a life of its own, as if the child of this magnetic attraction comes alive and experiences

itself as a unique being in time. A tremendous will is aroused. The body becomes filled with it. An unexpected and wondrous ecstasy is felt. Eventually, under ordinary human circumstances, this leads to sexual union.

Our will connects with this intense sensory experience, which dominates our attention. When this sensory stimulation reaches a critical threshold, orgasm occurs and the entire experience suddenly changes. The inner will is totally consumed and in a brief space of time there is only love. The union is completed and the being enters a void, or *bardo* (as the Tibetans call it), and becomes disembodied. Only after some time does the will slowly return.

This series of events repeats itself throughout the sexual lives of the two lovers and has numerous incarnations. This is a life (or lives) transmigrating through form and physical sensation.

2. Now, when a man and a woman, as two heavenly bodies, come into orbit, the magnetism that maintains this orbit is an attraction to Love itself. When these two bodies remain close and allow a steady connecting love to replace the repetition of births and deaths, defining separate lives, the eternal fire of Love is ignited and it permanently surrounds the inner Will. The two physical lives evolve into a steady orbit, and these heavenly bodies experience love and magnetism...unbroken...undisturbed. This loving presence, experienced by each lover, is his own physical form, resonating perfectly with the spiritual Design.

It is important to look deeply into the nature of sex until it is completely understood. In sexual union the three lower chakras...the "animal" centers...are awakened. Earth, water and fire are joined. When a deep love is there, the fourth chakra is also awakened and the attention and energy enter there. It is air-like. Here we experience ourselves (and our partner) as beings beyond the physical limitation of our bodies, and a deep bonding of hearts takes place. It lifts us into a new dimension of life. As we learn to maintain an unbroken absorption in this loving condition, our life is permanently elevated. We feel weightless...as if "walking on air."

In one sense, this is as far as the human sexual journey goes. For some, this may seem to be enough. The individual who recognizes that the spiritual journey is not yet complete moves on within his own being to the higher spiritual Centers. However, there is a remarkable correlation between these two passages.

As above, so below. "Below" is the physical evolution… "Above" is the Spiritual Involution. The physical conception of a child, marked by the willful journey of the sperm through the cervix, into the uterus, uniting with the waiting ovum…and the ascension of consciousness through the spine into the Spherical Center of Spiritual Conception… are remarkably parallel. It is a long, difficult struggle for the tiny, single sperm that will fertilize the egg. It moves with tremendous will and instinct. In a mysterious way it knows what it must do. Science alone cannot adequately describe how it knows this and why it moves with such a complete effort. A deep instinctive desire drives it toward the egg.

The egg remains still…waiting. It contains a whole life's potential, needing only this tiny sperm to penetrate its surface and complete the matrix. At the moment of conception, the fertilized egg surrounds itself with a membrane that ensures that just the one sperm can enter. This fertilization then triggers growth and division, and evolves into a complete human life. The Design requires the combination of the two essential parts…male and female. One without the other is not enough. It must have both. The human form, created by the union of these two essences, is the living matrix wherein Spirit can, first, express itself naturally, and then know itself completely.

Spiritual ascension and union with God, while dwelling within a physical body, involves the awakening of all the Centers and the movement of *Shakti* (the Goddess of Power) through the interior spinal-cerebral channel. Our consciousness focuses upon a clear and distinct Light within the Spiritual Eye and then, through a wondrous and liberating etheric force, is drawn into the exquisite illumination of the Crown Chakra. The movement of sexual function is normally the first sudden awakening of this shakti, even though it is partially exteriorized and, for the most part, outwardly directed. This ecstatic physical experience is a dramatic hint of complete Spiritual Union. This functioning is implanted in the design of life. Within the physical dimension it has a physical effect...within the Spiritual Dimension it has a spiritual effect. The physical experience is a dynamic and mysterious metaphor for our spiritual journey. It is an oracle heralding the path our consciousness will take as it returns to God.

In one sense these two expressions are parallel, but in a more important way they are opposite. Sex is evolution... the outward path of will, entering and enlivening matter. Meditation and the resulting conscious movement is involution...the inward path, where the will, which has become completely infused in matter, makes its conscious return to its Spiritual Source. Love works in both directions. In evolution, it permits the will to pass through its sensory apparatus into matter and create new forms. In involution, love permits this creative Essence to return inward and upward without resistance. Patience is that shepherding quality allowing this involution to carry on to its completion.

With the searchlight turned inward, love and patience reduce the friction to nil, and consciousness slips home naturally...without individual effort. God shall be the doer. God's Will evolved and thus created the Path. His Will shall draw us Home upon the exact same path. This is the "mystery" revealed...pure and simple.

The close correlation of these two experiences, separated only by the veil of physical appearance, offers a tremendous insight into how we may appropriate the essential qualities of human love and strength, and transform our attention into Spiritual Essence. We carefully observe our experience of sensory pleasure and the instinctive, outward path of will, and intuit a *sadhana*, our inner practice, which reverses these effects. Put simply, we allow a loving countenance to envelop, but not impede, the dynamic path of awareness. This becomes our basic nature. It is the form, merging with the Whole Being God Is.

Having discovered the basic design of ourselves as the inner and outer balance of the male and the female energies, we are in a unique position to understand how things become misaligned. Sometimes we forsake the design as a reaction to circumstances either real or imagined. We become hard outside for one of two basic reasons. We have become either offensive or defensive with our life experience vis-à-vis the outside world. We may try to compensate outside for a feeling of weakness within. Our ego attempts to assert itself by employing physical, psychological or mental toughness. This can happen as a sudden burst of emotion, or it can slowly harden our outer experience over a long period of time.

We may create this same imbalance as a reaction to the overall harsh quality of the physical life. We become defensive. The hard exterior then "protects" us from situations for which we have not found a more enlightened solution. Either way, our imbalance is self-created.

Another kind of imbalance occurs when we forsake the inner will. If we feel a kind of hopelessness and a lack of personal power, we may abandon the will altogether and become very soft inside. Instead of recognizing that God's Will is manifested everywhere, at all times, and accepting this in a loving way as our own inner strength, we react as if the dominion of His Will disempowers us. Here we fail to appreciate and accept the design of the dynamic inner will as our own. We then drift on the sea of life. We languish spiritually and abandon the Master within ourselves. Our physical experience moves forth only as a kind of lifeless momentum.

These are just some of the ways of ignoring or defying the innate design. But **know this**... There never can be any real inadequacy. The design is always there. It just appears lost because of inappropriate habit and incomplete consciousness. There is nothing actually missing. There is no way for it to be destroyed.

When we become too hard on the outside or too soft on the inside...if we lose touch with the design...the Asana of Form...human love and support is there to help us consciously reconnect with it. It is a matter of our own development. For some, this personal contact is completely unnecessary. For others, it is tremendously important. And for others, it becomes the outer expression of an inner realization. Each of us can see its purpose only by looking deeply within our Self.

Consider the lively topic of homosexuality for just a moment. If you will look carefully without pre-judgment, it is really not the sexual orientation that is any problem. A problem arises only when a person (man or woman) becomes hard outside, soft inside, or both. It is these misalignments that cause an instinctive negative reaction. Why? Because deep within each person is the knowledge of this primordial design. Within each of us is the understanding, whether conscious or subconscious, that our Divine Form is the aligned union of the male and female.

See if this is not so. How do you feel, for example, when you meet someone who is hard on the outside...totally inflexible? It feels painful and it seems clearly unnecessary.

I shall not elaborate on the great variety of possible misalignments and their causes. However, if we look carefully behind any human facade, we see two things. We see a mistaken identity **and** we see the Holy Spirit. As we focus on the Spirit exclusively, we help to ease the true identity into its form.

My daughter once asked me a very significant question. She was considering the many Indian gurus and masters revered through the centuries, and particularly six gurus of the Self-Realization lineage...Lahiri Mahasaya, Babaji, Jesus, Krishna, Sri Yukteswar and Paramhansa Yogananda. She asked, "Why are all these 'gurus' men?"

First, these six gurus are **not** men. There is only One Body. That Body is the Holy Spirit, which is experienced as the Holy Sound, Divine Light and Cosmic Vibration. That One Body is omnipresent.

Any human witnessing of the One Body may materially be of a man or a woman. This is just the physical appearance. It is not the Body! There is only One Body. That Body is neither female nor male. It contains both.

But our earth is a place where ignorance abounds. And ignorance is any experience of separate existence. One nuance of that ignorance is prejudice. When a witness to the One Body happens within a man, a male, a great silence surrounds him. That silence is unexpected. "Men act, women watch" is the ongoing prejudice of viewpoint. So, that silence is recognized. It is seen as unexpected, unusual. It is noticed.

When a woman is a witness to the One Body, that same great silence surrounds her. But for women, silence is expected. That is part of the prejudice. The Self-Realization goes unnoticed. A tremendous will resides within, but the human perspective notices the outer much more than the inner. The quiet is easily perceived…the deep inner strength and maturity can easily be overlooked.

This earth dwells in other kinds of prejudices as well. When a "young" witness experiences the One Body, he is not recognized. The "old" cannot accept the "young" as realized, because it admits to his own slow development. Hence there is denial. But the One Body has no age at all. It is ever new.

We have not incarnated for the purpose that we be recognized as individuals. We are witnessing separately in order to realize God from all perspectives. When this earth loses its prejudice, it will recognize all women and all men of all ages…indeed all Life…as the One Body of God. For now it is our effort to:

Merge with this Design … Return to the endless Light.

CHANGE &
THE CHANGELESS

A few days ago, my youngest daughter, Lily, asked me to join with her in a game. She is an exquisite child with a bubbly enthusiasm. Like many children, she loves games, but does not take them seriously. (Adults might be better served to play like this!)

She was in the back seat of our car as we were driving home from another city. She began to ask me questions about my choices in life. This was the game. The first question was, "If you could choose again, who would you marry? You must give me three names."

My wife, Holly, was sitting right beside me, so I felt challenged to be careful with my response. "May I pick Holly?" I asked.

"Sure...anyone...but you must make three choices," she replied.

The game wasn't going anywhere until I came up with my first set of answers...so I chose Holly, another woman, who lives nearby, and the actress, Meryl Streep.

Lily then asked, "How much money do you want to have?" Again I had to respond with three choices.

Then... "Where do you want to live? At what time in history do you choose to live?"...and so on.

As I gave my answers, she was recording them in a random grouping of 4 possible life scenarios...the three choices I offered, and one more that she whimsically added to each response.

Finally, after recording all my answers, she asked me to call out, "Stop," whenever I wanted. All the while she was

Jaia (the author's son)

Lily (the author's daughter)

swinging her finger back and forth over the four groups of choices. I spoke up, "Stop!" My die was cast. She now delighted in describing my new "life."

As it turned out, I would be married to a very unpleasant woman (Lily's addition), and I was obliged to live in Death Valley in the 14th century. Fortunately, however, I did have ten million dollars to make life easier.

I laughed and said, "Maybe I could give my new wife nine million and then move to Colorado... Alone!"

At this point, Holly said she had also played the game and wound up married to the Dalai Lama. "Nice choice," I thought.

As we drove on into the night, I began to imagine how this life might be, if I were with another partner. "Things" would obviously be quite different. I began to review the changes of my own perception over the past twenty years that Holly and I had been together. Three images struck me.

First: Our personalities and our day to day experiences had evolved considerably over this time. Our life views had each slowly drifted towards that of the other...like two ships on a sea, gradually adjusting their headings, so that they might sail together, side by side.

Second: The greatest and most endearing change in our experiential lives had come during the past five years, as meditation had become the single most dominant activity for both of us. Meditation had expanded our enjoyment of the details of life and released us from the "seriousness" of trifling matters. It had also liberated us from many earlier, disabling patterns of relating. In their place was a deep and abiding affection for each other.

Third: This last image, in a curious way, seemed to contradict the other two... namely... **That which we are in Reality had not changed in the slightest.** While our viewpoint may undergo considerable variation, our Real Self is completely immutable. A key to experiencing Bliss is to enjoy this realization, independent of any prevailing "situation."

When we first board a ship and sail out on a rolling sea, the way in which we must balance changes. We become softer in the knees, to allow for the swaying of the very floor below our feet. The sea rolls, the ship rolls with it and we must roll with the ship. The entire environment in which we have placed our body is constantly moving, swaying. We may try to steady our body. We may try to stand firm, but this will not work. We may even fall down. And while we are lying there defiantly upon the deck, our body will continue to roll.

When we disembark from this ship, for a time we continue to sway and roll as if we were still on the water. The earth itself seems to move.

When we look closely at the use of the term, *Sea*...as in "the Cosmic Sea," the entire universe of our Being...it becomes remarkably clear why this is such an appropriate and beautiful metaphor. Our entire environment is forever changing, vibrating, breathing. We must constantly make adjustments in every single thing we think and do in order to accommodate to the current circumstances. When the world is upside-down, we must stand on our heads to be right-side up!

The challenge of life, indeed the actual purpose or design of life, is to consciously evolve the way we respond to the movement, the variety and the uncertainty of the Sea. We must pay attention and we must become **involved**.

"Things" change. Every single material thing is changing right now. Our bodies are constantly changing. Even the thoughts that we hold as dear are changing somewhat.

If we look at but a few of the outstanding icons, events and popular themes of Western civilization over the past fifty years, we can see a variety of shifting images. This flux on the surface of our experience can be unsettling, even bewildering. For example:

The end of World War II brought on a general feeling of optimism. Collectively, we began to think that we might be able to experience peaceful coexistence and cooperation.

The United Nations was formed to help guide our planetary evolution with reason and compassion.

But in the late 1950's the United States and the Soviet
Union began to compete fiercely for superiority in nuclear
weapons and space exploration, creating a persistent threat
to everyone and everything on our shrinking home planet.

In the mid to late 1960's, a renewed enthusiasm of an
emerging generation was expressed very simply through
song...and notably by the Beatles when they voiced the
phrase, "All you need is love!" It was easy to believe
this...because **it is True**. We all know this is true...and yet
we often fail to stay with it consistently.

Some years later, the movie, *Wall Street*, issued the dark,
contradictory image that perhaps, "Greed is good." The
mind can make the dark seem light...and the light seem
dark. Truth found only in the mind can easily become
twisted through self-interest.

The reunification of Germany and the subsequent,
partial democratization and break up of the Soviet Union
dissolved some strategic alliances and created a more
localized, though uncertain array of others. The only
apparent constant in the world of politics seems to be that
nothing stays the same.

The most significant acceleration of outward human
change over the last half century, and quite possibly
throughout our planetary history, has come through the
proliferation of a network of instantaneous communication
via computers and the world wide web. The specific things
we do and the way we do them is being transfigured at a
pace unknown in the history of our planet. Communication now interconnects vast numbers of us almost instantaneously. But, for what purpose? What are we communi-
cating? What do we have to share with each other?

In the face of all this "change," we might wonder,
"What is Changeless?" And more to the point, "Who are
we?"

The current, obvious trend in movie making is toward
"virtual reality." Movie makers will eventually involve all
the senses to increase our viewing participation. They will

synthesize smell, taste and then touch, perhaps by strapping electrodes to the brain, or perhaps by creating holographic images that carry "information" relevant to each of our sense organs. Our viewing experience will seem more and more like the "real thing."

But this virtual reality has already been created. We experience it every day. It is called **Life**. Life as we know it now is not the "real thing" we think it is.

Life as we know it is a virtual reality.

How are we to discover that this statement is true? The only way to know if this "reality" is only "virtual" and not actually real is to stop participating long enough to remember how and when we came into the "theater." When this happens, we understand exactly what Shakespeare meant when he wrote, "All the world is a stage..."

For the average person the ego stubbornly binds experience to the incarnated dimension. Ego is the persistent thought-form that, "I am the body." Thus there is a constant uncontrollable need to respond, preempting bliss and the pure witnessing of our eternal vibrant Being. The original design is thus obscured. The yang, centrifugal aspect becomes assertiveness. The yin, centripetal aspect becomes withdrawal.

The fundamental way to dispel the ego of its false attachment is to recognize with utter clarity that this physical life is a virtual reality. It is a complete and accurate metaphor...an outward **expression** of the Real Thing. The metaphor decoded is that the outward changes form a constant proof that the inner Life is **ever new**.

All Master Souls keep pointing out the same basic premise: Do not attach your self to the outward appearance. The *Bhagavad Gita* iterates over and over again, "Don't become attached to the fruits of karmic existence. Awaken to the Life within."

Yet, from time to time, we think that it is significant to meet or hang out with well-known personalities. We even seek to become one of "them" ourselves. This desire is now deeply imbedded in Western civilization. We seek recognition in the eyes of others, as if this will somehow make us more real.

Those who reach the "top" often find life more fragile than before. Now they must maintain their perch. Deep within themselves they know that this perch is completely meaningless, and yet they can hardly admit it, even to themselves. This kind of vicarious living is appealing, because we persist in the false assumption that we have become something, and can thereby cease the struggle to become.

When we live vicariously, we stay on the periphery of life. We even want to hang out with spiritual personalities, in part to avoid the actual centering required to make our own passage to God...to know and experience directly what is Real. We are reluctant to allow the imaginary to pass away. Thus our experience is a paradise lost...lost in ignorance and misdirected attention.

The desire to achieve the outer, transitory quality of fame and recognition may have replaced the deeply implanted inner need for Self-Realization and Bliss, independent of circumstance. But even this is OK. We need only redirect that desire and attention to a new place, in a new way. We can use that struggle to enter the Path. At least we have overcome lethargy in the process. Now a refining process must begin.

We are also victims of our own habits. To cope with the challenge of life, we begin from the moment we are born to develop ways of automatically responding to certain conditions. The overwhelming number of choices available at every moment in time requires that some things we do become automatic. Early on, these habits begin to seem natural to us. They may seem so, but for the most part they are not. When we look closely at the myriad responses possible in every situation, the predicament of life becomes clear. There are too many possible choices at every moment for a finite being to be in control. It is impossible.

We develop a style of walking, standing, sitting, running, moving our limbs, our torso, our facial muscles and so on. The minutia of possibilities of operating all of our bones, muscles and organs is mind boggling. To accomplish it all, we develop habits. Each habit has its own definition of style and meaning...a kind of genetic code, the sum total of which is recognizable as unique to each individual. We form these habits, not only in our bodily movements, but also in the way we respond mentally and emotionally to the various stimuli contained within the Sea.

All of this is so obvious that it would hardly be worth mentioning were it not for the fact that we are actually capable of changing these patterns of habitual response at any time we choose. We are capable of becoming more Conscious and less a victim of the habits we have already developed. These habits were formed before we fully realized the importance of creating and responding in ways that are beautiful, loving, intelligent, harmonious, wise, humorous, peaceful and kind. **These more evolved responses precipitate Bliss.** Anyone can feel this. Anyone can know this.

We literally can recreate our style at any moment. However, to many the thought of doing this almost never arises, and when it does, it is forgotten quickly. For others the task of such a change is too daunting.

But a few understand the importance of recreating themselves. I trust that you, in fact, are among them by virtue of having this book in your hands. You are looking for a new mode of being...an expression of self that is more in tune with the Cosmic Design.

There are two somewhat complementary ways of proceeding. You can go about changing the particulars of the personality and its habit patterns, to draw it in tune with the Ideal as you perceive it...a kind of step by step approach toward perfection. This is the linear approach. You see yourself at point A and change or move yourself along to point B. The other approach is to trust in God's Design, and set out to see if that perfection is already a fact of your own Being. The only change that you "plan" to make is your **understanding** of what is. Any outer change that follows will do so as a natural result of what you discover to be real. This approach is called **Self-Realization**.

In the case of the former, you set out to change your habits one by one, using some set of intelligent suggestions. These suggestions may originate as someone else's ideas or your own. The key activating mechanism is that you will get the suggestion and act upon it. You are going to eat less, or eat better. You are going to watch your manners and watch your mouth. You are going to be kinder, gentler, neater, cleaner, stronger, more graceful, and so on. You may even break it down into just the way you hold your hands, your head, your feet, your eyes, and so forth. Or, possibly, you may decide to renovate your everyday way of looking at things, your ideas, your vocabulary... piece by piece. You will make new friends, do new things and go to new places. Essentially you plan to give yourself a complete "make-over" in thought, word, feeling and action. You are going to proceed toward the goal by adjusting your movement...changing your style...finding a new tuning, a new tone, a new song.

There is no problem with this approach. Time is infinite, after all. There is enough time to adjust and improve everything. There are enough lifetimes. You can recreate yourself endlessly until you finally get it right. This is, in fact, what we have been doing since time began. Let's look at some of the possible ways we might apply this technique.

To begin, choose one thing to change...just one. To attempt to completely change your entire persona in an instant is too much. Get yourself clear on just one thing... and you **begin** to clear up everything. So begin with one thing, and **get it right**!

The choice is yours. Make this choice now. Stop reading right now, until you arrive at the one thing you will change...the one kind of doing that you will do differently from now on. **Choose it now**! Write it down. Make the choice absolutely clear to your mind! Know exactly what the plan is, and begin to imagine all the ways in which this change will take place.

If you choose to read on, rather than to begin some activation of change right now, then at least recognize the kind of change I am suggesting. This kind of change requires a definite **plan** and a continuity of remembering that applies some kind of consistently different quality to your future experience and self-expression, based upon that plan.

Now, to adopt or apply the alternate, though completely complementary, plan for re-creation of our self, called *Self-Realization*, we must seek some definite understanding of what is happening here and now. In fact, we must begin with the clearest picture possible of What This Is.

I will offer one suggestion...one linear thing to do that may have a great impact upon your Self-Realization: Whenever you meditate, have a pen and paper just next to you. At the point your meditation is over, immediately write down what you are experiencing, imagining or thinking. Try to maintain the meditative quality of your experience as you write. Allow yourself to coast in the harmonic condition. **Discover the Truth in Harmony.**

If you adopt this suggestion, you will probably experience both an upside and a downside in this. The downside is that this practice of writing down your immediate impressions may cause you to think and store thoughts during your meditation in order to write them down later. You may begin to use meditation as a vicarious way of obtaining interesting ideas. Thought, itself, is a tremendous hurdle to overcome in meditation. This new practice may make the hurdle seem higher, or at least more clear and precise.

The upside to this is that you are now beginning to use your conscious constructive mind to seek out the most subtle and significant thoughts that are available to you. If you persist in this writing, almost surely a **plan** will begin to take shape.

It will be difficult to exercise this plan continuously, because your life experience passes through a vast number of distinct shades of sensitivity, from the exquisitely fine to the positively crude. The plan will seem to apply only in the finest region. Even if the general plan is for you to con-tinuously reside in the subtle sensitive realm and to elimi-nate the crude elements of your experience, the plan will have a hard time penetrating there. However, if you perse-vere in this practice and allow the plan to reach into your entire life experience...into the sleeping hours as well as the waking hours...into the physical, the mental and the emotional realms...into every mode of experience and every level of sensitivity...something quite significant **will happen**. Some Constant that you have discovered will begin to enter your life experience. Some control will assert itself. The Master will begin to guide your life. That which is Changeless will make itself known.

One word of caution... Do not allow the downside to dominate this practice. Do not become attached to this writing in such a way that it alone drives your meditation. Meditate for the sheer joy of it. Don't allow meditation... the single most important tool of evolution and involu-tion...to become a new cog in the wheel of life. Meditation is not a cog. **It is the Motionless Center**.

Now, after you have practiced this writing for a week, a month, a year, a decade...however long it is necessary to access the plan...then reverse the pattern. Instead of using meditation to access the plan, allow the Master of the Plan to guide your meditation. Write your impressions **before** you meditate. **Discover the Harmony in Truth.** Allow your finest ideas and feelings to precede you into the Cosmic Sea. Take the path of involution rather than evolu-tion. Seek the Center with your whole attention and leave the ideas behind you!

Consider this: All life, all things of the manifested world are in motion. That very movement has the quality of vibration, the quality of sound and the quality of light. It is a vibration of back and forth...coming and going...birth-ing and dying...breathing in and breathing out. All seems to be in motion. Everything is energy. But the Whole Thing is absolutely motionless. God is completely Still. To be in all places at once **means** to be completely still. To hear the

Whole Sound, we must be completely silent. To be "in the light," we must become transparent.

When Jesus said, "It is more difficult for a rich man to enter the kingdom of heaven, than for a camel to pass through the eye of a needle," He was referring to the Eye of Stillness...the unmoving, calm, motionless Center of conscious awareness.

The breath rises and falls, fills and empties about this Center. The mighty Cosmic Motor, this Music of the Spheres, issues everywhere as a majestic, symphonic Presence surrounding the Center of Stillness. It draws the infinite outer consciousness into a homeostatic harmonic balance. It calls our focus into the Eye of Superconsciousness...wherein we merge with the omnipresent stillness of the Whole Being God Is.

Each breath calls us home. Each outer sound is the reminder of the symphonic entry into the motionless Home.

The path to God is our appropriate response to the total outward manifestation. The path is centripetal. It is a conscious reawakening in the Center with a new and full understanding of the Whole. The path is the merging, arriving as witness, rejoicing in the stillness, basking in the complete Resonance.

The restlessness that is felt is the mistaken notion that our identity must remain in motion...that to remain alive, to hold on to that life, we must dwell eternally in the outer movement. Death is feared as the utter cessation of that conscious movement.

For the ego to survive, it must continue to move. Its very identity lies in the world of opposites. It is known by what it is not. It has its life, meager as it is, by being separate from something else...everything else. Its basic fear is Omnipresence...the One Wholeness. Thus it keeps moving. It keeps renewing its self-image. It keeps adapting. It even retreats from the Holy Sound. It retreats from love. It retreats from bliss. It retreats from every reminder of the One Whole Being.

If you will recall, in an earlier chapter we found Nan-in, the tea master, overfilling his guest's cup to dramatize the need to become empty. But, if we empty ourselves, what will rush in to fill us up? How will we change? Can we even know ahead of time what might happen if we practice such a technique? To change ourselves in this way requires great will, great effort and great faith. In a way, all we can know or even suspect at the beginning is that if we empty ourselves completely and maintain a vigilance in ignoring the false and the temporary, we will either remain empty, or we will be filled with the Real and the Changeless.

Ask the question, "What is Changeless?" It is tremendously significant for the soul to discover even one small thing that does not change, one constant. Your intuition will tell you that there is but one sure way of discovering the Changeless. You must become **still**. You must stop identifying with the changing part of yourself and merge with That which does not change.

It is not that this shell or "Wheel of Life" actually moves or spins, but rather, our consciousness moves out from the Center to individual points all over the wheel…thus life appears to move. This movement, this *Maya*, this entering into time, is the illusory quality of change. God allows His consciousness to enter this wheel as ourselves in order to experience some thing other than His own Oneness. His Oneness cannot be known in any other way. When He "tires" of this activity, He "retires" to the primordial Center.

After we have become still, we can then enter a complete **silence**.

There is a symphony of Sound, which you can hear, that has a changeless quality…a ceaseless, steady, harmonic Sound that you can hear from your Center. It is the complete energetic field that issues the manifested world. To hear this Sound is to under-stand the world of creation…to stand under it. To enter this condition of hearing is to approach God. From this Center each thought will appear as the still small voice, directing you ever closer to the

Father who is calling to you. The qualities that define your own individual personality, namely your own thoughts, must remain outside this Center...upon the outer shell. As you remain focused within this Center, you lose all sense of identification with the personality itself. You cannot hold on to your self-image. It will not pass through this Eye. Even one thought will not pass through. You can take nothing there but your Consciousness...your unqualified joy...your love. This open, blissful quality ushers you across the Cosmic Threshold.

We are always collecting, storing, saving. There is no problem in this. To some extent we must do this to survive. We must prepare for eventualities. Hunger will come, weather will befall us, summer shall give way to autumn...and then winter. All of this preparation is for body maintenance. Most of this appears essential. It is also completely temporary. Upon our physical death, it is all completely irrelevant.

Passage through the inner Eye, into the realm of Spirit, requires the "death" of the physical connection. Paul said, "I die daily." To enter meditation is to leave it all behind. To enter meditation is to become utterly silent, and the loudest, most persistent part of our self is **thought**. It is incessant...so much so that the Holy Sound, Om, is almost never heard. It has been drowned out. Activity and thought have erased the memory of its very existence.

There is no one on this earthly plane who can give this memory back to you. **You must silence yourself.** Others may give you pause, briefly, but the Silence is there only for those who seek it with great tenacity on their own.

As we persevere with our effort to attain a personal silence in meditation, we become surrounded by the Holy Sound, Om. Om gradually becomes the whole environment of our experience. Our identity then merges with this Current of Sound.

There are three primary qualities of the Holy Sound, Om, which can be known and experienced as we consciously merge with it. These are: Force, Intelligence and Love. These are not really separate qualities. They are more like the three, so-called primary colors. Each one gradually blends into the other, forming the entire spectrum of visible light. And, just like light, as each of these qualities blends with another one, the pair form another quality (or hue). This color analogy can prove useful in understanding the qualities of Om.

Suppose we assign each of these three primary qualities a corresponding primary color. Imagine force to be red, love to be green, and intelligence to be blue. When red light is combined with green light, the resulting color of light is yellow.[1] Analogously, when we combine the force and love experienced within the Sound, Om, we experience a transforming **fire** that burns the karmic seeds of our physical existence.

When we combine red light with blue light, we get magenta. Likewise, when we combine force and intelligence, we experience the divine organizational **matrix**. Spirit is thus able to create any form required for a particular manifestation, for any particular experiential need.

When we combine blue light with green light, we get cyan. When intelligence and love are combined, we experience a calm effortless **bliss**. All struggle ends. The spiritual plan is understood.

Finally, when all three primary colors of light are combined, we get pure white light. The complete assimilation of the qualities of force, love and intelligence dissolves all inner crystallization of matter and sets the Soul free to experience Spirit as itself.

---

[1] Here we are referring to the additive quality of light, rather than the subtractive quality of pigments. When we combine the pigment red with the pigment green, we get a pigment darker than either of the two original ones. When we combine these two lights, we get yellow. Unequal proportions of two or three primary colors create other colors as well. For example, when we combine certain unequal proportions of red and green light, we get orange. Most importantly, however, when we combine all the colors of the visible light spectrum we have an additive process which produces white light.

Once Om has silenced the "thinking man," its force begins to be felt as a deep inner resonance...a **vibration**... which breaks down the crystallization of matter as we normally experience it in the physical life dimension. An overall awakening shakes the body to its core, only... **There is no physical core in Reality!** Solid becomes liquid, liquid becomes vapor, and vapor becomes etheric light itself. This vibratory awakening redistributes our consciousness, and we dis-cover the Light Body...our Essence.

We are now prepared for the final step. The attachment to matter dissolves and we enter the world of Light. We become **transparent**. The Soul, that entered its prison of form, slips through the bars of its confinement and rediscovers itself as the primordial Spirit. The very life of that Soul is sustained utterly through the divine and eternal Presence of our Father, who is essentially unknowable in any other way than direct experience. All conceptualizations fail to adequately describe His quality.

This is the exquisite changeless condition that preexists all individual personality. It extends beyond the perceptions of time and space. Put simply... It is our Being. It is precisely **who we are**.

THE CALL

The very Thing that we are...
That which we have always been...
That which we will always be...
That which we cannot destroy...
That in which there lies no harm...
That, as Bliss, is Life Itself...
Unborn!

That Consciousness, though omnipresent, enters form to have specific local experiences. To understand the Whole, it visits a part. Because of that visitation, the Consciousness temporarily begins to think it is that form, itself. It imagines a local identification.

God, the unidentified, unembodied, formless Consciousness, recognizes this mistaken identity. So He issues a call for us to awaken...to disengage from form...to remember that we are pure Consciousness without form. This call is the issuing of a dual breath...into form–out of form. That which we analyze as death is not a death. It is the remembrance that we are unborn.

Paul said, "I die daily." This was well said. But Paul returns for an update, "I am unborn daily." The knot is untied. No thing remains. Glory be the unborn Son in God.

Yeah, though I walk through the valley of the **shadow** of death, I am always **unborn**. In all ways there is no birth. Breath issues as the call to dis-cover the unborn nature through the exit of form experience.

**Om is the unborn Sound of the Whole Being God Is…
into and from which the embodied Soul breathes.**

You are that Light
    Who wedded form
        and went to sleep
    Who dreamed in limits
        and postulated ends
    Who felt an edge
        and imagined a retreat
    Who collapsed in hunger
        and assumed He was dying
    Who battled demons of smoke
        and devils of vapor
        as if they could extinguish a Life
Who now sees the star Himself
        and the flower Herself
In transit
    from night …
      … to Morning!

Maya

Consider this question. Try to answer it honestly before reading on. Does the following more or less describe who we are and how we must proceed?

"I am a vessel, created by God. My purpose, my spiritual effort, is to allow God to flow into every part of myself. In this way I am raised into Him."

Before continuing on, read these three sentences again and consider them deeply. Is this the way you understand yourself?

The truth is that we are **not a vessel at all**. This idea that we are a vessel is the root cause of our suffering. We are not that which contains the Spirit. We are not a container of any kind.

We are the Spirit Itself!

We are Spirit. We have always been Spirit. We shall always be Spirit.

Through birth, we entered a field of delusion known as *Maya*, a disguise. We actually began to think, as we were taught, that we are the limited body that we entered. We entered this form with little or no conscious memory, but rather a manner of consciousness that has evolved as our own distinct pattern of habits, inclinations and tendencies. We became somewhat more deluded, by absorbing some of the assumptions and tendencies of those around us, caught up in their own delusive processes.

These others, too, are Spirit. But in this density there is great delusion. It reigns almost exclusively, even in the waking hours.

For whom is this not true?

What are we to do?

We must learn to **be** ourselves...Spirit. We must consciously discover this Truth and learn how to operate creatively within matter, throughout matter and...

INDEPENDENT OF MATTER!

To learn this we must study life in a deep way. We must be patient with our apparent slow progress...and we must **meditate!**

Adepts of *Jnana Yoga* (the path of wisdom) have delineated a chain of the twenty-four elements of the downward evolution of Spirit, into the delusive Mother-Nature of matter. It might be well to look briefly at these: 1) the Creative Power of God, 2) the Intelligence of the Design, 3) the ego, 4) the mind, 5–9) the five manifesting senses of perception (seeing, hearing, touching, tasting, and smelling), 10–14) the mental instrumentation of five bodily activities (procreation, excretion, talking, walking, and manual dexterity), 15–19) the five divisions of vibration, experienced as earth, water, fire, air, and ether, and 20–24) the active, somewhat automatic forces within the body that produce circulation, crystallization, assimilation, metabolism and elimination.

Chapter four in *The Revelation To John* (the last book of the Bible) relates directly to this Wisdom Yoga. It is a description of John's absorption into the Spirit, and the vision given to him regarding the **form** of matter. It reads:

1 ... I looked, and behold, a door to heaven was opened to me. The first Voice that I heard was a trumpet, which said, "Come home to Spirit... I will show you the nature of this life."

2 At once I was in Spirit, and there stood a throne, and One sat on the throne.

3 The One on the throne was bathed in pure Light
  like that of precious stones.
4 Around the throne were twenty-four thrones,
  each with one elder sitting on it and wearing
  white robes with golden crowns upon their
  heads.

John goes on to say that these "elders," having risen into
Spirit Consciousness, recognize their existence...their
manifestation in life...is completely due to the Creative
Force of God. Maya is thus seen as Lila, the dance that God
has formed to play.

The point here is not to create an elaborate philosophy
by which we can analyze the minutia of physical activity,
but rather to get an overview of the manifesting activities
of the matter-form of our incarnation. This is the **activity**
that proceeds all the time we inhabit the human form.
These are the elements of our identification. These are the
"things" that have made it possible for us to assume that
we are some "thing" of substance. **We have become
mesmerized by this relentless hypnotic activity.**

As we set out on our meditative discovery, we try to
understand just how we have identified with these qualities. A tremendous release comes as we recognize the ways
that an individualized Spirit (the Soul) has accepted each
of these elements as an identity...a false identity. Then we
slowly extract our self-identification from them. The one
doing this extraction is our Self...an exact microcosmic
duplication of God.

How are we to accomplish this extraction? ...By understanding the mistakes of our attention, and then turning it
steadfastly upon the Real. We can do this by meditating
upon Om, the primordial, eternal vibration of Spirit.

The intelligence of this yoga is this: The Essence of the
Cosmic Sound, Om, is the experience of the Soul as it exits
the unreal formulations of the three worlds of Maya, and
enters the ecstatic real existence that God Is. By choice and
the conscious renunciation of unconscious tendencies, we
begin to make this experiential transition. Things are not

what they have appeared to be. They remain as they were, however…once unknown…but now understood. This understanding is the basis of the path of Yoga. It is beyond the three worlds and quite Real.

Imagine being completely tied up with a rope. The knots are tight and thoroughly binding. After a long struggle, the knots are slowly loosened and one by one we untie them. Finally we are freed of the rope and we stand there holding it. Then the rope itself dissolves. The molecules of physical existence are rearranged and the matter of the rope simply evaporates. A realization comes that the rope was never actually real in Essence. It was an appearance! Matter itself is real, but the appearances it takes as form, and our interpretations and identifications with the form, mesmerize our attention. This is Maya. It is temporary and unreal in Essence.

An intelligence is dawning that understands the universe of matter to be just like this. It **is** like this! The prison has not been real…just imagined, and perpetuated by a basic assumption. The assumption was formed through lives of sense activity, resulting in thoughts regarding our "situation." Having dissolved the assumption, an inner preexisting freedom is recognized.

The gathering of matter into particular designs has no meaning in and of itself. However, the Intelligence, Love and Power cause matter to evolve in particular revealing patterns, initiated by our deep desire to experience our Self and to know it completely. The involution through a physical "reality" allows us to experience a completely irrefutable understanding, which serves to demonstrate our Self as a witness in joy. **The primordial purpose of creation is not "to accomplish," but rather "to know" and thereby experience endless Bliss.** Utter knowing does not begin until the false evolution of the activity of accomplishing completely dies out.

We are Conscious Energy, experiencing within a vessel. We are involving our attention in order to experience omnipresence. This can only happen when we drop even the idea of a separate consciousness and understand we

are the Ocean itself. This false perception is deeply imbedded in man's way of perceiving all things. We see events
and other people not as they are, but as they seem to stand
in relation to our self.

A fish knows little or nothing about water. He has no
reference. It is the only environment he has ever experienced. However, in the beginning there was just the
Ocean. Forms emerged within the Ocean...perhaps as a
whim, as Meher Baba has suggested. The Ocean then
began to think of itself as the fishes, and then as a particular fish. Now, as long as the Ocean sees itself as a part
(apart) of its entirety, it fails in consciousness, but not in
Reality, to be itself. There is and can be no failing in
Reality.

The individual is "initiated"...started upon the path of
observing that which is Real...when he discovers, or is
shown, a manner of **conscious attention** that directs his
focus continuously upon the eternal Reality. The Ocean,
which is always vibrating, emits a particular Sound. This
Sound is Om. The way into our Self and the way out of the
delusion is to consciously merge with Om...to recognize
without any doubt that we **are** the Vibrancy. We are Spirit!

We are more than just this Spirit as vibration, but this is
the first aspect of our three-part nature that we discover.

Ego is the imagination that the non-separate Whole has
a real division. We are not separate beings experiencing
God, but rather God has imagined parts in order to play-
fully view the Whole of Himself.

Ego is not a noun. It is not a real thing. It is a verb. It is a
way of viewing the Whole Thing separately, when in fact it
was never separate, is not separate and can never be
separate.

Intuitively our mind perceives the death of ego as immi-
nent, but it does not know the full import of this. It then
projects this impending inner passage in outward terms,
according to its acquired habits and thoughts. It imagines
that it might "die" alone, and thus invents ideas to soothe
or negate its imagined situation. Ironically it reinvents
itself in a false manner at the same time. It assembles the

physical appearance of cataclysm in assorted forms. Yet the only real "cataclysm" is actually the ecstatic entrance into Cosmic Consciousness.

Often we profess and cling to ideas and outward events, which become substitutes for the actual individual involution of spiritual consciousness...the inner conception and birth. We look to the outer world for events, in order to experience Spirit vicariously. Sex is not the only such event. People interpret unusual weather, earth changes, the siting of space ships, earth "vortexes," catastrophes and possible Armageddon (to mention only a few) as signs of a great outer conclusion, to substitute for a fundamental inner conclusion, not yet experienced. Our lack of patience manifests as an insistent urge to point to or execute a completion outside, while the inner completion has not yet been made.

Buddha said, "Birth is pain. Death is pain." And everything in between is pain. It's a jungle out there...literally. Slowly we begin to recognize this truth. Slowly we begin to find and travel upon this inner path. The outer temple serves no lasting purpose until the inner way is seen. Then the purpose of our birth is known. The gate is removed. The way in becomes wide and clear. As we stop asserting and resisting, the union commences.

But human cosmological thinking and planning, on the whole, is woefully inconsistent. In one minute we may agree with the premise expressed earlier..."We are Spirit" ...then in the next breath we are back in the ego. Someone "else" has hurt us... We don't have enough money... We "like" this, but not that. The options and the opinions go on and on. We experience a taste of our original Being and then become mesmerized again.

Maya is **deeply rooted** in our conscious way of experiencing. Yoga is the manner of deep, consistent, inner attention that allows us to remove the roots of Maya and secure our focus continuously upon the Real.

We anguish with the breaks in our conscious connection with God. We long for a continuity of grace. An inner helplessness is surely felt. We sense that we are incapable of making this transition using only the force of our own mind. We become acutely aware that we need help. **The deep and fervent need to discover and remain in the Real projects spontaneous mantra or prayer into our mind.** This is the condition that immediately preexists and prepares us for **devotion**.

We have made a great effort and repeatedly have failed, or at least we have fallen short. We begin to sense that the hurdle of our ego and its persistent outward focus is too much for us. A profound humility enters naturally. It is an honest acknowledgment of our seemingly perpetual, imprisoned condition.

Now there is a ripeness...a coming to fruition. Essentially we vacillate between two kinds of prayer:

1. Inner assertion: For example... *"Stillness, Silence, Transparency... Stillness, Silence, Transparency..."* repeated over and over...a mantra...a command. We claim our very Essence through mental assertion.
2. Prayerful acknowledgment of the limited power of mind itself: For example... "Lord, I am not worthy that Thou should come under my roof. Speak but the Word and my soul shall be healed."

These two blended conditions preexist Grace. God and/or Guru step into the attention **now**...and **only now**...for two fundamental reasons. **Now**...because we have asked with our complete attention, sincerely and with utter humility. **Only now**...because we have been given the freedom to experience that which we choose. That freedom is an endless reality. It is never abridged. Freedom requires that our entrance into Spirit Consciousness be of our own choosing. The reunion of Father and Son is the choice of the Son, not the insistence of the Father. The rebellion ends. There is a peaceful resolution...and the peace is lasting.

When the Guru, our loving brother, hears the inner cry of the one calling to be released from his self-asserted path of confinement and suffering...when that cry for help is not just a plaintiff wail, but the deep, undeniable Inner Voice of God, willing that the Truth manifest...and when this Voice is the only voice that can be heard...the Guru appears. His face is the doorway to a kingdom not of this world, but a home of endless joy. Maya, then, is seen as a dance. The music played...the dervish whirled. Now, utter Silence ushers in the Sound, and then the Light.

The rebellion began in the individualized mind, and that is where it ends. It ceases through understanding. It subsides in Bliss. The restless waves upon the Ocean lose their strength. Gradually a calm is felt across the surface and throughout its entirety. The whole energy remains contained within stillness.

In our meditations two qualities of our attention are significant: **depth** and **continuity**. Go deeper and deeper into the Medullary Center. Visualize this Center to be the womb of our birth into complete Spirit Consciousness. Exit this life, which is death, and enter the death, which is Life. A cord of imagination binds us to a life of sensory delusion. Cut this umbilical cord. Enter the womb. This is not a rebirth. We are not returning to a previous condition. We are entering an utterly new condition...a Life from which no birth will be required...total awakening into the state of real Being...Superconsciousness...complete Self-recognition and its unobstructed Vibration.

The effort involved with entering this spiritual womb, and remaining completely inside, tests our endurance. It tests our sincerity. It tests our will. Be prepared to give totally, without looking back. And take Heart! You have nothing to lose but your chains.

DEVOTION

The greatest truth is seen through the eyes of devotion. When we place ourselves first in the order of things, we fail to perceive it...for we have no eyes in the back of our head.

We are all devoted to something. In the West we are primarily devoted to ourselves, i.e., our perceived persona, possessions, level of convenience, wealth, status and so forth. It is so commonplace, that it normally goes unnoticed. In a somewhat extreme case, we recognize a person who is "egocentric" or "self-centered," but we barely notice that almost everyone is more or less like that. We even have an expression for this... "We are looking out for number one." This is taken for granted. It is basically accepted. This attitude is the driving force of our capitalistic economy.

And...we teach this to our children.

Deep within, however, we can know that this is ridiculous. The human life is tenuous and short. The physical entity formed by that life is extinguished at death. Only the underlying, interpenetrating spiritual Identity passes through the doorway. Nonetheless we remain self-indulgent, and we have made a tremendous effort to develop the skill of masking this devotion to ourselves.

The deep significance of this self-devotion somehow had escaped me until I visited India in 1971. When I stepped off the plane in Calcutta, I knew I had entered a completely foreign place...not just foreign, as in a different country, but more like another planet...a planet where most people are not devoted to themselves, but rather to something quite different.

The eyes are the "windows of the soul." Everywhere I looked, these eyes of India were different from those of the West. These eyes, whether of seemingly "average" people on the streets, of devotees in the ashrams, of travelers on the trains or of those in the market places, sparkled in a way I had rarely, if ever, seen before. They radiated a simple undisturbed curiosity and playfulness.

These eyes looked deeply into me, interested, but strangely unaffected by who I might be, what I might think or what I was doing. Whether I was a Buddhist, a hippie, a student, a monk, a seeker, a musician or anything else, was interesting to them, but whoever I was posed no inner threat or disturbance.

As I stepped off the plane and spoke with the immigration officer, I felt transparent and yet completely accepted at the same time. In the West when someone looks this deeply into us, we almost always feel some element of aggression, some form of judgment, some manner of acceptance or rejection based on the opinions, beliefs, intentions or agenda of the observer. It is as if something could be lost or gained with a particular observation, and one must actively pursue a position or stance to maximize the imagined gain or minimize the imagined loss.

To avoid this kind of endless confrontational condition, Westerners have developed social mores and codes of activity that permit us to contact each other with our aggressive selfishness intact, and yet create an appearance that is somewhat non-threatening. We play the social game according to rules we have been taught (or that we intuit from the interaction of others), but rarely express our deepest understanding and our greatest concerns. In this way we unconsciously create a continuous level of anxiety, because deep within we know that we are avoiding our instinctual, inborn desire to observe and experience the truth of the present moment. Gradually we become completely unable to search ourselves. The very process of doing so has been choked off by the social restrictions we have tacitly accepted.

To break free of this confining pattern of relating, young adults often become antisocial and hostile to society. This is quite natural, for they have been injured spiritually by a social prison, not of their own making.

A child who has not yet been conditioned to act within these guidelines tries to discover the truth naturally and directly. We are amused by his/her uninhibited curiosity, but for the most part we dare not act that way ourselves.

But these "eyes" of India are quite childlike, as if we are all part of some play...*Lila*, as it is known to them...some drama that is created by God for each of us to observe, experience and enjoy, but not to take too seriously. And since God is forever in charge, it must be a Divine Comedy. Very soon it became clear to me that **This** is their primary devotion. On the whole they are not devoted to themselves, but rather to God's Play. This is a tremendously different way of living a life than is normally experienced in the West.

Take a moment and consider just how you look at others. What is your purpose when you look deeply into another person? Are you trying to "say" something with each look? Are you "expressing" yourself? Are you trying to "achieve" something by looking (or even not looking) in some particular way? Are you secretly trying to generate a particular response? Most honest Westerners would have to answer, "Yes!"

This other way of consciously looking...seeing without expecting, acting without rules, watching without really doing anything...can only begin to happen when the self is rooted to the Center, when the being is devoted to God. He then recognizes that there is nothing pressing for Him to do. It is already happening now.

Sometimes this Indian devotion takes on a more active character. It is not uncommon to see people chanting or singing the praises of God, even while performing ordinary daily tasks. I saw two men passing each other in Rishikesh, one on a bicycle, the other (a swami quite famous in the West) on foot. The man on the bicycle sang out, "Ram, Ram...Ram, Ram," to the swami, in an ecstatic but controlled tone, openly expressing his devotion...his absorption into God's Being.

At night, when the oppressive heat of the day subsides, the Shiva temples come alive with powerful singing and chanting. Many devotees join in. The air becomes charged with devotional electricity. The chants repeat a basic phrase rhythmically over and over. Now and then the phrase is spontaneously altered in some subtle artistic way, to consciously increase the energy of the moment...to keep the mystery ever present in their attention.

The tone and power of these chants express a deep energetic interest in the essentials of our life experience. They also express a devotion to God that is total. These devotees enter into the process **wholeheartedly**. Their prayer is not a whimsical request that God show them some special consideration. There is no holding back. They enter...body, mind and soul...into a place of wonder and amazement.

The single, most amazing expression of devotion that I have ever witnessed occurred in the middle of a blistering day in Calcutta. I was walking through a park, in the heart of the city, heading for an office. The sun was high and very intense. I was anxiously anticipating the cool of the air-conditioned building. I began to hear an exquisite chant coming from a single man. I was drawn into the Source of the sound. As I approached him, I discovered that he was without a single normal limb. Both arms and both legs were grotesquely deformed (possibly a case of intentional disfigurement for the purposes of begging...possibly done to him by his parents or guardians at birth). Why and how this had happened, however, was irrelevant in that moment. He lay on his back, eyes wide open, staring at the infinite expanse of bright sky...chanting with tremendous force, eloquence and feeling. It is impossible to convey in words the joyous exhilaration that he was expressing. In a moment my complete smallness and pathetic dependence upon the comforts of this temporal life flashed before my eyes. I was both enthralled and humbled at the same time.

The gift of that moment remains for me a deep well of inspiration. It defines the essence of Devotion.

But...let us now return to our own habituated condition.

> What follows here is a self-test. To experience the full force of its purpose, I am suggesting that you continue reading until you get the "questions" and then stop and follow the instructions.

TEST

Before you begin your next meditation, have a pen and paper ready to respond to some questions immediately upon finishing. Don't try to anticipate the questions while meditating and don't begin to prepare any responses.

For those who practice meditation regularly, do this in your normal way. Pay close attention to everything that normally enters your consciousness. Be yourself. Meditate with full attention.

For those who do not meditate regularly or who have never done so, find a comfortable position for sitting that will allow you to be very relaxed. Keep your back straight and upright for as long as possible without strain. Just meditate and observe. Then, without disturbing the sensitive inner condition, answer the questions directly with complete openness. Be honest and forthright. The answers are for you alone.

Begin your meditation now.

QUESTIONS

1. Which people in your life (if any) did you think about? What was the tone of those thoughts, and what was the effect of thinking about them? Be specific.
2. What activities that you normally do entered your mind? What was the feeling you had toward them?
3. What activities that you do not normally do (or never have done) entered your mind? Did these

ideas present a new positive challenge, or were they in some way dreadful? Note each one that you can now remember.

4. Did you focus upon actual events in your past or your future?
5. Within your physical body, where did your focus go? Did this focus remain in one place, or did it travel about? Did it wander aimlessly, or did it move with purpose of some kind? What do you recognize as the purpose of this movement?
6. What did you hear within yourself? Be exact. Did you hear yourself breathing? Did you hear your heart beating? Did you hear a current of sound or a steady tone?
7. If sounds arose outside yourself, did you dwell on their source? Did you form any attitude about them?
8. What internal things, lights or forms did you see? How exact was this vision?
9. What vibrations did you feel, e.g., your breath, your heart beat, blood flow, the whirring or radiation of chakras?
10. When you finished your meditation, how did you feel? ...discouraged, neutral, content and uplifted, elated, etc.? Take the time to be precise.

These questions concern our actual, exact experience...not how we "intended" to focus. Our answers to these questions form a blueprint of the direction and extent of our devotion.[1] When we set out to meditate upon a particular sound, mantra, idea, person, feeling or any other focal point, the natural tendency is for the focus to drift

[1] This "test" can be retaken again and again over time. Even though you will know ahead of time that those things to which you are currently devoted will appear in your meditation, this will not skew the results significantly. For when we meditate continuously for a considerable period of time, say...30 minutes, the gravity of our ongoing devotional condition asserts itself again and again.

away. It gravitates toward those things to which we are now devoted.

If we compare our living conditions in the West today with those of just a century ago, one thing clearly stands out. Our basic material desires and needs are now realized much more quickly and easily. We have many, more refined, physical choices and opportunities.

If we want a cup of coffee, we collect our Mocha Java, French Roast or Colombian Supremo, put the grinds in a coffee maker, or even our cappuccino or espresso machine, and flip a switch. In a very short time...and for some, not short enough...we have just the brew we desired.

But what happens when some "accident" occurs...say the electricity suddenly goes off? How do we feel now? What happens when some thing we have grown accustomed to is suddenly gone? How do we bear up with loss or discomfort? How do we feel when the computer goes down? How do we take criticism? These are significant questions. Our "normal" responses to these events map our devotion. Our responses to these situations are much better indicators of our inner condition than our philosophy or our beliefs. Our reactions show us where we are now...without our physical, emotional and mental supports.

Deep spiritual devotion is so completely involving, that we hardly know any "accident" has happened. The scene changes, but the Play goes on as usual.

Our devotion is actually a collection of things, ideas and impulses that have become "normal" to us. Our **real purpose**, which we are yet to completely realize, is the wondrous discovery of Self-Realization...the definite involution of our consciousness into Spirit. This changing experience will naturally redirect our devotion toward God.

Here it is significant to ask, "Is God personal or impersonal?" I encourage you to consider this carefully. Clarify your own assumptions and conclusions. What is your underlying assumption? What is the color of your feeling? Is God personal or impersonal?

If you find God to be impersonal, then your devotion will surely be impersonal. It will be scientific. If He is beyond form, unmanifested and absolute, then your devotion will be saturated with those qualities. It is difficult to deny that in some way God is like this. He is beyond our scope...while we are definitely limited by our own "personality."

On the other hand, God manifested...and continues to manifest...every single personality that has ever existed. You and I are His manifestation. Thus He is an immensely personal Being. He has become billions and billions of persons Himself. Krishna says, "He who perceives Me everywhere and beholds everything in Me never loses sight of Me, nor do I ever lose sight of him."[1] In this light, devotion becomes highly personal...alive with affection and love. We feel His feeling directly in our own experiences. Why else would we have been created? We cannot be separate from God for a single moment. This exquisite realization is the foundation of ecstasy. It opens our heart to the Infinite.

There are many beautiful stories of saints who are so rapt in Grace that the physical and the spiritual are one and the same. Here are two examples:

Neem Karoli Baba was frequently fed *prasad* (consecrated food) by his disciples. Normally he would eat any and all that was offered. Such an offering, given with devotion to the guru, could be none other than a gift from God Himself. As such, Baba would go on eating, often without the faintest idea of how much he had consumed. From time to time his disciples would have to intervene and remind him that he had already eaten dozens of meals. Such is the ecstatic condition of one devoted to God and those sent to him by God.

Another tremendous saint is Francis of Assisi. Having taken a vow of poverty, he found it necessary, though difficult at first, to beg for his food. He placed utter trust in God that his real needs would be met. Of course, this would undoubtedly be a path that would redefine just

---

[1] *Bhagavad Gita*, VI:30

what those "needs" might be. Early in his days of poverty
he came to beg at the homes of those who knew of him in
his younger days...the son of a successful merchant. Those
to whom he begged for food were not always friendly.
Often they would chastise him severely for his "demise."
But Francis found God's instructions to him even through
the voice of condemnation.

"On one occasion at the home of a woman, who knew
his past, he was rebuked, 'So that is what has become of
you, sir Francis, noble troubadour!' And turning to the
maid, 'Give him the bones we kept for the dogs. Then he
has something to gnaw at and will not bother us any
longer with his presence.'

"But instead of being hurt, he responded, 'I thank you,
noble lady, for the bones and for the humiliation, which is
welcome food for my soul, for it wants to practice humble-
ness.'"[1]

True devotion to God is a scarce commodity in the
West. Instead of being primarily devotional, we have
developed many curious habitual tendencies that interfere
in a basic way with our Self-discovery. For example, one
habit of the "new age" community is speculation. Speculation is essentially a mask for our impatience. When we
insert ego into speculation, we formulate exaggeration,
superstition and misinformation. But when we let the
flame of Love light the fire of Devotion deep within our
heart, this fire will first burn out all this speculation. It will
spread to all the centers of our consciousness. God will
keep us informed. He will give us every thought and idea
that we need for our own experience, or that we might
need to share honestly with others. More importantly,
when no thought is given, we are free to bask in the ceaseless Bliss of His Being.

Devotion, however, does not spring forth from the
cautious man, the pundit or the one inflated with ego.
Constant dwelling upon the intricacies of mind does not
generate trust in the devotee. Thus, the Master will not fill

---

[1] Rene Fulop–Miller: *The Saints that Moved the World*, 1945.

us up with continuous idle speculation. A deep abiding **trust** gives shelter to even the most fearful of beings. It subdues the wildest animal and cools the angriest of men. It calms the heart of all who are nearby. Attract the Master into your heart, and His work will transform you completely.

The path to God becomes primarily devotional. It is the completely natural response of the seeking soul who recognizes directly that each and every soul life is continuously sustained and nurtured by God. As we begin to find our way in from where we are now, a Light begins to dawn. The scientific mind may still want its understanding. The organizational mind must see the intricate design. The artist will create the unique and beautiful. The musician will play a song to heal his own heart and the hearts of others. But devotion will be the environment in which all these activities take place.

Begin with the one Word that is His in the beginning:

Om

Let this Word light the fire of Devotion!

The heart can be steadied by devotion long before, and much more easily than, the mind can be steadied with any single idea. The Father, dwelling in the Formless, emits a Star at the initiating Center of the vibrational world, shining a perfectly steady, bright and distinct Light. A restless mind, however, flickers incessantly. It does not see or bear witness to this Star. Just behind this Center where the Star radiates, a Sound vibrates into all places. Om fills the entire world of manifestation. Yet, when the movement and sound made by our mind dominates the audible realm, Om is not heard…the Star is not seen.

From this same Center and from each other center having resonant capability, vibration forms devotional Spheres. But, if we fill these spaces with our own idiosyncratic noise and desires, we will not feel the bliss. And, if we exit these spheres along the sensory pathways, we lose contact with our essential, central, vibratory Being.

Deep devotion, combined with proper yogic technique, transforms each and every physical cell of our body in such a way that our cellular conscious attention is drawn magnetically along the open cerebro-spinal pathway to the Pole Star, like a compass needle is drawn to the north pole. The tool of mind is set aside and a joyous devotional quality replaces the pattern of endless mental habituation. Om is heard everywhere. The Star is seen risen in the Eastern Sky. Behold...the Father dwells within. The separate life dissolves. The path is clear. The body goes its karmic way, but we dwell in His Being, as in the beginning. This is the evolving process of Divine Illumination.

Your ecstasy can become so extensive you will not know the difference between deep meditation in infinite spacelessness and getting up and moving about the world of form. The union is with Bliss, regardless of the apparent outer condition.

This cosmic Flow can cure any disease or limitation and immerse you in immortality. Your eventual exit from form...viewed commonly as death...will be natural and un-resisted, because your will has merged with God's Will and choosing, just as Jesus did not resist his own physical trial and crucifixion.

This concurrence with the Flow converts the apparent tragedies of man's condition into a deeply abiding comedy. Laughter prevails in the heart. The illusion of a serious physical reality dissolves. The outer world is a "show" ...a "demonstration"...a "play." All the world (the physical one) is a stage. But the world of Spirit is not just a stage. It is a real, ecstatic, vibrant, eternal Presence.

The human being must shed his tears, but the realized Being can hardly stop smiling. It is all too much. And, it is Real!

Let the wildfire of devotion consume the wandering thought. Call on the Master to enter into your heart and live there until His light is your light...until His understanding is your understanding...until His experience is your experience. Then the Master has found a new home, a new expression, a new torch for the ever new age of Being.

Amen.

PRAYERS & SONGS

The Altar:

Lord, bring me to the altar of Life...
　　that interior channel of blissful Flow.
I welcome the Rise...
　　I welcome the Return.
From the lowest to the highest
　　and highest to the lowest
　　there is nothing but Your Dance of Joy.

Teach me the Path of No Resistance.
　　Teach me the Path of Love.
I shall serve You with place to dwell
　　as You do serve me with Life Itself.

For we are wedded in eternal love... You and I...
　　the Father for the Son
　　and the Son in Return.
And Spirit be the wedding Song.

Let this Song so fill each one
　　that even the deaf shall hear.
And let this Love so fill each heart
　　that even the numb shall feel.
And let this Light shine so full
　　that even the blind shall see.
And let this Joy so fill the air
　　that even the sad shall be lifted up.

And let Harmonic tones abide
  in every living cell.
And let a Home of endless Bliss
  unite the world of Beings formed
  to share the unexpected smile
  that comes in waves to understand
  and spreads its cooling fire throughout
  the endless Realm of Thee...
  having naught to do, but Play.

To Feel A Deep Humility And To Eliminate The Ego:

Lord I am not worthy,[1] that Thou should come under my
  roof.

---

[1] This prayer, and particularly the phrase, "I am not worthy,"
will undoubtedly raise some eyebrows in the "new age" community and among those who eschew the "power of positive
thinking." In these two environments the command or prayer of
the day is often to assert, or even demand, our inalienable worth
and worthiness. This is appropriate for some people, particularly
those who have, throughout their past, chosen to live with considerable inhibition. In the extreme our inhibitions can lead to an
emotional implosion that appears to imprison the soul in a realm
of utter restriction. If this is your temporary condition, (indeed, it
cannot be permanent) then this prayer may not be particularly
useful at this time.

However, in this prayer it is important to understand a different nuance of meaning for "unworthy." There are those who
have swung to the completely opposite extreme...who think
they can only achieve through their own efforts, and thus proceed in life as if in an endless stream of self-assertion. Here the
balance is achieved by recognizing that God is the Doer of all
things...that we could not even take a single breath of life were it
not for His Cosmic Breath. This recognition leads inevitably to a
deep abiding humility, but definitely not a feeling of humiliation.

Return to this prayer from this perspective and its purpose
will begin to clear.

Speak but Thy Word and my soul shall be healed.
Lord I am not worthy, that Thou should come under my
    roof.
Speak but Thy Word and my soul shall be healed.
Lord I am not worthy, that Thou should come under my
    roof.
Speak but Thy Word and my soul shall be healed.

To Release A Fox:[1]

The clever will outfox a life
    by missing love from the start.
For mind is but a map to read
    the journey of the heart.

To say that, "I have naught to do...
    that all is done" is reason true.
But till the heart be soft as air
    knowledge takes us nowhere.

For this Design in moments see
    a mind without a Heart to feel
And such is not the Life to Be
    but just the spinning of a wheel.

Lo, he who separates himself

---

[1] A monk, through a misunderstanding, had become reborn as a fox. His life as a fox continued for 500 incarnations. Naturally, the monk grew tired of this form of life and finally made his way to the Zen Master, Pai-chang. He said, "Master, eons ago I was asked the question, 'Does a Yogi who goes through great spiritual training live beyond the Law of Causation?' I then replied, 'Yes!'

"I ask you now, to answer this question for me."

The Master replied, "He does not obscure the Law."

At this the monk became enlightened and was released from form.

as something special to behold
Does shine and shine a luster life
    into the bitter cold
    into the bitter cold.

For there is naught in ego's realm
    a single place to find a home
But endless toiling mind in strife
    that struggles all alone.

Yet open up that dungeon heart
    until a friend of Light to meet
Does silence every anguished cell
    and I to wash His feet
    and I to wash His feet.

So lest it seems we think our way
    to His eternal Ground
Be sure to let the Silence reign
    into His Holy Sound
    His Endless Holy Sound.

To Reach A Continuous Awareness Of Spirit:

Stillness, Silence, Transparency
Stillness, Silence, Transparency
Stillness, Silence, Transparency . . .

The Western Yogi:

Inspired by the One
    Mesmerized by the many...
        Truth is beset by
            Excitement - Irrelevance - Delusion
            Keep It Simple... stupid!

Balanced between the One and the Many
    Krishna's flute is dancing yet
        Beyond the vastness
            Rest at Ease.
Western Time
    is overcoming the fruitlessness
        of excitable, faddish information.
The western Yogi
    eyes the Calm
        as a whirling Dervish.

Ecstasy Awaits:

Having slept for eons
    a child is born
    into a world without certain definition
    amid countless other children
    with no real clue of direction and meaning.
Meaning, itself, is born a search
    as yet an infant.
After a time of wondering
    ... and wandering,
    this same One falls into a deep sleep
    the imaginary life of ego
    ... a separate existence.
In this sleep, myriad dreams pass through the senses
    each one suggesting some reality
    only to vanish without a trace
    like the mist of dawn dissolving in the heat of the sun.
Stirred by ego, the vessel of transit,
    the brave step out
    to uncover the Real.
A long battle ensues... lifetimes
    ages of darkness

save a lone Star shining in the heaven of intuition...
out of reach just now
but offering real wonder to the mind's eye.
The child then pauses to contemplate
and waits.

Faintly a Sound, like no other, is heard...
a Sound without beginning or ending...
vague... ethereal... but undeniable.
The Sound Itself, though imitated, cannot be spoken.
It is the Whole One Itself in Ecstasy!

. . . OM . . .

standing alone.

The Path is thus heard for a first time.
A Way faintly clears.
The ego begins its dissolution
into the Real Being.
Gradually the Sound becomes louder
the outer world more quiet.
Differences...
once thought to be significant
sustaining the temporary illusion of self-definition
recede.
The many emerge as the same...
All One Being
All One Sound.
The outer dance stalls
... the inner Ecstasy begins.

"Look," they say, "he's lost his mind."
Yet a blessing beyond imagination.

At the Crossroad:
> To listen to the One
>> or
> To listen to the many?

Choose the One.

Ecstasy Awaits!

For Brothers:

> If you wish to teach him to love, then love him.
> If you want to change him, then first change yourself.
> If you wish to teach him humility, then be humble.
> If you want him to be kind, then treat him with kindness.
> If you wish to transform him, then first transform yourself.
> If you want him to be perfect, then perfect yourself.
> If you want him to leave you alone, then leave him alone.
> If you want him to understand you, then understand him.
> If you want him to appreciate you, then appreciate him.
> If you want him to trust you, then trust him.
> If you want him to know the truth, then first find it yourself.
> If you want him to discover beauty, then become beautiful yourself.
> If you hope that he finds peace, then be peaceful... trusting that
>> He shall find it too.

A Prayer: [1]

Thou art my Devotion
Thou art my Love
Thou art my Wisdom
Thou art my Joy
Thou art my Feeling
Thou art my Sound
Thou art my Light

The Father Loves The Son:

Long before a Son became
    the Father dwells in Bliss

But Urge did move inside the Heart
    a gentle thought
    an aerie wisp

A sense creates
    the Sound of sounds
        a Blueprint of soft insistence
        buried alive in Earth's glowing

Inside, the Essence
    begot a Seed
    to plant the Wonder
    and share the Joy

---

[1] Repeat three times.
    1st time—to awaken to the understanding.
    2nd time—with deep feeling and force of will...simple and joyous.
    3rd time—softly...dissolve into each quality.

with some One else
And Love it did Conceive

Upon the Birth They do rejoice
        the Father loves the Son
        the Mother loves the Son
                and bear They deep
                the burden share
                to make a smile
                and wonder new

But then did find this Pair of Love
        the sense to let Him Know
        unto Himself alone He Be

When seen as Two a Path does form
        Father to Son
        a stream of Light
        and wave of Sound
        to move upon
        to find Himself

(When seen as Three a Union makes
        Thy Holy Trinity)

But separation does
        within the Son
        an Urge create

Now...
        reverse the flow
        upon the Path
        and see Thy Self
        before this Birth
        in Bliss Original

After a time
    of no real space
Inside a space
    of no real time

Lo,... I See
Forever Free to Be
I Am He

Invocation:

The Source of every expression is the Life.
This Life breathes my life as Its own.
I willingly attest to Its Will.
I lovingly attest to Its Love.
I thoughtfully attest to Its Intelligence.
    Now & Always
        ... as best I can.

LOVE

An essential purpose of embodiment is to feel. The most meaningful feeling we can have relative to our self is joy... or bliss. The most meaningful feeling we can have relative to another is Love.

When the Father and the Son feel this love for each other, they experience the bond of the Holy Spirit. The Holy Trinity, *Sat – Tat – Om*,[1] is the triune Being of God, alive in form. All particulars issue from this Trinity. Anything and everything experienced as an "event" is simply a brush stroke on the infinite canvas by the Artist in love. "I believe a leaf of grass is no less than the journey-work of the stars."[2] Once this feeling opens the Heart, the Sound radiates its ecstasy into all places and all times. The purpose of this life is finally uncovered. Only tears of joy adequately express this feeling.

"Divine am I inside and out, and I make holy whatever I touch or am touch'd from ...Now I will do nothing but listen."[3] This Song has no ending.

The resonance of love drives the poet's pen. It opens the heart of the female in love and raises the phallus of her male lover. It bursts forth as song from the breast of the lark, the nightingale and the sparrow, stunned by the exquisite return of the warm and lighted sun. It is the force that puts the hum in life and makes the entire process of creation worth its effort. This is what unites all Life.

---

[1] Father – Son – Holy Spirit.
[2] Walt Whitman, *Song of Myself*, (from *Leaves of Grass*), stanza 31.
[3] Ibid., stanza 24 & 26.

ᘀoᴠe, ᘀoᴠe, ᘀoᴠe!

This is the Song of the Heart.

So, what has happened upon this earth?

In our attempt to secure a more permanent place here... and earth is not our true home...we plan too much, we talk too much, we attach ourselves to things and ideas. We fall deeply into a pattern of need and temporary gratification. All of this is the vain attempt to materialize the Self. But...**the Self is not material!** This misplaced desire creates and sustains a life of habitual activity, thinking and desiring, which disturbs our original Harmonic Condition. We disturb the silence...and the Sound is not heard. After a time, we are unaware that any such Sound exists. We go about our business, "living" and seeking a completely material life. We inhibit the bliss, buried deep within our very own heart.

As we dwell upon our **image**, rather than the underlying **Reality**, we miss our Being. We remain snagged in the net of Maya and temporarily miss a great opportunity.

We create our own apparent fragile condition. We misplace basic priorities. In one moment we might place love...as an idea...foremost in our mind and, perhaps, even feel it in our heart. But a time comes when something of lesser importance steals its place. As our displacement persists, we may, in utter desperation, strike out at someone...even at the one who is dearest to us. The mind creates all manner of false reason to perpetuate confusion. Strange! Yet it happens.

We argue over ideas or what needs to be done. We drown out the preeminent harmonic Sound with the tone of our disappointments and our misdirected expectations. As our humility dissolves in waves of anger and resentment, fabricated in thin air, we perpetuate the false sound of discord.

Harmony is natural. It is primordial. However, within this dense earthly domain, as we lack **attention** upon its resonance, harmony mysteriously vanishes. Paradise is lost. Harmony must be reabsorbed from the infinite domain. "Things" will always be present to sub-plant love into a lower priority, until this divine **resonance** permanently cements the ecstatic vibration within the Heart. This resonance within the Heart is the basis of divine life. To enter this life, Lord Buddha discovered that we must make the right effort.

Upon this earth, we are immersed in confusion. Consider one of our primary sources of "information"...the daily newspaper. It is a black and white metaphor for our apparent condition. It is filled with the self-perpetuating trauma of our mis-conceptions. What do we find there?

Section one describes the lives of those making national or international "news." Everywhere there are attacks... nation against nation, organization against organization, people against leaders, and leaders against each other. There are descriptions of the violence and disasters befalling unknown people and the strife caused by economic uncertainty.

Section two describes these same dramas occurring within the state.

The opinion page includes the cutting imagination of razor-sharp intellects. Such a mind often has a single, thinly veiled agenda...to promote itself through the criticism, and even the humiliation of others.

The sports section describes winners and losers in a day after day struggle for physical dominance. Each story ends in a score or a price tag, as if a tally defines the participation of souls. Each competition is presented as a battle, as if Life is naturally warlike. Yet, strangely enough, the roots of our language can illuminate a higher purpose. The word, *competition*, is derived from the Latin *cum*, meaning *with* or *together*, and *petitio* or *petere*, meaning *to seek*. Thus the original, deeper meaning of competition is to *seek together*. Why then, do we derive and perpetuate the very opposite meaning? We view sports as a way of struggling separately...punctuating the whole effort with a final score.

The business section reads like a sports section, whose sport is money making and money dominance.

In other sections there are things we can buy or sell, places where we can go, meetings we can attend and dramas we can watch. Within every large newspaper there is simply a vast array of ideas expressing, in large measure, the lowest common denominator of the **dream** we are all having.

These "facts" are not really facts. They are a woefully incomplete interpretation of what is going on. They mirror our own pettiness and confusion…and perpetuate it.

We forget that we are the one, primordial, vibratory, Spiritual Being, facing a peculiar dilemma. From birth we have forgotten who we are. This forgetfulness causes us to interpret the "events" of this world in a way that is not in tune with what is actually happening. But the consummate intelligence, love and will of the cosmic design inexorably drives and guides each of us home. To know this, aligns us with the strength needed to take each step. This knowledge is our strength. Our effort and attention revive the resonance.

A simple direct way to enter the path is to love.

The challenge of love is twofold. On the one hand, we must love one individual completely. Then, after recognizing that the whole creation is non-separate, we can no longer love just one. So we make a simple adjustment: We expand this feeling to include everyone and every thing.

The reverse also applies. As we learn to love the whole, we must find a way to love each one. Jesus said, "Love your enemy." But there is no way to do this until there is the deep and full recognition that the "enemy" and the "friend" are not separate. They are the same Whole Being. To love the enemy, we love the **Being**. So our love must evolve in creative ways, through temporary conditions, to reach each and every one we meet.

We have all heard this before…"Love unconditionally"…but certainly we have had difficulty finding our way through the particulars. How does it feel to love this way?

There is a Radiation through the physical condensation of matter, through the astral condensation of emotion, and through the mental condensation of imagination. It penetrates all three bodies and is undeterred by what is there. Its persistence and its purity dissolve form into Essence. Sight and Sound pass right through to God, waiting patiently behind the veil of our material perception. She breathes the love into us...and draws it back out. **The residue of our self is Bliss.**

In India, *ghee* is the cherished oil for the preparing of cooked foods. It is clarified butter. Heat has extinguished every last impurity of the churned milk of the "sacred cow." Thus we may prepare a meal for Krishna, whose Heart is just this pure. His Divine Flute issues forth the sweet Music of the Spheres. He pours this Essence into the ears of anyone who has the empathy to listen. His ecstasy is irresistible. The Heart of Love begets another. His Song becomes our own.

The full Heart can no longer contain itself. It spills over with ecstasy until it finds another. Krishna must have Arjuna as much as Arjuna must have Krishna. Completed love is always mutual. It is the essence of our search, our quest and our path to any other being. **No relationship is complete until love is experienced mutually.**

Love is the natural intelligent feeling of communion with another. Love is the Holy Spirit, vibrating the first cause. It sustains the design of the entire universe of dual creation. On the most simple, biological level, a single cell expands through wonder, until it can contain itself no longer and, upon reaching a harmonic threshold, suddenly divides into two. At once a natural **relationship** emerges that is the wonder of love. It is the birthing of a consciousness into empathy, now alive and veiled as separate within each of the two cells.

Flame lights flame. Love passes from one soul to the next through a luminous Resonance that eventually becomes super-conscious. It moves like fire. He who does not experience love is self prevented by a resisting, anti-inflammatory condition of mind and habit. Giving this up, we open and the fire spreads, illuminating all parts of our

Self. The fire is love. It is completely irresistible. Gradually we enter a Divine Nexus with every other Heart.

Of all the facts that can be unearthed by geologists and archaeologists, or measured by physicists and biologists, or surmised by philosophers and mathematicians...not one fact can ever be uncovered or created that approaches the gravity of the undeniable manifesting force of Love. It is our beginning, it is our preservation and it is our completion.

In a quiet space within the heart of every human being there is a Sound, waiting to radiate in tune with love. It is life's spiritual gyroscope. As we hear this Sound and feel its Current, our path is clear. Our path is love.

To uncover this requires that we become the persistent and ultimate scientist of our Self. We dive deep into our own heart and become immersed in its feeling. Every last discord will exhaust itself and die for lack of purpose. Deep courage and trust sustain the immersion until the time arrives when the only wave that survives is the vibrant, omnipresent, eternal Sound of Love, radiating from the purified Heart.

The actual truth is amazing...endlessly surprising...and much greater than our stodgy finite mind can grasp. And it is **easy**. It is not complicated. It is immediate and continuous. It issues with the Sound.

The innocent Heart feels no edge. It sings into the Infinite.

> Silence begets the Sound
> and the Sound is Love.
> This is all I know
> and all I need to know.

So, dear reader, witness this Love!

All descriptions, all techniques and all directions of meditation lead directly to it. It is the object and it is the subject. It is non-dual. It is omnipresent. It is OM. It is Amen. It is a command. It is observation. It is the way in. It is the way out. It is Christ. It is He becoming our self.

It only appears dual as form. As the breath that blows through a flute may create different notes, owing to the length of the resonant chamber...so it appears as many. But the breath and the life are the force of Love, dividing the One into two, so that we may "see" it, "hear" it and "feel" it.

The Breath gives conscious awareness and is awareness itself. It enlivens form and empowers lives. And yet, this Breath is omnipresent...not just the breath within a body, but the Breath that breathes all bodies, that sustains duality and separate awareness. It is all One Breath. It is Love manifesting. Love is the entry into meditation.

> In as breath... I thus do rise
>   in cooling rush of Lighted birth.
> Then down as breath... I thus do fall
>   to warm the heart and wed the earth.

We breathe Love in...and we breathe Love out. Love saturates the entire universe of duality. It is the Essence of the Divine Mother. Bliss is the primordial Essence issuing the Sound...interlacing the Hearts of those in Love.

WISDOM

It may surprise you...it certainly surprised me when I first discovered it...but virtually everyone thinks that he is wise. Most everyone has observed life in his own way, and has drawn one basic conclusion: "My approach to life and my understanding of life is essentially correct, appropriate and, for the most part, superior." Strange! This is the prevailing opinion. It is the primary assumption of the ego. Those rare individuals who do not share this assumption are called **devotees**.

Wisdom has more to do with what is appropriate than what is "right." It has more to do with effectiveness than pure reason. Appearances are deceiving. The deception of Maya...the illusion that things are just as they seem on the surface, that physical stuff is the essence of creation...is the primary reason why man wanders this earth with no true direction. He has not glimpsed the truth of his "situation," for he has no idea **Who He Is**!

There is a special personal quality that dawns upon anyone who carefully observes the unreality of the physical world. Life becomes imbued with the appreciation that, "Everything is always new!" The heart becomes full of compassion, resulting naturally and effortlessly from the deep understanding of our true condition.

This changes everything...our plans, our purpose, our attitudes and so on. It bestows **humor and kindness** upon all situations. Wisdom blends **understanding** with these two qualities. This blending is tremendously important. Buddhists call it *skillful means*.

I'll share an incident that happened recently. I was standing in line at the grocery store. A family of three, a father, a mother and a young boy, entered the line directly behind me. Suddenly the man broke into an arrogant rage about a string of things that were, for him, stupid and ridiculous.

First it was our small town. Then it was a neighboring city. Then it was the owner of this particular chain of grocery stores. Finally it was a notice, attached to an adjacent cash register. Something was wrong with everything, and he felt compelled to voice his contempt to anyone within earshot.

What to do?

In the path of this hostile barrage, I felt an instinctual urge[1] to turn around and level a string of surgically chosen "insights" about his crude behavior. The habit of the ego laden mind is to assert the superiority of its own understanding. Before I could speak, however, I was simultaneously imagining what this conversation would produce. The tone of the imagined dialogue was manifested in the urge itself. A battle, which had already taken root within myself, would ensue for the two of us as well. No. That would not do. Still, a need persisted for me to do something appropriate...to be effective.

So I listened for the Master's response. What would He say? How would He say it? Slowly, His Presence entered and replaced my own stock responses. His words and tone began to take form. An **innocence** unveiled itself.

What is required in the face of such a blind fury is not an equally opposite fury, delivered with sharp surgical intelligence, but rather an innocent response with healing qualities. What is required is something so skillful that it encourages comfort and truth. It is not simply information.

---

[1] I was raised in a family of seven sons. My parents were highly educated. My father, a "self made man," was also very competitive and demanding. All seven boys, though fundamentally kind and "intelligent," developed a strong rivalry. Often there arose a battle of wills over the slightest of issues. Owing to this family environment, somewhat naturally I developed a facility of verbal repartee...the kind of facility that makes a lesser man proud, a greater man ashamed, and a wise man silent.

It is a demonstration of the Way itself. If the time is not ripe for such a healing to occur, then silence is the only skillful expression.

Wisdom is the active use of an appropriate, skillful response that demonstrates Truth and Bliss.

How we understand wisdom must undergo a fundamental change. Its meaning must be enlarged. The paradigm is expanding and shifting. It must include the perception of the preeminence of the Holy Spirit. Our view must become **All inclusive**.

Wisdom is usually thought of as a wedding of intelligence and experience. It is that, but it is much more. It extends into a vast range of personal capabilities. It includes a number of different ways of experiencing and the integration of experience and usefulness.

Consider the following list of partial descriptions of wisdom:

1. The ability to focus upon one thing at a time, excluding all else.
2. Focusing upon the Source and power of a single intelligent thought, to access a deeper meaning.
3. Experiencing the illuminating force of spontaneous and persistent prayer.
4. Trusting our own capacity to intuit the Spiritual Design, imbedded within us.
5. Experiencing Divine Vibration as meaning unto itself.
6. Hearing Mantra and feeling its power.
7. Expressing that power skillfully.
8. Discovering how the breath initiates a standing wave of sympathetic vibrational resonance within the inner cerebo-spinal Channel.
9. Knowing the consciousness of matter to be vibrational Essence.
10. Merging with the Oceanic Sound.

11. Refocusing the Sound Vibration into higher octaves of visionary Light Presence.
12. Feeling the permanent inner leap into Omnipresent Spirit.

These descriptions should help to expand a sense of the entire realm of wisdom. This is only a partial list. Take one at a time and let the full meaning of it begin to take shape. Wisdom has more the quality of feeling than simple intelligence. It evokes change. Wisdom has a radiant quality, often producing a sympathetic resonance within others.

Intelligence has a well ordered and often intricate structure. It can sustain us through a complicated labyrinth of thought and eventually deliver us to some goal. But wisdom is more simple. It views the maze of life as a comedy...not a problem. It immediately **delivers us to joy**. It is the approach itself. It is the way of ease at the outset... allowing us to use intelligence, when this has some use... but its scope is larger. It causes us to act, when action will work, and it causes us to be silent, when action will fail. Intelligence allows us to use a formula to complete a task, but wisdom is the knowing whether to follow the formula or to throw it out. It refines intelligence with tone and service. The "Wisdom of the Buddha" is the compassion of skillful means.

Wisdom cannot be contained and it cannot be grasped, yet it can be expressed in everything we feel and do. It is open, receptive and flowing. It has the quality of beauty and the fragrance of a flower. Its sweetness is like a mother suckling her newborn.

Wisdom is not necessarily slow, but it is always patient. It does not force an issue when a prolonged kindness will work just as well. There is no sense of inhibition or urgency, but rather a continuous opportunity to be appropriate and effective.

The first time I ever recognized a man of wisdom was in 1971. A whole new dimension opened for me. Suddenly life was not a linear journey between desires. Time stopped for a moment. And there I was, simply partaking of another man's easy way of life.

The meeting could not have lasted more than a few minutes, but it stands out for me as a rare and treasured moment.

I had been living in Japan for a year and a half. My friends were an assortment of Westerners and a few Japanese. My closest friend was an English-American, who had been initiated into a yoga of Sound by Charan Singh, a Sat Guru living in Beas,[1] India. Through the influence of my friend, I decided to make a trek to meet this Master. My companion, Futaba, a wonderful, young Japanese woman, decided to make the journey with me.

We had very little money...enough, perhaps, to get there, live simply for a few months and, hopefully, get back home to Japan. There were, however, a number of ways to help subsidize such a journey. Travel over long distances in India is commonly made by train. If you go third class, the fare is remarkably low. Of course, the accommodations are very basic and often crowded. At that time, if you had a "student card," it was possible to get the fare cut in half. Such a card could be bought for a couple of dollars on the black market in Calcutta.

Futaba and I arrived in Calcutta and eventually found our way into the market place, where we got our student cards. A few days later we proceeded to the Howrah train station.

The next step on our discounted journey was to get a pass for the train, permitting us to travel at half price. To obtain such a pass, it was necessary to see the railway inspector.

We entered his office apprehensively...prepared with a description of our lives as "students." We sat down. He smiled and asked simply, "What brings you to India?"

Trying to hide any nervousness, I began with my prepared explanation. He listened for a few sentences, smiled

---

[1] A small town in the Punjab, about twenty miles from Amritsar, on the border with Pakistan.

again and waved his hand. "No...not that. What is your real purpose?"

His tone was so sweet, sincere and endearing, that I could do no other than explain our real mission...to see the Master. He continued to smile and wished us well. Then he stamped our passes, and we were free to go.

In the presence of real wisdom, one feels unmasked, naked and yet unashamed. There is no danger lurking. There is no threat. Your exposure is not exploited. There is no vulnerability. The only challenge is to enter the under-standing...to merge with the feeling.

Despite the apparent chaos and poverty in India, there is an ongoing selective process for individual advancement in business and professions, that is somewhat different than our own. In the West, the pressures of corporate life and demanding stockholders have produced a greedy acceptance of the importance of the "bottom line"...in the "short term." By contrast, in India the path of management is infused with other values as well. In part, the chaos, which "seems" to be prevalent there, weeds out those who have no humor or patience. And the almost universal acceptance of the transmigration of souls supports a sys-tem of values that awards the growth of soul qualities over a singular facility with money and efficiency.

India is a land of many wise men. It is a primary part of its heritage. I first saw it in this railway inspector. Then, as I looked intently, beyond the limiting physical conditions, I began to see a simple, yet deep understanding in almost every face. My three month visit there left me stunned and forever changed.

Circumstances prevented Futaba and me from meeting with Charan Singh in person. The Bangladesh War had broken out, and we were not allowed to remain in Beas, owing to its strategic location near the fighting. However, from his devotees we discovered one particular principle that he expressed as axiomatic to the spiritual life: There are three fundamental conditions that should be met before we speak. What we say should be **true, necessary and kind**.

Imagine a community of people who use these three criteria faithfully. First of all, there would be plenty of silence. We know so little of what is actually true. Then, as we gain a brief impression of the real **Truth,** we are normally struck dumb by its scope. Silence becomes our natural environment...a continuous blessing that caresses us and those who are near.

We are normally full of plans, full of desire, full of intentions. To what ends? So much of this apparent need is falsely imagined. It is the foam on the surface of the Ocean, filled with air, having little or no substance. It prevents real introspection. Below the surface of our activity and our intentions lies real purpose. This is the gem we are after, even if it is not yet clear how to acquire it. As we become more calm, the "foam" on the surface dissolves naturally, revealing our deeper Essence. Then, what is **necessary** in each moment becomes clear and natural.

The human condition is sometimes called a "rat race." What a strange comparison. However, this description need not apply. As we allow ourselves to be filled with **kindness,** instead of nervous haste, we begin to taste a tremendous sweetness. A deep caring is born that each may experience an unbridled enjoyment of this wonderland of Being.

Truth is the Vibration of the Holy Sound, Om, resonating in the **Mind.**

Necessity is the Vibration of the Holy Sound, Om, resonating in the **Will.**

Kindness is the Vibration of the Holy Sound, Om, resonating in the **Heart.**

As we allow this **Vibration** to expand into all the Centers, every action becomes appropriate. All doubt dissolves. When the flow is full, wisdom is the environment itself. It is the experience of Om, vibrating in all the Centers simultaneously.

I had an experience recently which made this utterly clear to me. Holly and I slipped into a misunderstanding. An argument arose with sudden, unexpected force over a very minor, but sticky personal issue. With very little warning, we became mired in a maze of intellectual combat. The faucet of love was shut off by one turn of Maya's grip. We both struggled to resolve the disagreement, but the issue itself took on a life of its own. In a very short time we found ourselves confused, deeply divided and miserable...caught in the quicksand of heartless opposition.

This division persisted for several hours without relief. When the disagreement first began, the Holy Sound resonated in all of my Centers...from top to bottom. The entire length of the inner Channel was alive with the Current. But, as the distress of our opposition continued, a hole began to form within my third chakra, the center of will, fire and power. Then the Current began to leak out. The Sound remained resonant in the other Centers, but the Flow had stopped.

In a very short time I became psychically disabled. Will completely left me. Love was still there...basic intelligence was still there...but the will was gone. In its place came an overwhelming sadness. Sadness is essentially the absence of will. It is a break in the cosmic Current, commonly felt as an emptiness in the pit of the stomach.

As this condition stayed with me for a second day, a desperation began to assert itself. Late in the day Holly and I found ourselves thrown together by karmic circumstance...riding in a car...trapped...nowhere to go but together, down a crowded highway at 40 mph.

In this tiny confinement, my sadness eventually exploded into deep, seemingly endless tears. All I could express was that our love and our friendship were so important, that anything that interfered with it was completely insignificant. My tears flowed and flowed. I cried and cried in anguish. "Why, oh why, have we forsaken each other?"

Then a healing slowly began for both of us. Our purpose became clearly identified through my plea. Our purpose for each other is Love.

During a storm, the surface of the sea becomes waves of water and foam, building force, in search of land where it might express its fury. Finally, each wave crashes upon the shoreline. This is the end of its journey. But deep within the ocean there is a stillness, and within that stillness there is a Being. The purpose of that Being is Love. This is ours to discover in any way that we possibly can.

When I rose on the third day, the Current was restored. I was whole again. Holly and I rediscovered the purpose of our friendship...the purpose of our partnership. With this came a special revelation to me!

The night before this disagreement started, Holly, Harmony and I were out walking together. Harmony, our eldest daughter, was a sophomore in university, taking a class in world religions. While studying the life of Jesus, she became deeply puzzled by a difficult question. As Jesus was suffering on the cross, He spoke, "Eli, Eli, lama sabachthani."... "My God, my God, why hast Thou forsaken me."

"Why is it," she asked, "that Jesus said this? After all, he raised people from the dead, had tremendous powers and also had claimed, 'I and my Father are One!'"

It is a troubling question for anyone who sees Jesus as more than just a man. What could have happened to him to bring about this despair? I thought to myself, "Why don't I know the answer?"

Then, on the third day of my painful ordeal with Holly...as the Current of Life returned within me... I knew the answer to this question, without any reservation. I had just had the same kind of disabling experience. Jesus must have experienced a very deep sadness. All his devotees and close friends had abandoned him at the time of his greatest challenge. Even if these events had been known to him in advance, the shock of it actually happening was still tremendous. The purpose of his entire earthly life was to help these devotees and followers experience the joy and

freedom of the Holy Spirit. His Heart was an endless well
of compassion. And now his "friends" retreated from the
Essence of the teaching, when facing a great moment of
truth. Conclusion: The Current within him must have
temporarily been broken, in the wake of such disappointment.

When sadness enters deeply into our life, the Current of
Life…the Current of the Holy Spirit…leaves us through an
opening in our emotional body, a tear in the etheric web. A
psychic hole develops and we are drained, sometimes
quite suddenly. In the extreme, we become emotionally
dead. In a short time, regardless of what has been our past
experience, regardless of our level of intelligence, we face
our profound physical limitation. We become dis-eased.

Disease takes one of two forms. Either we absorb some
"foreign," discordant impulse within our current of life
energy, or some of the energy itself is drained off. Often it
is both. The "secret" of good health is to maintain the
Harmonic Current. One very effective way to help accomplish this is to develop the ability to actually **hear this Life
Current, feel it, and then see it**. In this way we can recognize immediately when something begins to go wrong. We
stay on top of our health. This overall condition of the
awareness of the Holy Spirit and the ability to remain in
the Flow, fully conscious, is the essence of wisdom. It is
our use of skillful means within our self…and it is completely natural.

Within this kingdom of Heaven on earth, all is made
clear. Ask of the Spirit anything, and in an appropriate
time it shall be revealed to Thee. Stay in the Grace of the
Holy Sound, Om, and the revelation shall come with due
haste. Listen deeply, openly and with the innocence of a
child, and no secret shall be kept from Thee.

OM

Human life can be slippery. One minute a way seems clear. The next minute something "happens" to cause doubt or confusion. Quite naturally, we seek to understand ourselves and our environment. To uncover a true Path for ourselves requires that we formulate some basic decisions about our condition. If we decide too quickly, without sufficient clarity and reliability, we will likely cut short the search and misjudge the Reality somewhat. But, if we remain undecided too long, we may become ambivalent. We need sufficient Light to reveal enough of the Whole Being God Is, to create an opening through which we may enter. How much Light is that?... Quite a lot!

There is a wonderful Zen *koan* that suggests how much Light is required:

To achieve the Buddha Nature, first maintain a vision of our sun...
a huge ball of fiery essence.
Now... Swallow it whole!

There is a great need for us to discover two basic things. First, that a path to God exists in Reality, and second, that each one will eventually make the journey. The discovery of the first establishes a real purpose for this life. It initiates the quest. The discovery of the second allows us to relax, and thereby effect a way to merge with the path itself.

There are many ways to characterize this path. At times, life seems to be utterly complex. The religions of the world, most of which have encountered a long evolution, began with dramatic simplicity from the life of a single charismatic individual. In general, the older the religion is, the more complex it has become. A variety of interpretations and refinements enter into the teachings. The study of religion then becomes interlaced with the beliefs of other, less realized individuals. Doctrines evolve. Canons are pronounced. Church laws are dictated. All of this complicates the Spiritual Reality and tends to distract our attention from a direct perception of the truth, inhibiting the path of Self-Realization. Complex ideology can also lead to a web of self-righteousness and guilt, veiling our original, pure and innocent nature.

Great care must be taken to sift through religious and metaphysical teachings to discover the path for our self. When Moses went up to the mountain to hear the Word of God, he was first given one single commandment: **"Love!"** However, when he returned with this news, it was not adequately understood by his brothers and sisters. They could not appreciate the depth of this simple truth. So Moses returned to the mountain. And God gave him ten commandments...to replace the single one. This was the first of a vast complex of inclusions and expansions made upon the original vision.

Buddha, whose early life was filled with great searching, became united with Spirit in samadhi under the bodhi tree...utterly complete. But after attempting to share this union with others, he found that most could not understand, and could not duplicate his experience. They were too far from the door. For them, the necessity, intensity and clarity of the quest was not as keen. So he taught them the Eightfold Path.

Buckminster Fuller, referred to by some as an "American Mystic," generated literally thousands of principles of synergy, which attempt to describe this reality surrounding us. Among the simplest of these principles are: 1) All that is physical is energetic. All that is metaphysical is synergetic; 2) There are no solids or particles, no-things; 3) There is no dimension without time; and 4) The only reality is the abstraction of principles, the eternal generalized principles.[1]

So, in some way, the path can be made to appear complicated. On the other hand, we might effectively describe the Spiritual Life simply as a singular journey through ecstasy. This alone may be a perfect road map for some... all that is needed. A simple elegant truth is often the most useful. For most, however, something with a little more detail will help.

There is an elegant description found in *The Holy Science* by Sri Yukteswar. He describes the path as having just three parts: 1) Deep Study, 2) Patience, and 3) Meditation upon Om. It is simple and easy to understand, yet challenging to follow.

Deep study requires of us to know ourselves in ways that we presently do not. It will require that, from time to time, we cast out some of our present conceptualizations and open to a larger view. Sometimes it will demand that we leap into the unknown...to trust that we can enter a much more wondrous version of ourselves and to abide by its vision.

A key ingredient of this leap is that we respond more appropriately to our intuition. For some this means to go with a feeling more readily and with greater dedication. For others it will suggest that they relax, stop lurching here and there, single out a primary impression and **move with it**. Intuition can make life slippery, but it is also the grease that allows us to glide smoothly upon the path.

In any event, there is no substitution for knowing ourselves better. There is a great deal we do not know. And we cannot simply wait to be informed. We must search for it.

Life is like a game of hide and seek. It is curious and indeed somewhat profound that children discover the archetypes of personalities with tremendous ease and embody them in simple games. In the game of hide and seek,

---

[1] Published on the World Wide Web at: http://www.rwgrayprojects.com/synergetics/synergetics.html

one person is "it." He must blind his eyes for a time and allow all the others to hide. When he opens his eyes, he begins his search to find them.

Through life, gradually we fall into one of these two categories. Either we are seeking or we are hiding. We will tend to hide if we sense there is something to fear in Reality. It may be best not to know everything. Deep inside we feel we may be disappointed if we discover too much. So we put our inquisitive nature on the shelf.

If we are to seek, we must have courage. We put appearances on the line and move into the unknown. A definite urge impels us to discover what is Real...at any cost.

Meditation is the ultimate method of seeking. It is how we peal away the layers of our ignorance. We know from extensive trial and error that the surface of life holds no hope for permanent joy. And pure reason is a lot like a deck of playing cards, one stacked carefully upon another, on end, to form a fragile house of ideas. There is no real ecstasy waiting there, only moments of pleasure and moments of pain...sometimes contentment and sometimes angst. So, an irresistible need is born to "get to the bottom" of life. The seeker **must** find the simple Truth underlying the whole thing.

Sri Yukteswar loved two books, the *Bhagavad Gita* and the *New Testament*...so much so that he challenged Paramhansa Yogananda to go to the West and demonstrate that the teachings of Krishna and Jesus are more than just compatible...that they arise from the exact same Spiritual Essence. But he didn't allow the complex web of conflicting church doctrines to interfere with the simple direct perception of real insight. Far better to find one specific suggestion...one meaningful parable...one basic truth...and allow its fragrance to waft through the pores of the body in meditative bliss.

Consider, for example, the well-known verse in Matthew,[1] "If thine Eye be single, thy whole body shall be full of Light." Better to study this one phrase thoroughly,

---

[1] Matthew 6:22

then to spend an entire life arguing the nuance in scores of "infallible" doctrines.

As we seek, we must recognize clearly what we know to be true **and** get a feel for what we do not know. What we intuit as significant may dawn in a delicate way. It must be pursued carefully, until either our intuition is proven to be correct, or discovered to be whimsical. When we first begin to hear the Sound, Om, we are naturally in this same state of uncertainty.

Om first enters our consciousness in such a subtle way that it can easily be dismissed. After all, our world is full of sounds. How does this vague sound differ from all the others? There is only one way to find out. We must listen very tenderly and wait for its effects…with great **patience**.

Sri Yukteswar recognized patience as so significant, that when he reduced the path to just three essential elements, patience was one of them…right in the middle.

Most of us do not know the meaning of the word! In just the same way that most everyone thinks he is wise, most everyone thinks he is appropriately patient. In a way, we define patience as the way we deal with life already. When we are listening, we are being patient. But when we "appear" to be impatient, we have "good reason" not to be. The conditions require us to "act." So by our own definition, we are patient. However, anyone who looks deeply within himself, without ego or prejudice, discovers beyond any doubt whatsoever, that he is impatient. **We all are!** Dear reader, do not think you are exempt.

There is a definite, though subtle contradiction in the first two parts of this three-fold path. First, we must study…we must seek to know. There must be a great effort here. But then we find that we must be patient as well. The effort must calm down. We must make inner adjustments of attitude that allow us to make our greatest effort, and yet not be attached to the results. We simply relax and carry on.

This is the entire theme of the *Bhagavad Gita*. Krishna tells Arjuna that he must go out and do battle.[1] He cannot allow himself to hide. Arjuna has every argument "in the book" ready to suggest that it is futile to do so. He does not see the point of entering the fight, of making this kind of physical effort, because in the end all flesh dissolves. The physical life has no permanency. Why bother? Arjuna's voice is the voice of "reason," infused with apathy.

But Krishna is there at every moment, exhorting him to rise up and make the effort required to overcome the habits of sensual indulgence and the lack of will. The higher voice of intuition is always with us, yet speaks with a sweetness that is so subtle that often we fail to hear it clearly.

However, what begins as a still small voice, through time and yogic effort, becomes the unmistakable vibrant

---

[1] The *Bhagavad Gita* is both a historical account and an allegory. Historically, Krishna tells Arjuna that he must enter the battlefield of the Kurukshetra War, which took place at least 500 BC, and possibly as much as 5000 years earlier.

The war arose over a dispute between two families, the Kurus and the Pandus, over the rights to the kingdom of Kurukshetra. Arjuna, belonging to the Pandus, had acted as a mediator in the dispute to no avail. Even though the Pandus had a rightful claim to the land, the Kurus refused to acknowledge any part of their claim. The Gita begins as the two armies are lined up on the plains of Kurukshetra to begin battle.

Krishna exhorts Arjuna to join his own family in the legitimate struggle to recover their homeland. Even though Arjuna recognizes his family's rightful ownership, he cannot bring himself to enter the battle on either side. He is not afraid for himself, but rather sees no good in the act of war. The entire account of the Gita is the dialogue that ensues between these two.

Allegorically, the dialogue is between man and God...the lower self and the Higher Self. The battlefield is the body of life. The Kurus represent the body nature...the senses and the ego. The Pandus represent the higher faculties, discovered through the practice of yoga. Krishna is the clear voice of intuition, imploring Arjuna, the Soul, to overcome the sensual orientation through yogic effort, and thereby return to Spirit.

Sound of the Holy Spirit. The intelligence needed to respond to this Voice already lies within us. We need only join with its frequency and harmony. We allow the Music to play and we make those inner adjustments that expand the range of the tones, the location of the resonance and the overall volume that we hear. We become a conscious radio. **Tune in, turn up and bliss out.**

After Krishna has logically removed every reason to hesitate, he then adds this injunction, "Act, but do not be attached to the fruits of your action." Relax. Be patient. Do not fall into the trap of trying to command your own future. It is in God's hands.

The dilemma of how to achieve an appropriate balance, between human effort and the will of God, finds its way into every religion and every yogic discipline. A wonderful Zen story illustrates this predicament.

In the 8th century AD, when the 5th Zen Patriarch, Hung-jên, was nearing the end of his days on earth, he called together his disciples to determine who would be his successor. It was decided that the one who could compose a poem that best demonstrated an understanding of his teachings would be chosen. It was generally accepted that among his disciples, Shên-hsiu was the most scholarly, and thus would surely become the successor.

Shên-hsiu's poem read:

> This body is the Bodhi tree,[1]
> The soul is like a mirror bright;
> Take heed to keep it always clean,
> And let not dust collect upon it.

Hui-nêng, a quiet monk with little special training and education, saw the poem and decided it was not adequate. Underneath it he wrote:

> The Bodhi is not like the tree,
> The mirror bright is nowhere shining;
> As there is nothing from the beginning,

---

[1] Enlightenment.

Where can the dust collect itself?[1]

When Hui-nêng was chosen as the rightful successor, Zen Buddhism broke into two rather distinct schools: The schools of 1) gradual enlightenment and 2) sudden enlightenment. Shên-hsiu became the proponent of the gradual school, and Hui-nêng became the patriarch of the sudden school.

If we had to choose the one of these two schools that is best suited to our own disposition, we would probably choose the wrong one. Only when our intuition is very keen, and clearly independent of our ego, could we make this choice appropriately. Those who are ambivalent, lazy or unmotivated would normally choose the gradual school. Apathy and procrastination are already part of their nature. Those who are impulsive and impatient would naturally choose the sudden school. They want it all, NOW! And yet, the opposite choice for these personality types would be more effective.

Those who are not motivated would do well to find purpose...and move with it! And those who are generally demanding and impatient need to discover the continuous state of mind that accedes to God's will, and then become comfortable with it.

However, as we look carefully within our self, we can discover that these schools are not two separate paths, but rather a single path with two lanes. On a highway, the outside, moderate lane is for normal driving and the inside lane is for passing. At every moment we must choose the lane that is appropriate for the conditions at that time.

Gradual enlightenment "happens" through steady effort, discovery, training and technique. We bring everything available to our quest. We take it all to the limit. We persevere. Spirit eventually unfolds Her wonder for us.

Sudden enlightenment "happens," because the future is out of our hands. We can in no way preempt the will of God through some ultimate effort. The leap is done in

[1] D.T. Suzuki, *Essays in Zen Buddhism*, second series, p. 45–46.

partnership. We leap, and God creates a place for us to land. Suddenly we are Home.

The need to make the right effort does not cease, even for those who have entered some higher state of consciousness. The bliss felt in these regions can be wonderful... even intoxicating. But the journey is a long one...very long indeed! When we assume it is virtually endless, we are on the right track.

There is an interesting account in *Autobiography of a Yogi*, by Paramhansa Yogananda, of a dialogue between the author and his guru, who has returned from the grave in a perfectly physical form. Sri Yukteswar relates that his own work has taken him to a heavenly plane, where the souls are so filled with blissful experience that almost all desire to attain Self-Realization has withdrawn. Such an environment is fraught with its own hazards. If complacency sets in too deeply, the Soul will eventually be forced to take a rebirth on a lower, more dense and painful planetary environment, in order to re-ignite the fire of inner effort...the desire to be One with God.

The description of this condition applies well to those on this earth who have attained tremendous wealth, and thereby have available all the pleasure and power that money can buy, and yet no longer have any desire to proceed with a spiritual discipline. The life ahead will prove to be a shock when the body begins to wither, or when another, more difficult incarnation is at hand. This is why it is so difficult for "a rich man to enter the Kingdom of Heaven." He has settled into the ease of his life, without first understanding what his Real Life is.

The third part of the path as described in *The Holy Science*, by Sri Yukteswar, is **Meditation upon Om**. Om is the fruit. Om is the sweetness. **Om is the path itself.**

There exists in Reality a vibrating, resonant, omnipresent and omniscient Sphere of blissful Experience called Om, or Holy Spirit. Leading to the center of this infinite Sphere is a path within each of us, through a resonant Heart, into the spherical Eye of consciousness. In the middle of this spherical Eye is found a central radiant Star of perfect Light. Its eternal radiation is unaffected by the physical life. The **conscious** journey to this Star takes us beyond karmic bondage. This path cannot be destroyed by any means.

Om is the doorway to God. It is the Voice of God. In meditation, once Om is heard, it becomes intuitively known that this Sound vibrates at the juncture of two worlds, the physical and the Spiritual.

We first hear it coming through a very tiny "hole" at the back of the head, entering the medulla oblongata, where the brain joins the spinal column. Its prominent upward flow is heard on the right side. Over time, as we meditate upon this Sound, Om gradually begins to resonate throughout. It caresses and soothes our three bodies. Little by little our prison feels more tolerable...even comfortable. As we learn not to interfere, and as we dismiss the habit of endless conceptualization, the doorway opens wide. There is room enough for Om to come in. Our prison dissolves and we find ourselves in Bliss.

This resonance awaits each of us. The Cosmic Sound is forever available. The extraordinary truth is that it is the resounding Voice of God, that cannot cease. It is the very Force behind, within and underneath the entire creation. It issues forth an utter oneness and sustains the building blocks of matter at the same time. This "material" is nothing more than the energy of God at its coolest and darkest edge...its condensation.

The Way is utterly simple. **Let the Sound in!**

All true religious paths lead to love. When enough love awakens in the heart, we begin to hear the Sound of God. It is really very simple. As we open to love, we begin to fill with this Sound. In time it begins to displace our habit of physical identification. Eventually we know our Self as Om!

"In the beginning was the Word, and the Word was with God." This is completed by the experience..."and the Word **is** God." To discover this, creates endless amazement. There is no way to fully comprehend the Source.

We can look at specific physical and psychological effects within this earthly domain and find the relative causes that brought them about...one by one. We can trace events backward in time to understand why and how one thing evolves from another. But, when we reach the edge of time and matter, we can no longer search step by step. We either retreat into what we already know, or leap into the Cause itself. Such a leap goes beyond explanation... and such a leap is required.

Each one of us appears to be standing upon a unique point of this spherical and solid earth. No two people occupy the same point. Some may be quite close to one another, while others are very far away. Within this earth there is a point called its *center of gravity*. Each and every one of us is mysteriously pulled toward this central point. Gravitational force creates a peculiar phenomenon, that we all take for granted. Despite the fact that I may be standing in America, and another person is simultaneously standing at the completely opposite side of the earth, we both appear to ourselves as being upright, and we both experientially feel the gravitational pull directly toward the same central point. The only thing preventing us from flying toward that center...and colliding there...is the "solidity" of this physical creation.

This is a simple, but exquisite metaphor for the path to God, which is experienced uniquely by each and every one of us.

There is a Central Point within each of us that has this kind of magnetic quality, inexorably drawing our complete conscious attention towards it. Were we not so "thick," the conscious experience within every cell would fly there in an instant. Some feel the pull only slightly...others feel it intensely. Still others feel it **and Hear It!** The pull toward this Center can be heard as a definite Sound. Depending on our conscious condition and the degree of thickness residing in our self-experience, we may hear this Sound in numerous ways.

It can sound like a motor humming in a steady continuous tone. It can sound like a trumpet, or the rush of wind.

It can sound like the hiss of a snake, particularly within the first chakra. It can sound like a bell of perfect pitch, endlessly resounding in the Heart. It can be heard resonating in various parts of the body, separately or all at once. When it is heard as a full symphonic sound, it is called the Music of the Spheres. All of this is Om.

The actual path to the Center is unique for each of us, by virtue of our individual patterns of inner adjustment to this centripetal Force. At the same time, it is utterly identical for everyone. We have all been poured from the same mold. We are all formed as complete microcosms of the same identical Being.

As we "gravitate" closer and closer to this Center, we meet other evolving beings who reside there almost exclusively. Those who have passed completely through dwell utterly as Spirit. But the Elder Brothers, Buddhas, Masters, Bodhisattvas and Saints who have not exited this life dimension...who remain just on this side...are completely available to us as we near this Center. In fact, the Bodhisattva has vowed not to make this final outgoing passage until he has assisted all others through as well. When Jesus said, "No one can enter the kingdom of heaven except through Me," this is exactly what he meant. Hence He is known as a shepherd. He dwells at the Center and draws us there with his magnetic personality. He is calling us hOMe.

The effort required to travel this path consists of those adjustments of attitude, habit and tendency that allow this Force, pulling upon our conscious identity, to freely draw us into the Center...the womb of our Spiritual Birth. Once we have been consciously drawn into this central place, Master and God manifest directly, without a trace of ambiguity.

Our involution to Spiritual Consciousness reads like a "good news, bad news" joke. The "good news" is: We cannot possibly fail for eternity to recognize and conjoin with Spirit...our Essence. This simply cannot fail to happen eventually to each one of us. The "bad news" is:

There is a great effort to be made. It shall not be easy...and it will take time.

Our being has the metaphorical "shape" of an hourglass, having a very tiny opening in the middle, dividing us, apparently, into two separate parts. Our physical nature, the sand, fills the top half. Our true, spiritual, etheric Essence dwells temporarily in a prison...trapped in the bottom half. The top-heaviness of this shape creates an instability of experience, causing a persistent, though often vague demand upon us to find the right effort or technique that will let the sand pass through...thereby allowing Spirit to rise. Natural life demands a stable living condition.

For this metaphor, the tiny opening between the two worlds is the biblical "Eye of the needle." At the beginning the sand is so course that not a single grain can pass through it. However, the grinding of our continuous life experience inexorably makes the sand finer and finer until, almost imperceptibly, a single minute grain passes. The refining process continues, and the grains become smaller and smaller. Gradually the grains begin to slip through the tiny passageway. As this happens, our Spirit "flows" upward through the opening. This flow eventually becomes audible. We can actually hear it!

Dear reader... This is the Path! **Listen deeply!**

Each of us might describe it in a different way. We might emphasize one or another need as crucial. We might list one thing as the quintessential precept or delineate dozens, even hundreds of transformational requirements. Regardless of the variations of descriptions, the path is the same!

If our life were a science fiction novel, it would read something like this:

> We have been sent on a mission to planet earth, to discover and experience directly the nature of the physical, psychological and mental landscapes that abides there. We had to travel across a vast stretch of space and time. Thus we were first placed into a deep sleep...a state of suspended animation...in order to arrive on

earth in a refreshed condition. This sleep wiped clean our memory banks, that we might experience this earth without prejudice.

After our long dreamless voyage, we land in the womb of an expectant mother and soon become "born." Our birth completely immerses us in the earthly realm and, indeed, we begin to experience **exactly** what life here is like. Actually, we do not experience what life is **like**, we experience what it **IS!**

Time goes by. We grow and expand into all three bodily realms in order to collect the experiential information we are seeking.

There are a few important covenants for our mission, given to us by our Commander. These too have been forgotten, but they can be retrieved with the simple and clear sight of intuition. Everyone "knows" them, unless (and until) they become brainwashed by human attachment, or distracted by earthly noise:

1. Every single inhabitant on planet earth has been given the same basic mission. It is not the responsibility of any one to tell another what he must do. Each has a mission of his own undertaking. Each one is free to experiment and experience as he chooses. However, all the others here are our brothers and our sisters. If they seek our help, **we must not refuse it**. If they want to know our experience, it is theirs for the asking...but **their will is as free as our own**. It is not our purpose to use force upon others in any way, except in the event that they have run amok...and have chosen to abridge the freedom of others in their pursuit of earthly experience.

2. Our own children present us with special responsibilities. From the beginning they require nurturing, to allow them to develop their ultimate potential to complete their own missions. We are to guide them in love, with as much insight and **as little force as possible**, to set them surely and gently on their way.

3. The sole purpose of human laws is **to improve the opportunity for all** of our brothers and sisters to have a successful mission. Those guided to participate in both lawmaking and law enforcement must fully understand this basic purpose, and be true servants of

all people. Human law should never be designed or enforced to exact advantage or revenge for anyone, at any time.

At some point during our earthly experience, due to our memory loss, we begin to wonder what it is exactly that is going on here. It has become unclear that this "birth" **is** a mission. We have become absorbed in, and disoriented by the particulars of the events that surround us. We sense that there is more to this "life" than meets the eye...and the other sense organs as well. Eventually our wonder becomes intense, even crucial. **We must know!**

When our space journey began, a number of safeguards were put in place for our assistance. The instruction manual for the operational system of our planetary vehicle, and our return flight, were encoded within our higher conscious mind. If we have trouble contacting this mind, or have trouble decoding the information that is there (and indeed, most of us do have these troubles from time to time), there are three ways of proceeding: 1) We can contact a mission Captain for specific instructions; 2) We can repair our own electro-psychic equipment through quiet contemplation, ridding our self of the earthly static that interferes with our proper functioning; and 3) We can radio back to our Commander for help.

We can employ all three methods of troubleshooting and repair, separately or together.

Our radio is part of the innate missionary form, which is itself a body of vibration. It has both a receiving and a sending mode of operation. We receive transmissions at approximately 124 Hz (cycles per second). We broadcast at a lower harmonic frequency of 93 Hz.

A beacon exists on our Home Planet, broadcasting and receiving an uninterrupted stream of electro-magnetic waves throughout the entire Cosmos at three basic harmonic frequencies. The primary outgoing broadcasts are made at 124 Hz. The incoming transmissions are received at 93 Hz. A third frequency, 1488 Hz, is used as a background signal to initiate contact with those who are sweeping the electromagnetic spectrum in search of other intelligent life-forms. Often a resonance is acti-

vated at harmonic points, both above and below these
three frequencies. These are the natural overtones of the
primary sound waves. In fact, the resonance extends
beyond sound, into the spectrum of light and beyond.

We can even create a "mind meld" with the Commander himself, by tuning in to both of the two lower
fundamental frequencies, simultaneously. This is not as
difficult as it might seem. We simply have to learn certain techniques of resonant teleportation, using the notes
B and Gb on the musical scale for our harmonic attunement and energy absorption.

The transmissions can be either audible or telepathic
in nature. The system is actually a fully operational television system as well. The radio function has the simplest operating mode, and most transmissions to and
from the Commander are made via the frequencies of
sound. Light transmissions require much more power.
Usually these are accomplished only by the most adept
Captains or other officers of the fleet. However, anyone
capable of activating, and then fully charging his operational system, can use the television for sending and/or
receiving full video telecasts, conjoined with the audio
messages.

To begin or end any single transmission with the
Commander, different code words are used, having the
general meaning of "come in" and "over and out." The
Captains of the West often use the signal, "In the name
of the Father, the Son and the Holy Ghost," in the case of
the former, and "Amen," in the case of the latter. Some
Eastern Captains simply use "Mu" or even "Kwatz" for
both. The most widely used code words in the East are
"Sat, Tat, Om" for tuning in, and "Om, Tat, Sat" for sign-
ing off.

We understood, before our sleep, that whenever it
became time to make our return trip, our earthly body
would drop away, much like a booster rocket does when
the fuel has been exhausted. The radio then automatically activates to its pre-tuned return frequency (93 Hz),
and we are transported Home naturally on its Tractor
Beam. This happens whether we are aware of it or not.
This procedure cannot be circumvented by our own
ignorance or forgetfulness. Essentially we have an auto-
pilot system for space navigation. It is, however, useful

(even fun) to know this and to remain awake. It allows us to be more at ease with our mission. It also gives us the freedom to enjoy and play throughout our entire voyage.

But, if we forget or fall asleep, there is no problem. Beyond the flesh that we have come to inhabit, the memory and function reside...perfectly intact. Our original, pre-space flight condition remains as it was from the beginning. Do we really think that our Commander would actually let us wither on some planet in a galaxy near the edge of the universe? Not a chance!

We need not wait to become disembodied to make our report. Whenever possible, we can transmit a clear and present picture of this planetary life. **Indeed, this is an important part of our mission!**

Every Captain in the fleet has all of this information. In part, their mission is to pass this on to us whenever we request it, provided our communication system has been adjusted within our own individual physical vehicle. These radios and televisions have no "on" or "off" switch. They are always on. However, the full recognition of the sound and light transmissions, received by our consciousness, requires a "translator." This part of our basic equipment is usually activated on earth by a Captain, or by one of his officers, after a preliminary maintenance checkup has been done. For some curious earthly reason, a ceremony is often performed at this time. The ceremony is generally called "Initiation." Some Captains prefer to use the term, "Ordination."

After that, we are on our own. We can serve the Captain, if he or she needs assistance, or we can go about our way performing our own mission. However, it is generally understood that it is best to keep close to the Captain for quite some time after our initiation, to be sure that our system is operating at peak efficiency. And at no time should we lose contact with the Commander himself.

Frequently, when I contact the Commander, he sends me the same simple message, "Enjoy your mission and have a pleasant flight home. Over and out."

Om is the continuous, energetic tractor beam emanating from our Father. So sweet and full is His Voice, that once it is heard, we cannot fail to know His Purpose and feel His Power. He is our Path Home.

Because this Path has a definite audible quality, and because the Sound itself is quite subtle at first, it is tremendously important to find a quiet place. A noisy environment will not allow the Sound to be heard. While it is true that Om is vibrational and visual, as well as audible, the prominent expression of the Holy Spirit to the initiate is **its Sound**.

If you wish to enter this path, and yet your living conditions are full of noise, the effort required to get on with it will be to change your environment. You may need to relocate, or you may need to rise early in the morning, before the drone of human activity begins. There is no adequate substitute for peace and quiet. This is the essential environment of a spiritual retreat. **Dear reader, do whatever is necessary to find silence…and enter into it…over and over again!**

Once Om becomes integral to our spiritual discipline, then begins a refinement of how we hear the Sound and feel its Flow.

To help understand this refinement, let's begin by looking at the kinship of Om and the Hindu Trinity of God: Brahma, Vishnu and Shiva.

There are a number of ways we might understand these three aspects of God. Classically speaking, relative to the outward manifestation of life, Brahma is the Creator, Vishnu is the Preserver, and Shiva is the Destroyer. If life were just as it appears, then these descriptions would serve quite well. It appears that we are all born, we live for a time, and then we die. This is the basic life-cycle of form. But, Om vibrates beneath form. As we begin to appreciate the fundamental unreality (or virtual reality) of physical form, contrasted by the enduring Reality of the Holy Spirit, the Gods of the Hindu Trinity take on a deeper and more immediate meaning.

The Holy Sound, Om, (sometimes written Aum) has no beginning and no end. It contains all the tonal qualities from A (ah), through U (oo), to M (mm)…as one continuous vibratory Sound. It would not be totally accurate to divide Om into exactly three "parts" and label each part separately. However, there are three distinct tonal frequencies that can be heard.

1) A high pitched Sound,[1] that appears to circumscribe our whole body. This is the Sound of Brahma. Brahma is known as the Creator. He might just as well be described as the Initiator. Relative to our entry into the Sound, His vibration is normally the first one heard. It may be said that when we first recognize this Sound, we have received our first initiation upon the path of Om.

2) A much lower Tone,[2] which resonates with the incoming flow of pranic essence, from God, through the Soul, into man and his sensory organs. This is the Sound of Vishnu. Vishnu is the Preserver. He is heard and felt as a cool, preserving flow of vibratory Essence that sustains the life force in the body. He breathes His life into our own.

But exactly what does He preserve? Energy cannot be created or destroyed. It is transformed from one state into another. At certain times it may be active. At other times it may be dormant. But the potential never passes away. **Vishnu preserves the Design**. At the time of cosmic dissolution, form returns to Spirit. Vishnu then sleeps, waiting for the next age to commence, when He will redistribute the energetic design of duality.

3) A deeper and lower Tone,[3] resonating with the outgoing pranic flow. This is the Sound of Shiva. It is heard

---

[1] Vibrating at the frequency of Eb on the musical scale...almost three octaves above middle C...and having multiple overtones.

[2] Vibrating at the frequency of B, one octave plus a half step below middle C. Some may experience an overtone one octave higher.

[3] Vibrating at the frequency of Gb, a harmonic third below that of Vishnu. Some may experience an overtone, one octave higher.

Note: The values for these frequencies are both approximate and relative to the observer. They were measured by the author, from his own inner listening to the Cosmic Sound. A significant feature of these three Sounds is their relative frequencies. The ratio of the frequencies of these three notes within the same and felt as a warm flow of vibratory Essence. As the prana flows outward, our visual attention remains upon the inner Eye, the door to the Infinite. Shiva is known as the Destroyer...the force of God that dissolves form from our consciousness. We survive the dissolution, but the body must eventually lose its grip and return to "ashes."

Shiva is probably best understood through marriage. One of the most beautiful, and possibly most misunderstood of the Hindu Gods is the pair, Shiva and Kali. Kali is Shiva's wife. In this context, She is the Cosmic Vibration, Om. Through Kali all form is materialized. As the devotee begins hearing this Cosmic Sound, he finds himself at a bottleneck between form and formlessness.

The place where the Sound is first heard, the medulla oblongata, is known as the "mouth of God," the residence of Kali. From there initiates the flow of Cosmic Vibration into all parts of the body, thereby sustaining a "separate" and temporary, conscious form. Through Kali, all beings come into the mayaic existence.

Kali's husband, Shiva, is the formless, vibrationless Being...God beyond materialization. He is not residing in a "place" as such. Yet, within the body of man there is a correspondence which "places" His Essence in the Crown Chakra.

Kali is devoted to Shiva. She focuses her attention upon the spherical Eye, instinctively drawn to His Being. When certain vibratory conditions are reached, the Star within the Eye rises high into the Heavens, the attention then is drawn upward with tremendous force and purpose, and Her Essence then rises. This is the Ascension...the dissolution of form into the formless.

Kali and Shiva are wedded. These two are opposite poles...and this polarity exists within each human being. Each of us resonates the perfected microcosmic design of

---

octave is 4 : 5 : 6. The actual notes form the B Major chord. All major chords have this same ratio, which is the most fundamental resonant feature in music. These notes and their overtones create the Music of the Spheres.

God. Shiva is the Destroyer, in as much as He initiates the return to formlessness. Samadhi occurs as human consciousness passes out of form, by merging with the Cosmic Vibration, and then dissolving into formless Being. **This is the destruction...the de-materialization of the conscious attachment to physical life.** It is useful to understand this as Spiritual Awakening, rather than physical death.

Essential to the Hindu description of God is the Trinity of Being that exists during the cycles of manifestation. At these times, God (Brahman) takes on three primary attributes: Father, Son and Spirit (or Holy Ghost). Hindus have named them *Sat – Tat – Om*. When the cycles of manifestation conclude, God remains absolute and formless. This is known as Para-Brahman.

Each person is a single unique expression of this manifesting Trinity. Within each of us, *Sat* resides in the thousand-petaled Lotus in the brain. *Tat* forms the Spiritual Eye. And *Om* manifests the entire body of vibration.

Thus, as we intone the words, "Sat – Tat – Om," we are expressing the manifestation of God as form. When we reverse these words, "Om – Tat – Sat," we are expressing the return of form into the formless Infinite.

Now, let us pause for a moment...This cosmology is essentially useless information, until we let the Sound in! It is pointless to adhere to the idea of the Trinity of Om as Sound, without actually entering the Domain of the Sound. **The theory must not become a substitute for the Experience!** There is no worthwhile substitute for the Hearing of this Holy Sound, Om. The trap of all cosmology is that we become absorbed in the idea, rather than the Essence. We must remain vigilant to stay with the Sound itself.

Likewise, to consider the Trinity of God...Father, Son and Spirit...as some form of theoretical distinction, existing outside our own experience, is basically useless as well. These are the three fundamental manifestations of our Self. We can locate and experience them within our bodies. Otherwise, we fail to recognize Who We Are and perpetuate our own delusion. Meditation upon Om is a yogic discipline leading to the realization of Om – Tat – Sat.

To initiate our conscious union with God, we learn and practice those techniques that allow us to tune ourselves to the Resonance of Om. The transference of rhythmic breathing into a steady, continuous presence of the incoming and outgoing...upward and downward Currents, and the advancing techniques of *Pranayama* usher the fully conscious man into Samadhi. At the end of a long practice...years, perhaps lifetimes...and with the sure-handed guidance of the Master, we enter a condition where breath ceases, heartbeat ceases, and the still, eternal Being is experienced. This is where the path is leading.

The awakening of the *Kundalini* initiates two primary currents of prana within the body. The *apana* current flows downward from the Crown Chakra to the coccyx. Shiva initiates this current to dissolve the body consciousness.

The other current is called *prana*. It is the upward flow from the coccyx into the Eye Center. Vishnu sustains this current by drawing our consciousness into the Eye of God. Initially prana "pauses" within the Eye, and then begins to bridge the gap between the Eye Center and the Crown Chakra, completing the circuit.

These two currents, acting in opposite directions, create the duality of breath...the inhalation and the exhalation... and attach the otherwise pristine consciousness of the soul as Spirit to the conditions of the body. This is the primary situation experienced through incarnation. It is the fundamental, yet temporary environment. Until an adequate flow of prana relieves the body of its persistent physical functioning, the consciousness of the soul cannot perceive its Self with omnipresent clarity.

Yoga leads to the effortless and blissful experience of stillness within this dualistic flow.

When God breathes us, and we stop interfering, we slowly attune to His Rhythm. The breath gradually slows and will eventually cease, without causing physical death. Consciousness is then joined completely to a finer and more etheric Vibration. God's Bliss manifests throughout. Our conscious attention translates from the physical form to the etheric Essence. It is our persistent attention upon this real Essence that allows this transformation to take place.

Breathing is actually happening simultaneously in two ways, as two distinct kinds of experience. The process and the manner in which they overlap is, quite possibly, the most significant information needed to understand this Life. We then know how to proceed from human form into Spirit. Pranic breathing is what God is doing in all parts of Himself to allow His bliss and awareness to interpenetrate His Mansion.

The point between the eyebrows is the point where the life of man joins the Omniscience of God. The Energy of God is continuous...and utterly harmonic. The experience of man, however, vacillates with his breath. The Will of God is perfectly steady. It can be heard as the continuous harmonic Tone. The signal to breathe is initiated at the spiritual Eye, and the physical form of man is sustained. Vishnu is at work. But hear the Truth: Shiva is ever waiting to usher us Home.

I can do no more, and no better, than to share this permanent news. My repetition is a meager attempt to approximate its endlessness. Each time the sound of these words subsides, the spherical Sound is left alone... exposed...drawing the listener Home...hOMe!

All roads lead to Om. This is where we are going. This is the secret path leading to our fulfillment. This is the meaning of, "Thy Will be done on earth as it is in heaven."

Once we find this path, and apply the continuous effort required to know, in an utterly resolute way, that This is our own conscious Soul experiencing God, Life is completely transformed. The meaning of the "events" of this life become clear. The need to get information about this mind stuff can be fulfilled directly and completely within our Self. Eventually, however, even this need dies out. It vanishes. The outer life glides on with an easy dynamic momentum. Friction ceases to restrict our creative efforts. All things proceed as they will. The Calling of God for us to return unites with our own conscious attention, initiating the uninterrupted Flow of vibrant Energy, Sound and Light.

Om - Tat - Sat

PRANAYAMA

Prana goes to the heart of yoga. It is the very energy that is our life. It is the "substance" we use to attain our goal... to leave body consciousness and enter Divine Realization. It is the ever present Force of God in manifestation.

As we shall see, there are two types of prana. The causal connection between the prana existing everywhere, in all the "things" of creation, with the unique and surprising energetic **flow** along the interior cerebro-spinal channel... is real and yet mysterious. As we discuss this, however, we must take care not to isolate this as an idea. It is experiential. We can find scientific words that indicate, in some small way, the nature of this flow and the transition that happens to us, but words alone are inadequate.

It serves us to be aware that the three bodies form the scientific laboratory wherein this energy exchange takes place. At all times it will serve each of us to **protect, nourish, cherish and properly use the body** we have been given...and to treat all other bodies as sacred. A Divine Purpose is contained in each one.

In India the common everyday greeting of two people is, "Namaste." This literally means, "I acknowledge (or 'bow to') the God within you." When this acknowledgment is our real everyday recognition, then we shall be ready to begin the transition of prana that delivers us consciously to the feet of the Master. A single touch upon these feet enlightens the flame of Divine Illumination.

The exact techniques,[1] which greatly assist the devotee in his individual metamorphosis of Divine Realization, are

---

[1] There are many schools of yoga, which employ varying techniques and/or initiations. Some employ rapid and highly force-

demonstrated in a special way at an appropriate time. There is an intimate and private quality about the transmission that is not commonly available through written words. There is also a question of timing. As we prepare for this Divine Transition, we reach a definite threshold of understanding, commitment, devotion and physical conditioning, that can be recognized by the trained Eye. At the right time, the techniques are given...and the way opens up. Most devotees have a definite appreciation for this timing.

But a great effort will be required. This is not a pathway of idle curiosity. Old habits die hard. Until they do, and until a time comes when the effort to be with God totally consumes us, we cannot hope to make the energy transition. It simply does not happen until certain conditions are right. We must ask ourselves... Are we ready to have no further **personal** use for the life of the flesh? Are we ready to put ourselves through an initiation of fire? When we

---

ful breathing techniques, sometimes referred to as "fire breathing." The intention of these forceful techniques is to mechanically raise the kundalini. I would like to caution the reader not to practice any technique which uses any such extraordinary physical force. All yogic technique should be applied with a calm devotional attitude, under the direction of a qualified instructor or master. The kundalini will awaken naturally in the proper environment.

The qualities which color the attention, attitudes and vibrational environment within the disciple should be essentially in tune with the seven qualities which have been listed on the cover of this work: Devotion, Love, Wisdom, Joy, Vibration, Sound and Light. Our bodies are the sacred ground for our evolving experience of Spirit.

Unfortunately, some schools also employ the use of hallucinogenic drugs (e.g. peyote or LSD) which chemically and forcefully separate the Soul from some of its physical moorings. When the etheric web, binding soul and body together, is prematurely and somewhat arbitrarily torn, grave problems within all three bodies may ensue. Such drugs can seriously disassociate the Soul Consciousness from its natural path.

reach the edge of the world where matter and Spirit lose their separate qualities, do we retreat into the small, temporary, "safe" life we once thought of as our individual self, or do we joyously enter the Essence…that which has no limitation and no definition as well? This is the ecstatic experience of effortless non-separation from the Whole, which allows no further body or place to which we may lay individual claim. This is how ego evaporates, leaving only the Presence of the Self, which has always been and will always be the exact Essence we have been seeking.

This book has been written to awaken a keen interest in the path…and to open a way to the **edge** of a precipice, into which the devotee must leap. We shall now journey together to that edge…to look at the Essence that forms our life. We will put our toes into the primordial flow to get an initiating feel for where we are going. We shall stare together at the endless expanse that is our destiny.

On the ceiling of the Sistine Chapel lies the marvelous painting by Michelangelo known as *Creation of Adam*. Near the pinnacle of the chapel dome is the central focus of the painting. The Father, accompanied by a choir of angels, is reaching down to his son, Adam, who halfheartedly is reaching up. Their outstretched fingers almost touch…almost! This is tremendously significant. They are so close…yet not quite connected. There is a gap.

Why is Adam separated from his Father? Why is he so nonchalant? It is not because the Father is making an inadequate attempt to reach His son. Intense concern is clearly written all over His face. He is reaching down with his complete attention and effort. No…the distance is not yet bridged, because the son is not making the necessary effort. He has not yet perceived the importance of the connection, and thereby has not summoned the adequate force. He is drifting on a cloud, unconcerned about his situation. He seems unaware of his separation.

We are Adam. We are drifting. But, lets say that we are somewhat "aware." Either through our intelligence or through our pain…and almost certainly through both…we have discovered that we are separate. Wherever we now are, we are certain that it is not exactly Home. If this is the case, how will we get Home? By what force will we make such a return? And if such a force exists, what will be our measure of control?

Prana is the primordial energetic Force of the universe. It is the essence of all force. It is the force of Life itself. Without this force there would be no movement, there would be no thought, there would be no matter, there would be nothing...no thing at all. We are intimately reminded of prana through each of our three bodies. The physical reminder is food and water. The emotional reminder is breath. The mental reminder is our conscious attention. **Conscious control of this force within our own body is called *Pranayama*.**

There are two distinct ways to absorb prana, corresponding to the two distinct arenas of experience...matter and Spirit. The incarnated being experiences the world of the three bodies. The entire manifested cosmos is an active, organizational, energetic dimension wherein all bodies reside. We shall call the energy of this entire dimension, ***Cosmic Prana***. Herein, there is a matrix of energy conservation and energy exchange, which can be described somewhat by the laws of physics as we know them.

Every physicist today recognizes that this field of energy is, in some mysterious way, constant. The sum total of all the energy in the universe does not increase or decrease. It also has no known limitation or boundary. It is always here and it cannot dissipate. It can undergo transformation, but there can never be any absolute loss or gain. Our bodies are minute fragments of that manifested energy. They respond within this field in ways that are recognizable, once the laws of manifestation are known.

Cosmic Prana is the underlying force that supports the appearance of all matter. As such, it is present within our food. It is the Life of the food. It is contained in greatest measure and quality in live, ripened fruits, vegetables, seeds, nuts and grains. As we cook these foods, some of the life is lost in the heat. Of course, some foods (particularly grains) must be cooked to absorb water and become soft enough to be absorbed by our digestive systems.

Ample descriptions of proper dietary habits fill the bookshelves. I only want to emphasize that the prana we derive from food is maximized in quantity and quality by a diet of sensible moderation, with a definite emphasis upon the simple, wholesome life quality that we can absorb from organic plant life and pure water.

Our emotional body absorbs and processes Cosmic Prana primarily through breathing. If we could see the dynamic molecular, atomic and subatomic activity of the air we breathe, we would begin to appreciate the vast amount of energy entering our body with each breath. Yet we assimilate only a tiny fraction of that potential through oxygenation.[1] The effort of our breathing is highly inefficient. Mostly we proceed through life absorbing just enough prana to get by. The amount, quality and direction of the force that becomes available to us is affected by the pattern of breath, the deepness of breath and the conscious attitude we maintain in the process.

There is a tremendously close connection between the way we breathe and the way we experience. Every kind of emotional state regulates, or is regulated by, a distinct pattern of breath. When we are tense, our breathing is quick. It has a kind of desperation in it. We can hardly take in enough oxygen to satisfy the need. As fast as we can draw it in, the tension burns it.

When we are sitting still and quietly thinking of something pleasant, our breath is slow and shallow. We do not require a great deal of vibrant energy in this condition, and

---

[1] The normal molecular content of the air we breathe (dry air at sea level) by volume is approximately 78% nitrogen (N_2), 21% oxygen (O_2), 1% argon (Ar) and traces of other gases. Normally, carbon dioxide (CO_2) accounts for approximately 0.03%. Water vapor is found in variable concentrations.

The air that we exhale contains about 16% oxygen and 5% carbon dioxide. Thus, we actually absorb only about 25% of the oxygen that is taken into our lungs, or about 5% of all the air we breathe.

the stillness allows us to access the more subtle regions of the brain that store memory and stimulate our cognitive faculties.

When lovers are making love, the breath at the beginning is very slow and deep. The slowness is a response to an inner, joyous feeling of the love they share. The deepness of breath is a response to the overall enlivening that is felt, and the eventual energy requirement needed in the orgasmic state. The breathing gradually becomes faster and more deep, to fulfill the energetic need.

When we are exercising intensely, we breathe quickly and very deeply...sometimes we are even gasping for breath. As we rest for a moment to catch our breath, slowly we begin to feel the power return to our limbs and clarity to our brain. We regain our mental and physical balance. We have all experienced this.

We could go on and on, describing different breathing patterns associated with different physical, emotional and mental states. However, the state that is significant for our purpose is meditation and the corresponding subtle, energetic, interiorized attention.

All aspects of our essential Design have a hierarchical categorization. The maxim, "As above, so below," always applies. The physical, the etheric and the causal lives are each a metaphor for the utter Spiritual Reality. So, if breathing is "below," what is "above," and how are they connected? This is tremendously significant.

Breathing can be seen as a series of births and deaths. There is a lifelong relationship between breath and incarnation, from the first in-breath of a newborn to the last out-breath of the dying man, where the quality of each breath mirrors the quality of each moment. It will help to grasp intuitively the import of this statement. It will lead to the understanding that **how we breathe** determines, in part, our experience of **who we are**.

Why and how we breathe is very mysterious. As long as we are "alive," it just happens. When we "die," it simply stops. Each and every breath we draw inward and release outward is a natural resonance of the incarnated soul-body with some primordial force. From this force arises a dual quality...the yin and the yang. This two-part reverberation within us is our own microcosmic activation within the eternal, bipolar, energetic field of nature.

If we watch and listen to the breath very carefully, we may begin to recognize some subtle yet significant details of the design of this life, which hitherto have been unknown. Gradually we may experience each breath as an inner responding to an ever present need to awaken...to know our Self and the entire environment more completely. We begin to merge with a new found feeling of joy. In short, we begin to heal. As this happens, we may witness our Self as an effortless drop in the Ocean of Life.

Slowly we wake up to experience something quite marvelous and unexpected. We come to discover each breath as our own individual resonance to a deeply wondrous **calling**. In fact... **This is exactly true!** A totally awesome purpose is making itself known...a purpose that only a "child" could suspect. **We are being called away from the dual expression of life, into the central place of cosmic awareness**. This passage is greatly accelerated by pranayama, which is often defined as the control of breath, but its actual meaning is "the control of Life."

Under normal human circumstances our body distributes Cosmic Prana as a complex organization of swirling energy. We shall call this energy field, *body prana.* This body prana is to Cosmic Prana, what noise is to music. It has a chaotic, disturbed quality, which interferes with the natural flow and the intelligent design. Ego is the act of creating and sustaining body prana and not allowing Cosmic Prana to manifest as it will in its natural way. Ego creates a stagnant, partially closed energy system. Ego circumscribes what appears to be "itself," and thereby partially separates from the whole life force. It does this because of an ignorant and habitual lack of trust in the natural process. **Yoga is the practice of allowing the body prana to become reorganized and redistributed according to the original design of Cosmic Prana.**

Our physical body is a partially closed energetic system. Prana enters our body in small measure through food and breath. However, there is a more direct way to absorb Cosmic Prana. In most humans this is not known, and underdeveloped. The primary place within the body where Cosmic Prana enters and feeds us is in the area of the medulla oblongata. In the Bible this area is referred to as the "mouth of God." Through yoga technique, this becomes a wide open area of entry. From there, prana is distributed to the energy centers (chakras) through an etheric network.

There is a subtle, yet very significant, inter-dimensional channel within each of us, wherein is made the energetic link between the world of the three bodies and the direct energy of Spirit. It is the tether or etheric cord that maintains the nexus of the Soul Life and the physical body. The Soul that sleepwalks through this human life has little or no awareness of this cord, because the energy exchange along its path for him is very weak and subtle...normally below the threshold of conscious awareness. **Kundalini Pranayam[1] is the yogic process of consciously creating**

---

[1] The word, *Pranayama*, is sometimes written *Pranayam* (without an *a* at the end). Sanskrit scholars and accomplished yogis describe how the meaning changes with or without the last *a*. Swami Satyeswarananda Giri, for example, indicates that the correct spelling for this Kriya technique of breath ends in *m*. (See *Kriya: Finding the True Path*, p. 298–299.) In making the choice between these two spellings (and pronunciations) I faced a dilemma common to all devotees. When we are uncertain, whom should we trust. Satyeswarananda's argument is quite convincing, and very likely correct. Yet the writings of the one I have met upon my inward journey suggests the other.

I then took a tangential, and somewhat intuitive tack on the question. I listened to the pure sound of the two pronunciations. First: the **sound** of the word, *Pranayam*, is vibrationally more consistent with the **interiorized** experience of the **stillness** itself. Yet: the **symmetry** of the word, *Pranayama*, is vibrationally more consistent with the dual flow of the in-breath and the out-breath. (The mother tongue, Sanskrit, carries a vast blend of meaning through sound itself. This description only slightly intimates the

and sustaining a definite ascending and descending flow of Cosmic Prana through this cord. This opens the three bodies to the natural, blissful qualities of Cosmic Energy.

As we become more and more **quiet and still,** we may begin to hear and feel this flow. Through the practice of this yoga we do two things. We increase the pranic flow itself...by practicing certain exercises...and we hear and feel this flow with greater intensity as we become more still and silent in our meditations. We are moving toward a state of complete stillness...a state of suspended physical animation...whereby our conscious attention can be released from its prison of constant activity.

We are approaching a condition where Pranayama becomes an energetic substitute for both breath and pulse. To help visualize this, consider the following metaphor. Imagine a being of two dimensions only...a "flatlander." He moves along a single plane, east and west, north and south. But that is it! There is no depth. This is his entire universe of experience. Then something unexpected happens. Suddenly he discovers a new dimension...up and down. It is a total surprise. Life as he knows it completely changes.

In a parallel way, the mechanism whereby we may redistribute Cosmic Prana according to its Divine Matrix is tangential to our everyday experience and control. Instead of being energized solely by breath and the flow of oxygen

---

intricate nuances that are available to the scholar of this language.)

I made the simple choice of accepting both...each for slightly separate meanings. I use the word, *pranayama*, as a general term for the action of the balanced inner movement of prana associated with each pair of breaths...in and out. The association is dynamic, in that prana moves between Centers, yet static, in that the action is balanced and observed from stillness. However, when distinguishing between each of several separate poised actions of prana, (to be discussed in the final chapter) I have chosen to use the term, *pranayam*. Thus the plural of the term is *pranayams*.

through our bloodstream, we access Cosmic Prana directly through an innate Spiritual Form. Using a special, non-forceful yogic technique of attention, the physical breath stimulates the "interiorized" flow of Cosmic Prana.

The application of this technique is analogous to the way we prime a water pump. A small amount of water is poured into the system and the handle is pumped until the water begins to flow. (This comparison is surprisingly close.) Once the flow of water is established, the priming action is no longer required. The water flows naturally by the siphoning force of the water's momentum and the air pressure upon the reservoir of water. The flow of Cosmic Prana along the interior channel has much the same feel, with one significant difference. The water flows in one direction only, while Cosmic Prana flows in both directions...more like an alternating electrical current.

There is a change of dimension, because there has been a change of conscious attention. The body identification slips away and a cessation of urge commences. The dualistic mind rests. All scientific forms of meditation arise from the recognition of this non-movement. We have long identified our self as being **on** the "Wheel of Life." All the while, the Center has been there. We have simply not gone there. We have been too busy.

In one respect our entire life of meditation is directed toward this transition. We are in a state of half sleep, groping for a way to wake up, but it is difficult to get a handle on it. We are blindly approaching a moment when our life will suddenly acquire a new dimension...a dimension of pure awareness, where conscious attention and Cosmic Prana merge.

To acquire the ability to redistribute Cosmic Prana within the cord, we must first learn how to enter the cerebrospinal channel consciously, and remain there for extended periods of time. The only way we can begin to achieve this entry is to remove our attention from the senses. **This is the single greatest challenge of the spiritual life.** It is the sense organs, themselves, which have drawn our attention outward in the first place. These sense organs, by design, require a steady distribution of oxygen for their use. This is achieved by breathing and the flow of oxygenated blood. However, when we **completely disengage** our attention from the senses, this blood flow is no longer required. Instead, the entire vehicle is enveloped in an energy field of Cosmic Prana.

The yogi disciplines himself to make this cerebro-spinal entry again and again. He learns to make this his home. Eventually he becomes adept at watching...**and thus causing**...Cosmic Prana to flow within himself as is its design. The cord within the body enlivens with resonant energy. A wondrous, soothing Current awakens along the spine and brain. It resonates sympathetically with the Holy Sound, Om. As this happens, the yogi gains an immediate insight into the path of incarnation. Consciousness firmly attaches itself to the body through the breath. This new flow dramatically alters the way his consciousness perceives this attachment. For the moment, he becomes a fish out of water and begins to understand the "water" for the first time.

It is important to emphasize that while we can describe Pranayama in certain mechanical terms, it should not be considered purely mechanical. The multi-dimensional qualities of Spirit cannot be circumvented. The qualities of devotion, love, wisdom and joy must be part of the human equation of Transformation, because these are the Essence of the experience we are entering. This is why the Master's Presence is so essential. He has manifested these qualities to perfection. Until we absorb these qualities, the mechanical functioning of techniques will have little or no effect upon our transition. This transition is not from one physical experience to another physical experience... **We are moving into a new Dimension entirely.**

The meditative process ripens slowly. After the specific yoga techniques have been practiced for some time, in the Presence of the Master, a point eventually comes when we acquire "Life control." We pass into this new dimension... the paradigm shifts.

Let us now turn our attention to the relationship of our mental body and Cosmic Prana.

We are largely unaware of the significance our conscious attention plays in energy conversion. Normally we imagine that there is a long, involved, forceful manipulation that intervenes between a good idea and a finished "product." This is the nature of the physical life. Patience and perseverance are required in this slower, murky dimension. As the attunement to Spirit progresses, however, inexorably we begin to slip into a conscious realm, where life glides along a path of no resistance. Materialization progresses more naturally and with greater ease.

Psychologists and philosophers, like Nietzsche, Freud, Jung and others, have opened discussions in the West regarding an undeveloped state of mind called the *superconscious*. However, they failed to describe any simple, straightforward plan to experience it. Yoga is that plan!

Our mental body experiences prana as thought and conscious attention. There is a deep and utterly direct relationship between conscious attention and pranic force. We are familiar with the idea of the "power of positive thinking," but it is usually pictured as some vague quality that directs "us" to use force, and not the actual direction of the Force itself.

Every pulse of the centrifugal flow of attention directs prana into the physical, emotional and mental landscape. All of this is the endless creation of Spirit Force in evolution. The use of our sensory mechanisms continuously draws Cosmic Prana downward, forward and outward in order to experience the environment itself. This outward evolutionary path of the senses, through the design of nature, always brings us to an experiential edge beyond which there appears to exist some "other." Each and every such experience reinforces the idea that we are one thing, and everything else is not our self. All sense bound activity thereby supports the collective mis-in-formation of the individual ego. This, in turn, leads to codes of behavior, patterns of relating and a general consensus that nature... the externalized design...is the Essential Reality.

We dwell just between two realms. We are quite familiar with the physical realm, where we have learned to direct our attention outward for success. But we are infants in a Spiritual Realm of which we know very little. Thought, however, can balance, redirect and then reverse the flow of attention. Cognitive reasoning is the first step of a newborn Spiritual Being...a Son of God. The **direction** of that new birth and its manifestation is the reversal of the outward evolutionary path.

How does a salmon know to make the arduous and "life" ending return upstream? It is a knowing identical to the knowing that the spiritual infant discovers. It is intuitive. It is unrelated to the everyday rationale of the thinking man. The searchlights are reversed.

We are beginning to uncover the single **greatest misconception** regarding the spiritual journey. This misconception is largely unconscious and habitual. Our physical birth brought us to our senses. Slowly we developed control of our sense experience and thereby awakened... actually, reawakened...our cognitive facility, centered within the brain. As our thought patterns evolve, they maintain a connective relationship to form. Hence, despite the fact that the location of thought is near, or partially within the region of the Spiritual Womb, the pattern of thought itself is endlessly directed **outward**. It remains habitually linked to physical form. Instinctively we all seek God in a virtually continuous way, but for some peculiar reason we seek Him in the **wrong direction. We seek Him in form**, because we are firmly attached to form as experience.

Nature and Spirit are thus confused in our minds. Nature and Spirit are not the same. Nature is the creative blueprint of the outer appearance of Spirit, while Spirit itself is neither manifested nor unmanifested. To oppose nature is the way of illness and death. To identify with nature is the way of Maya (delusion). To simply allow nature to operate in its domain is the wisdom available to all who recognize the forming of physical manifestation **and** the Source of Life. Nature and Spirit have no real relationship. Yet we can use nature to assemble things, thoughts and energy in a way that allows us to approach, and then experience, the primordial qualities of Spirit. We can involve inner Light, Sound and Vibration to resonate within our form, connecting us to Bliss. This is the path to liberation.

Through deeper and deeper meditation, we discover the path **to** liberation follows those vibrational qualities that emanate naturally **from** it, but **in reverse**. It is a two-way path. This discovery leads to practice...cellular practice, atomic practice and eventually complete "control" of Life...**Pranayama**.

The Zen Masters have recognized our misdirected attention. It is our fundamental disease. If left untreated, the patient becomes terminally ill...ill for a term...one life's sentence. Hence the Master shouts, "Mu!" He initiates No Mind...which is really "conscious attention not attached to form." This fundamental spiritual discipline allows the **resonance** to enter. Resonance is the environment of Illumination. Spirit is forever here, prepared as Essence to manifest.

Consider the experience of Hui-nêng, (638–713), the 6th Zen Patriarch of China. One day, before he had ever studied Buddhism, he was passing by a place where the *Diamond Sutra* was being recited. He overheard a single passage, and suddenly he opened. He experienced *satori*, an utter oneness with Spirit. The phrase that triggered this release from the limited human condition was, "Awaken the mind, but fix it nowhere."

We are in the way of Spirit. Our specific mental solutions are largely the problem itself. To pass into ever greater illumination, we must acquire an alert and utterly open condition through trust, into which this unlimited bipolar resonance will enter.

The Master thus strikes to eliminate the disease of mind by making the disciple absolutely aware that he is not yet cured. He is not yet free. This yoga is the practice of those attentive inner adjustments that permits the consciousness to come alive with resonance. This initiates its return...

inward, along the cerebro-spinal channel connecting Spirit and form...Heaven and earth.

When focused narrowly and applied continuously, thought actually becomes an integral partner in the opening of the inner etheric pathway. Devotional thought refines and empowers the body circuitry. It prepares our circuits for the impending resonant force. Normally we experience our self as in a sealed chamber...vaguely aware of a vast energetic Being of Spirit "outside." However, we are somewhat ignorant of the completely benign and nurturing nature of this Being...the Whole Being God Is. There is more... This Being of Power is not simply benign. God as Spirit is the irresistible vibrational Force, which inevitably transports us into blissful illumination. Mind, however, beset with the fear of its own annihilation, fills the interior with the incessant pressure of its own thought, thus jamming the door shut and temporarily preventing the resonant entry.

The great drama that is about to take place can do so only upon our invitation. To invite God within is the prayer. To release the interiorized pressure and open the door is the practice of yoga. Illumination is the inevitable conscious result.

There is, however, a word of caution that we need to understand and heed. The Spirit Force is essentially benign, and yet it has tremendous...actually **unlimited**... power. When a diver has been very deep in the sea for a long time, he cannot suddenly return to the surface without adverse affects. As he descended, his body made a gradual adaptation to a great external pressure. As he rises, he must go through a careful decompression, or face serious internal injury or death. Spiritual decompression is exactly like this.

Our conscious entry and evolution in the world of the three bodies has been effected through a gradual adaptation to an environment of tremendous density. The physical density is relatively obvious. We are essentially confined to a single place in time and space. When we fall asleep, an exit is made, but we lose our conscious condition, or drift in a semi-conscious dream state. Only rarely, if ever, do we leave our physical prison fully conscious.

There are highly confining densities in our astral and mental bodies as well. We have become conditioned to patterns of suffering and limitation, through years of bondage to feelings of sloth, anger, fear, jealousy, resentment, irritation, dissatisfaction, anxiety, expectation and so on. This is a vast array of confining attitudes. We cannot suddenly burst into unrestrained, ecstatic and ceaseless joy. It is unfamiliar territory for us. Normally we make a slow adaptation in this direction, characterized by one or more leaps into the waiting arms of this God of Joy.

Mentally we have constructed a framework of thought, more or less in tune with the prevailing thought patterns within this human family. We have no real appreciation for **unlimited thought**. To burst upon a consciousness of omnipresent and omniscient quality would suddenly tear apart the well defined, self-constructed fabric of mind, that now envelops us. Our mental hospitals are overflowing with individuals who have virtually no way to cope with this kind of sudden and continuous mental disassociation.

It is not enough to simply formulate a philosophy or belief system to accommodate an infinite and unlimited mind. It is a start to imagine such a "Thing," but our adaptation to the Reality of this primordial, joyous, omniscient condition should not be underestimated. Tremendous inner work is required, and a guide is virtually essential. Find this guide…this Master…and prepare for something utterly marvelous…indescribable.

For now, there is this simple description: Unlimited, vibrant, conscious Force enters the medulla, moves up and down the spine and awakens the Eye Center, where the physical-astral-mental circuits conjoin. There shines the Cosmic Star from which our bodies are formed. It shines within a Blue Sphere surrounded by a circle of Light.[1]

---

[1] The Circle of Light is the sphere of Cosmic Essence (Spirit). The Sphere (deep opalescent blue in color) is the domain of Spiritual Reality or Christ Consciousness. The Star is the visual registration of our Father.

Slowly this Star comes into focus. As the flow of inward conscious attention progresses, we pass through the Star and complete our joyous union.

May the peace, joy and eternal bliss of the One Spirit of God fill you and make you Whole. Amen.

Kundalini Pranayam:

In as breath... I thus do rise
    in cooling rush of Lighted birth.
Then down as breath... I thus do fall
    to warm the Heart and wed the earth.

And let this practice so extend
    to move as smoothly as a breeze
That even as the grasses bend
    they welcome it with ease.
    I welcome it with ease.

A rhythm like poetic verse
    touches deep the Heart to feel
And loose the chains of anguished cells
    revealing waves of Joy to heal.

And on this wave a Word resounds
    deep into the Eye to know
That each may see the passing life
    is his to make the wonder show.

And grip not to the Word in stream
    lest ye leave the Heart aside
But join into symphonic play
    the coming and the ebbing tide.

To hear upon the current still
    a whisper call, a friendly Voice
Making clear the Path remains
    until I make the choice.

In as breath... I thus do rise
    in cooling rush of lighted birth
Then down as breath... I thus do fall
    to warm the Heart and wed the earth.

Resonating Sound of Thee
    for each and every cell to find
The inner flow along the spine
    an involution of a kind
    where sings the heart of Joy
    where sings the heart of Joy.

And when the flow of Love is full
    without a single thread to miss
The coming and the going join
    tender as a kiss.

Thus in time a ripeness comes
    where inner and the outer see
Without a trace of doubt to know
    that there is naught but Thee.
    For there is naught but Thee.

Into the Voice that You do speak
    to shape a Sound of Love to hear
A home in every place to be
    within a Heart that You did steer
    the Endless Sounding Love to hear.

A laugh to think someone might fail
at passing through the door to come.
The Tallyman, Him smile and say,
"Welcome every single one...
Welcome everyone."

MEDITATION

Divine Light
Sound - Sound - Sound
Vibration - Vibration - Vibration
Joy - Joy - Joy - Joy - Joy - Joy - Joy - Joy
Wisdom - Wisdom - Wisdom - Wisdom - Wisdom
Love - Love - Love - Love - Love - Love - Love - Love
Devotion - Devotion - Devotion - Devotion - Devotion - Devotion

Om, the Cosmic Sound-Vibration, is the continuous, impelling force-field of Spirit, acting through the medium of mental, astral and physical manifestation. It enlivens matter into relative aspects...yang and yin, in-breath and out-breath, male and female, the subjective and the objective.

The return current of force is heard as continuous Sound and seen dancing as a river of Light, while life is endlessly expressing its design throughout the physical universe. Remove the dams of emotional inhibition...and awareness easily returns to its natural state. Pure and completely joyous witnessing commences. The yogi attunes to Cosmic Prana. The conscious Being returns hOMe along the current.

When God enters the human form, He functions in a way that does not oppose nature. With each in-breath a life is born. With each out-breath a life ends. Yet He remains still...not manifesting...witnessing. The physical breath is guided into a design, sympathetic and resonant with Cosmic Prana, flowing within the inner channel. He indwells, unidentified with form, centered within Om, viewing the Cosmic Eye, feeling the vibrant flow. Holy Spirit fills the infinite space, manifesting through the matrix of nature. Through deep attention and nonresistance, matter is known to be Spirit.

Direct the will to flow as one with the Sound Current. The Father dwells above. His Son waits within the Eye Center. The Soul experiences nature's design and responds to the Father's call. The flow nourishes the Heart Center, where a wondrous Bell sounds. Om is the traveling medium, illuminating the Eye and translating the sound experience into light experience.

Permit the flow.

Om resonates in all Centers. Conscious awareness slips gently into this Sound. Devotion sweeps clean the home. The outer world dissolves in transparent Light. The Light coalesces as a central Star, seen rising in the East. Behold the transparent gaze of the Master! Thus the way is made clear and certain. Praise be to God.

Amen.

JOY

The Master experiences himself as an infinite bubble of joy. He is completely amazed by who he is. He may now be "used" to it...at home with himself...but it is still a source of wonder. This experience arrives only after a tremendous effort, yet effort itself cannot sustain it. Deep within, the urgency that drove him to make his unique discovery is now extinguished. There is a beautiful Zen story describing this:

Tê-shan (780–865) was studying under the master Ch'ung-hsin. While sitting outside the master's room, Ch'ung-hsin invited him in. Tê-shan responded that it was so dark that he could not find his way. The master then lit a candle and handed it to him. As Tê-shan was about to take it, the master blew it out. Suddenly the bottom of life fell out for Tê-shan. The urgency disappeared. The need disappeared. As the attention shifts from a linear searching to the primordial and appropriate place of Being, the problem of life dissolves.

That candle is blown out. The outer need is gone. All that remains is the undeniable joy. The smile cannot come off. To do anything other than laugh, makes no sense.

I invite you now to look at your own "situation" in life. Look deeply into those conditions that precede any serious state of mind. Is there not a way to find humor?

Start with something simple...not a big issue...not world hunger or the death of a close friend or relative. Begin with some single recent event that "caused" you to become angry or discouraged. Look at it closely. What is the big deal? Is this pre-condition permanent?

No! It cannot be. There are no permanent physical conditions. Each and every thing shall change, and then pass away. New forms will arise in their place. The localized pain itself shall pass away as well. It is your choice how to deal with it. It is your choice how to react. Even when a smile or a laugh seems insane under the conditions, it may be the only truly sane thing to do.

Look around you. Some people have a smile that hardly ever comes off. Why are **they** laughing?

The Master appears like the cat who just swallowed the canary. He has one persistent, irrepressible, psychological condition. He has just experienced (and continues to experience) something very funny. He does not want to make fun of any seriousness you might be feeling, but it's hard for him not to. It's almost impossible for him to contain himself.

Don't let his humor pass you by. It's contagious…if you put up no defense. What is making him laugh can make you laugh as well. Go with it. See what happens.

No Big Deal

God Is.

Life and death are all you know,
> but these are no big deal.
Samadhi is the only worthwhile pastime,
> but it is no big deal.
The gurus and saints are the only company having worth,
> but they are no big deal.

Big deals are impossible.
> You cannot climb a fence you have made too high.
> You can only meet the Real.
Your descent into matter is your only pain,
> but ascension is no big deal.
Remember…

God Is.

Nothing happens.
There is nothing to Be excited about.
    You overreact to a meaningless Play.
Between tragedy and comedy is the slightest move...
    a minute shift of view.
See the Play,
    but it is no big deal.

Your parents think they made you.
    Are you deceived by them?
Meditation is the Only Way to awaken the sleeping hordes,
    but this is no big deal.
It changes nothing.
    No Thing can be changed.
The Recognition Is...

God Is.

The Recognition seems like some Big Deal.
    If it were like That, it would be impossible...
        beyond reach.
    Yet wandering thoughts assume it is so.

If there were a Big Deal,
    it would be Calmness,
But don't get excited.
    It's no big deal.
What excites you, holds you back.
    Meet a Master calmly.
        It's no big deal.
Were it Big,
    you could not endure your smallness.

Listen... It's Krishna's Flute.
Two Buddhas meet.
    Two chuckles and off They go.
Two Christs ...
    The slightest smile points to the dross.
    Habit clings like dust to the sheer
        Light of Being.

The "things" of this world are more like events than actual things. "Things" can cause trouble, but "events"... we just watch them. We observe them. Once done, they are but a memory. What's to worry about?

When you set out to meditate, try slipping into a condition of unqualified mirth. Let yourself become the event that you are. Light permeates the physical "suchness" you seem to be. In this condition tremendous joy radiates from the Centers.

Look once again at the cover of this book. In the middle of the pyramid of God's manifesting qualities is **Joy**. It is the last of the qualities that has an emotional compartment. Vibration, Sound and Light are qualities of pure dispassionate experience. Joy is the highest and final human experience. From joy springs enlightenment. From joy springs omnipresent bliss. Joy and mirth are the afterburners that send experience beyond the gravitational pull of matter.

Shui-lao became enlightened through a "kick" given to him by Mat-su (an 8th century Chinese Zen Master). This kick was the Master's way of shaking Shui-lao from his serious state of mind. Shui-lao was later asked to share his understanding. He simply remarked, "Since the kick so heartily given by the master, I have not been able to stop laughing."

So begin laughing yourself. And do not stop.

Bertha had been "born again." She loved to go to revivals and get absorbed in the high praises of the Gospel.

It was Saturday night under the big tent and the preacher was doing his thing... "I'm here to tell you of the wages of SIN."

"AAAAAAMEN," she cried.

"I'm here to tell you that you must REPENT of your sins...get down on your KNEES...and stop your EVIL ways!"

"AAAAAAMEN," she echoed from the back of the big tent.

"I'm here to tell you that WINE and all the alcoholic SPIRITS are tools of the DEVIL!"

"AAAAAAMEN," she cried, without dropping a stitch of her knitting.

"I'm here to tell you that the evil of SEX will curse your SOUL and bring about the wrath of ALMIGHTY GOD!"

"AAAAAAMEN," she repeated... "AAAAAAMEN!"

"And, I'm here tonight to tell you that DANCING to the GYRATIONS of Rock 'n Roll is EVIL in the eyes of the RIGHTEOUS!"

"AAAAAAMEN!"

"And finally, BROTHERS AND SISTERS, I'm here tonight to bear witness to the fact, that TOBACCO is the DEVIL'S favorite implement of DESTRUCTION!"

Bertha's mouth came wide open. Out dropped the cigar from between her lips...and it fell to the floor. She stood up, slowly crushed out the butt, put down her knitting, turned to Maude, her loving companion, and looking up over her reading glasses, she declared, "Now...he's meddling!"

For years, before he passed away from this earth, I had a very dear friend, Glenn. He was irrepressible. He lived a varied life. He had been a successful businessman and had raised a family. For almost fifty years he had been fairly predictable and "normal." Then a wanderlust set in. He reinvented himself.

When I met Glenn, he was roaming the Southwest with a business card that seemed curiously vague. It suggested that he was ready for anything. He was wide open and available. It announced that he was a trader. In fact he was ready to trade almost anything for anything else. Curious "deals" seemed to be his forte. His card read, "Glenn Newell, The Indians' Friend." It was never clear exactly what that meant. (He frolicked in a kind of happy ambiguity.) But one transparent purpose was to avoid business relationships with anyone having a prejudice against Native Americans.

When Glenn dropped by, he was always ready to find the heart of experience. He would get to the point quickly. He would not avoid any issue. He was not afraid of unpleasantness, because he recognized that each of us is responsible for our own reactions. Every thought, every possibility was fair game in the Play. We would discuss "Life" for hours, until we were either blissed out with understanding or exhausted by thought. One never knew the course that was coming, except that it would be necessary to stay on your toes and remember to laugh.

If you were noticeably uncomfortable, he might break the ice with a joke. But if you were complacent or overly self-satisfied, he would test you. He did not view life as a careful path of avoiding trouble. He evolved many ways to stir things up...just to be sure a calm surface wasn't masking a suppressed inner disturbance or a tentative apathy.

To some, Glenn was a guru. To others, he was just quirky. To me, he was a friend and a great comedian. He was also a voracious reader. The works of Gurdjieff and Ouspensky opened his experience to a larger view. But it was in the books of Sufis that he discovered himself. That is probably where he found so many funny stories.

From the collective consciousness of every culture there arises a comic figure...a buffoon...who is so simple, natural and yet understated that we hardly know what he is about. He is a clown. He may be called the "village idiot." And yet sometimes he seems wise in a simple, direct way. For the Sufis, he is Mullah Nasrudin. Glenn reveled in the vagaries of Nasrudin.

> One day, Mullah was hanging out with two friends, when one of them asked, "What is the greatest invention of mankind?"

The other friend responded, "Electricity! It has so
much power, serves so many purposes and yet remains
a mystery."

The first friend suggested, "I think it is the printing
press. Before Gutenberg, the exchange of ideas was so
slow that humanity could just barely evolve. Collectively
we just inched along for millennia. Then, suddenly, there
was this explosion of ideas and production...one idea
feeding another...one invention suggesting a dozen
more."

Seemingly lost in thought, Mullah emerged to
announce an alternative choice. "I think the greatest
invention of mankind is the thermos."

The first friend broke out laughing. "All a thermos
can do," he chuckled, "is to keep hot drinks hot and cold
drinks cold."

"Yes," Mullah responded, "...but how does it know
which one to do?"

When Glenn passed away, I was asked to speak at his
memorial service. There was a rather large gathering of the
"new age" community of Sedona atop a beautiful knoll,
surrounded by a forest of junipers and mountains of red
rock.

What to say?

What can one say at the passing of a close friend? Glenn
had left us all laughing in life...so I related the last story he
left with me. Never mind that it was slightly off color. A
blend of truth and humor was the finest part of his human
side. It was this blend that was his springboard into the
Infinite.

An old man and his grandson set out on a long journey with a donkey. In the beginning, the young boy rode
on the donkey's back and the old man walked alongside.

Soon, people started to talk... "Look at that strong
young boy, riding the donkey, while that feeble old man
has to walk!"

Having heard these remarks, the young boy got off
the donkey and the grandfather got on. They continued
to travel on.

It wasn't long before people were talking again, "Look! That man gets to ride on the back of the donkey, while that poor young boy has to walk!"

So they both climbed on.

Still the talk persisted... "That poor donkey. He has to carry both those guys. Have they no heart?"

At this, the grandfather and the boy got off. The grandfather put the donkey on his own back, and they proceeded on their way.

They came to a narrow bridge, hanging over a deep gorge and river below. The old man, still carrying the donkey, struggled to keep his footing over the precipice. Suddenly he slipped and fell down. The donkey fell off his back, slid over the side of the bridge and dropped to the rocks below. He was killed instantly.

The moral of this story:

If you try to please everyone...you'll lose your ass.

Glenn left me a tremendous gift. Every time I remember him...I smile.

Two questions arise: How do we attract the Master? And how will we recognize Him?

The secret to this is really very simple. The way we attract Him is exactly the same way we make a friend. Like Glenn, like any friend, as we accept him, he feels the magnetic pull. He feels welcome. It is the same with the Master. He will always enter, wherever He is welcome.

To make a friend of a new acquaintance, we must make no assumptions. We meet him exactly as he is. If we listen openly, if we do not prejudge him, invariably we will draw him near. He will feel comfortable. A Master is a great listener. He is a true friend, who is also capable of seeing through any facade we might construct. He sees who we are without prejudice. Our sincerity and open honesty are sufficient welcome. He will enter. We attract Him long before we even know who He is.

To recognize Him is more difficult. We must feel His Flow. We must become this Flow. It is not sufficient to simply be "open." We must develop adequate powers of discernment to make good, consistent, vibrational choices for our self. We must study the course of the karmic river very carefully, so that we learn to merge in the Flow that is endless...the one that pours into the Infinite Ocean.

There are many currents that divert our direction. When we find our self on a tributary that dries up, or in an eddy that swirls endlessly, but leads nowhere, we must return to the primary Channel and reconnect. When we are steadfast in the primary Flow, we recognize Him in a direct and certain way.

When we are unhappy, we seek out things, called vices, to console ourselves...to ease the pain temporarily. Consider some of the things that we "enjoy": smoking, drinking, sex, uppers, downers, overeating, becoming absorbed in movies or sports, etc. When these enjoyments become obsessive, they are poor and addictive substitutes for the Real Thing...unqualified **Joy**.

Why are these kinds of enjoyments troublesome? Because they require specific conditions to be repeated over and over. We are not deeply refreshed, just temporarily satisfied. Look at what happens. Most of these alleviate tension for a while. They satisfy a need, but do not extinguish it. We relax for a moment or two. The surface is calmed. But an inner deficiency soon aches again under the facade of habitual activity.

Now, if our memories were better, if our attention were keener, if our consciousness were more continuous and complete and, most important of all, if our intuition were fully awake and in control, then after one inhalation of a cigarette, after one sip of alcohol, after one drug induced, out of body experience, after one loving sexual experience, after one good joke...we would come away with a profound glimpse of the Path. That glimpse would remain and expand into a continuous **Vision**. We could then spread our wings and fly into Life.

When we first begin to feel this Flow as a dynamic personal Presence within ourselves, we normally will feel a great burst of enthusiasm. As our heart opens into the radiant, blissful and wonderfully vibrant Center of our life, we can taste an endless enthusiasm. When the clutter has cleared and the primordial nature is revealed, we can feel a tremendous blissful Force that is new in every moment.

In order that we might understand this whole enthusiasm, we are given situations and experiences, through which we are free to experience emotion. We are free to respond any way that we choose. As we adapt to each and every situation in a way that brings us the greatest inner satisfaction, we feel this wonderful enthusiasm for the particular moments, but an even greater enthusiasm for the Whole Life.

When the Vibration of Om is felt as a continuous flow of sound, joy, power and bliss, we become "natural." When that Vibration resounds in our Heart, we experience true bliss. This is the central purpose of yoga...**to feel and to know our true nature**.

All descriptions begin to fail. Even the greatest poetry falls short of capturing this wonderful Presence. The Presence itself cannot be captured. The Heart extends way beyond the boundaries of our physical body. It permeates and sustains everything physical. It colors every thought we may have, every feeling we may experience.

Be still. Enter this radiant Flow. Merge with this endless enthusiasm. Do not settle for a trifle. Become it All!

> "Row, row, row your boat
>   Gently down the stream,
>   Merrily, merrily, merrily, merrily.
>   Life is but a dream."

The Cosmic Sound, Om, is the sound produced by the spinning of God's wheels. He is playing. It is all for fun. There is no "solution" to the problems of the world, for there is no problem in Reality. It is a game. It is not a problem. It is all play. The "rules" of playing are quite simple:

1. Discover that this **IS** a game.
2. Play!

Sounds simple enough. But if it is so simple, why is it so
rare among men and women? Because it is tremendously
difficult to make the initial discovery. It requires a very
definite effort and search. We must move through the idea
of solid matter. We must move through the idea of our
pain. In general, we must move through our ignorance.
Until rule # 1 is understood…is experienced in the core of
our Self…really, all we can do is apply the second rule.
Play! So lets begin by getting the feel of playing. Let's
become like a child. We row our boat gently down the
stream. And let's not make some serious thing about it.
Let's play with the ever present awareness that whatever
This is…it is a game.

"…Merrily, merrily, merrily, merrily…" There is no
more sensible way to experience this Life. Thus we can
easily find our part. It comes naturally. There is no need to
force an issue.

We must always begin where we are **Now**, and find our
way in. It may seem serious at this moment. It may seem
peculiar. Surely it is part mystery. Through practice and
effort…and the good fortune of this particular incarnation
…we find our way to the feet of the Master. He nurtures
us through our misconceptions. This nurturing may take
years…lifetimes. But it is leading to something marvelous.
Suddenly, without warning, the boundaries of our life
shatter. Everything is a thought in the mind of God. This is
the dramatic, uttermost Truth, known directly only
through actual experience…God's demonstration.

"…Life is but a dream…" in the mind of God. There is
no more sensible way to understand this Life.

It literally blows the mind. It shatters the mind's fabric.
Matter is the fabric of the mind. Yet even this is but a
dream in the mind of God. This demonstrated Reality
opens an infinite vista into endless freedom.

**Yoga is the deep inner attentiveness to Reality, lead-
ing to the discovery of the evanescent quality of all
things.** Everything has been materialized by God's mind.
It is all a play.

Tremendous humor enters our life as we realize this. Our participation becomes more beautiful, graceful and effective as we eliminate the desperate struggle between witness and participant. Once we know this, our participation becomes the intelligent and effortless unfolding of the design as Lila...cosmic play...cosmic dance.

People who are accomplished in sports, music, acting or dance, to name only a few areas of play, have found a singular expression in which they allow the innate intelligent design to express itself. They have accessed or developed a poised response, in tune with the design, within a particular defined portion of the physical life. The access is learned through practice, conditioning, focus, imitation and intuitive feeling. Moments of perfect adaptation are acquired through egoless attention. The witness uses a biofeedback mechanism, allowing this design to be effective...to manifest a unique and graceful expression.

Our three bodies operate with three intelligent designs having an innate independence. Ego is the act of making the Soul, and one or more of these three bodies, interdependent, binding the witness to particular habitual thoughts, emotions and physical experiences. A mouse is scurrying around in the maze of these bodies, tying them together in knots. This supports a belief that the knots themselves are the Being itself. In reality, God is playing.

Most people love to talk. It gives them comfort. It supports the appearance of being in control. Usually when we talk, we are somewhat unconsciously placing our "self" in a finite world (Maya) of our own making. Security is felt. Thoughts and words circumscribe a world we are trying to contain.

The way of yoga circumscribes no part of the Whole. It is not a path of containment. It is not a path of vicarious enjoyment. The Infinite cannot be contained. It can only be **entered**. Once this entry is made, the appeal of endless chatter ceases. The innate limitation of description drives the talker into song, and then into silence. It drives the writer into poetry, and then into pure awareness. When we meet a lover, words will not do…an embrace…perhaps a smile. Our Heart becomes radiant.

The Infinite cannot be expressed, except in deep silence.

Om is the Great Silencer. The current of Sound flowing through the Heart and the higher Centers, coursing through consciousness, arrests the mind of thought. It draws the attention into the amazement of the Present. Each moment is like that of the child taking his first look into a kaleidoscope. He is transfigured by its beauty.

So what is the size and weight of man's thinking? It is but a speck on the infinite landscape of God's Mind. This small understanding may lead us in one of two directions of our own choice. We may retreat within the tiny shell of ego and deny the Whole, or we may leap into the Infinite Path. We may look within and see the Whole contained in the part and the part within the Whole. As we enter within, we merge with the Whole Being God Is. We thereby discover the deathlessness of it All, and awaken to an exquisite joy. We become Bliss itself. This is our choice, and this choice will forever be here.

So…hesitate no longer. The door is open.

Come Inside!

A RECIPE FOR BLISS

Early in 1978, two things happened that changed my life in a profound way.

In February, while temporarily living in Santa Monica, California, I was awakened in the early morning by a distinct voice, speaking inside my head. In a gentle, but firm tone I heard, "**Holly will soon be conceiving a child. His name is David.**" Then the voice evaporated. In its place was a vibrational hum, surrounded by stillness and quiet.

Holly awoke a few minutes later and I shared the "news" with her, but I did not tell her the name. I wondered if she could receive it on her own. I asked her to tell me the name if it came to her.

Holly and I had never discussed having children and had never discussed any possible names either. At the time, we had almost no money, no home, and no clear idea of what we were going to do or where we would live. We were drifting through life, waiting for something to happen that might suggest our next direction.

About ten minutes later, she replied, "David!"

I was stunned. Even though I had half expected her to receive the name, I was nonetheless bewildered that this whole thing had happened.

Owing to our transient nature, however, it was not long before the thought of having a child slipped away. Our immediate attention was drawn to our basic "needs." We certainly did not want to conceive a child under these insecure conditions.

But...one month later it happened. At the exact moment of conception, Holly began to cry. She poured out deep feelings of helplessness, wonder and joy, all at the same time. She knew a child had come to her... I had no idea.

We received the medical confirmation a few weeks later.

We still did not have any clear idea of where to go and how to earn a living. We continued to linger in the Los Angeles area for about another month, waiting for some sign...some indication of what our next move should be. On occasion we would attend a spiritual group session in Santa Monica, where we could spend an interesting evening with friends, and sell a few crystals to help make ends meet.

On one such evening an older gentleman, who usually opened our meetings, was introducing a psychometric, biofeedback device. It was quite basic. Two metal cans had electrical wires running from them through a sensitive ohmmeter. If you held one can in each hand, the meter apparently measured your inner resistance to whatever was verbally suggested by a facilitator. For example, if he asked how you felt about your parents, your deep level of acceptance or rejection would affect the natural flow of current through yourself, and thus through the loop. The meter would indicate your level of resistance. Whether this device could or could not accomplish such a measurement was unclear to me.

If this device could work as he suggested, it occurred to me that it would be easy to allow our intuition a free reign and read the "results" in a spontaneous way, much like dowsers take readings with pendulums or other similar instruments. Simply take hold of the cans and watch the meter respond to our thoughts. We might even discover directly how subtle emotional states affect the currents of energy through our body. The possibilities for self-discovery and healing seemed far-reaching.

However, the moderator had determined that we must use this tool in a very specific way...through a facilitator, asking specific questions and receiving specific answers. This seemed narrow and unimaginative, but I resisted speaking up in deference to him. I sat there edgy...but silent.

Gradually a Force began to stir within, disorienting my "normal" way of perceiving and experiencing. It felt as though some tremendous implosion was about to happen. The force generated an electrical flow through my limbs and into my spine. It became quite intense. Silently I prayed that the meeting would end, so that I could get outside without causing a disturbance.

As though an answer to my prayer, the meeting quickly came to a halt. With Holly's help, I struggled to get outside into our van and lay down in the back. Holly drove away and stopped at a park where we often would spend the night.

My physical condition then intensified. The energy that was bottled up was seeking a path to exit. However, this energy appeared to be **my self**, trying to escape from my own physical prison, rather than something foreign that I might expel. In fact, I had the distinct feeling that I was about to die. There seemed no way that I could remain within my body much longer. A great conscious force was building inside, trying to flow through these limbs and spine, aimed straight toward the top of my head. This force was either my individual identity itself, or it contained "me" as part of some larger, more powerful entity.

For a few minutes I held on, but the pressure would not subside. Finally I allowed myself to let go completely. The force, issuing a very loud Sound, suddenly raced through this body, drawing me upward and out the top of my head. As I was exiting, my inner voice called out to the one person in whom I had the greatest trust in that moment... "Jesus!"

Instantly I was somewhere far outside of my body, standing before two radiant and peaceful individuals. One was Jesus and the other was Paramhansa Yogananda. They stood side by side. Yogananda looked exactly as he did in his last days on this earth. In a calm, yet insistent way, they both looked directly into me. Not a word was spoken. No question came for me to ask. In fact, not a single thought entered my mind. I was simply **There**, overwhelmed by

ecstasy. I deeply appreciated the sanctuary. Their omniscience was obvious to me.

A short time later I gently slipped back down into this
body, and I was on earth once more. An afterglow radiated
in me. Never before had I felt so radiant and peaceful. This
blissful feeling was exquisite. Every cell danced. I seemed
to be floating within my body. In that moment I realized
how utterly safe we all are, despite the anxieties of our
conscious mind, trapped in this temporary physical frame.
From this new reference point, the "things" of this world
lose their grip. Maya may seem compelling and unrelent-
ing...but it is nothing but evanescent form. The degree of
our own incarceration is self-caused through our attitudes,
thoughts and tendencies as they coalesce in all three
bodies. But there is no Reality in these limiting formations
of experience. We are Consciousness itself...unborn and
unlimited.

In all, my out of body experience lasted no more than a
few timeless moments, perhaps twenty seconds at the
most. Yet it remains utterly vivid to this day...and far
more significant for me than any physical experience I
have had. It left me with a completely new appreciation for
this life experience...and one piece of invaluable information: Our elder brothers are watching us, ready to assist us
in moments of dire need. Certainly they could materialize
at any moment...or, more appropriately, dematerialize us
at any moment...and tell us directly what we should or
should not do. But generally, they allow us to find our
own way. Why? Because... **Life is a journey of Self-
discovery.**

From that point on, my outlook and direction changed
in a fundamental way. This extraordinary experience and
the impending birth of our child were clear indications
that I needed to find, or create, a sanctuary on earth to
allow these two conceptions to be born in tune with the
etheric Reality.

Holly and I soon shifted into a domestic mode and
returned to Sedona, Arizona, where we had been living a
short time before. We both felt the womb-like quality of

this beautiful and quiet, rural community. It was not yet the tourist Mecca that it is today.

The vision of the two Masters became a central focus. A deep purpose began to grow for me to somehow establish and maintain this vibratory quality on earth. I have found that this requires great attention and a consistent willingness to apply an appropriate natural effort. Oddly enough, being perfectly natural on this earth is not "natural" at all...except, perhaps, for children.

The birth of our first child was a heart opening experience for me. On the morning of December 27th, Holly went into labor. It was intense and very painful for her. I was captivated by the forceful reality of the moment. Holly's stress intensified the significance of the birth for me. I tried my best to help her through her pain, but there was very little that I could do. She had chosen to have the birth at home with a midwife and without anesthesia or drugs. We both felt that this would be best for the child. For Holly there was a definite price to pay.

When our newborn finally emerged, a great relief came. Suddenly we all were floating on air. Then came a moment of ambrosial cosmic humor. We discovered our child, "David," is now a girl. This was an unexpected delight. During the entire pregnancy, I had assumed we were having a boy.

I had been raised in a family of seven boys. I was the second son and had attended to many infant brothers while growing up. How we all longed for a sister, who might soften the pervasive masculine, competitive nature of our family life. But it was not to be.

Now the feminine was embodied before me. I was ecstatic. She did not make a sound. The room became utterly silent. She stared into her new environment easily with a natural curiosity. The three of us stared with her.

In the first minute she took no breath at all. Her conscious attention drifted about the room through her eyes. I was entranced by her beauty and her innocence. Our midwife soon insisted that we come down to earth and help her start breathing. She gently massaged her chest and spoke insistently, "Come on, dear... **Breathe!**" We all passed through a few anxious moments as our daughter seemed to resist these intrusive efforts. Harmony's first breath startled her slightly. We all drew a breath at the same time. After a few inhalations, she accepted it and returned to gazing around the room.

She was a little shy at first. She would look into our eyes only for brief moments and then look away cautiously...as if to say, "Who are these people, and what do they want with me?"

For an hour or more, the four of us simply hung out. A bond of joy and affection began to form. We could see her developing a trust that her situation was safe and inviting. We washed her and wrapped her in a blanket. I was completely wrapped in wonder.

Several of our friends had been waiting quietly in the next room throughout the labor and birth. Finally we decided to bring our daughter out. To this point, the only sound she had made was the sound of her first breath. Her utter quiet had been extraordinary.

I picked her up and carried her gently into the next room. The first person she saw was our friend, Malachi Israel...a towering man, about six feet four inches tall, weighing 250 pounds or more. He had a full black beard and steely eyes peering through a maze of tangled hair. Our daughter took one look at him and burst out crying in fright.

When a birth is "normal," a wondrous innocence and curiosity fills the newborn. As the child first nestles in the arms of his or her mother, he re-experiences the bliss of the womb and now feels an externalized resonance, vibrating between the two hearts. In this timeless moment the world seems perfect. Mother and child make a sweet and delicate connection. The natural Design of Love is easy to feel at this time.

But situations change. Life evolves. As each child grows, Consciousness, hungry to experience, moves outward into a maze of dual forms. Some of these forms and experiences, however, become definite "problems."

Harmony

If we carefully watch infants growing up, invariably, interspersed with a natural love of playing, we will see a rebellion. We want them to do this or that. Often they don't want to. A resistance asserts itself. Why? Because they have an original understanding that they are free to do whatever they want. But they find themselves confined in a small body, completely helpless, save the few instincts that allow them to suckle milk and express delight or discomfort. Gradually they discover their parents want them to do **this**, but not **that!** Right away, they **know** something is wrong. Heaven was not like this. Freedom and bliss are the essence of the etheric domain...the essence of the primordial Reality. So, when these conditions are removed, infants are disappointed and react negatively. It is natural.

Infants and young children begin to learn early on that they must forego some particular freedoms to get some others. Parents either punish or reward them, depending on their own preferences. For the child, strategies begin to form. In order to enjoy **this**, I have to do **that**. I might not like that, but I definitely want this. So I do that.

Now things become complex. The child does not have social ideas about all this stuff. He doesn't know, for instance, that we are not supposed to play with our genitals openly...so he does. It is a curiosity to him. He is investigating himself. He enjoys something about it, so he goes ahead. Then social restraint comes crashing down, and he must develop a strategy.

Maybe he reserves this activity for when he is alone. Maybe he gives it up out of utter fear. Maybe he can't do either of these, and goes ahead with it, suffering the consequences anyway. In life's forward search for understanding and return journey to Bliss, all manner of complex subplots are set in motion.

Each child enters with an understanding that seems to be part instinct and part intuition, not yet colored with language and operating instructions. Each infant is solely self-aware, with no established relationship, except for a vibrational attunement with the mother. Put simply, the infant is a foreigner...an alien.

By the time the child becomes a teenager, the original Design and Purpose are buried in a complex web of desires, strategies and habits. The pure joy of the formative years is replaced by an intense struggle to recover from this imbalance. But there is no clear direction. Often there is a definite rebellion, equal and opposite to the restricting forces of the parents and other "authorities." The Cosmic Plan is thus lost in a maze of strategy. Lost in the study of mathematics or English or physics or cultures or automobile mechanics or cooking or whatever, is the original purpose of birth. We are here to find our way to Bliss...our way to God...and to proceed consciously on that way.

Many of us never quite recover from this early misdirection. Our orientation somehow hardens. And it does not melt easily. Years of struggle and pain have created emotional grooves that now seem normal, despite the discomfort. The possibility is always there to slip into Bliss, but the choice is short circuited over and over by habit and misconception, now deeply entrenched in experience.

Yet Bliss is just nearby. The warmth of one spring day can undo an entire winter of frozen thought. One kind word from a true friend can ease us into life's next joyous experience. The Holy Sound, Om, is issuing just behind the mind...waiting for a single silent moment...waiting for the Heart to reopen and feel unconditional joy. Once this Sound is heard, an understanding of our original **purpose** dawns. Over time, listening to this Sound deprograms the congested complexity of our personality. Our Original Condition gradually appears through the mist of confusion.

Each of us eventually discovers, beyond any doubt, that our entry into the conscious conditions of this earthly realm is caused by our desire to know our Self, and to use that understanding to enter Bliss...if not now, then later... if not in this life, then sometime in another life. It must eventually happen. All conscious experience points to this inevitability.

Merging with Om is a simple, uncomplicated, direct way to achieve this. A progression of Master Souls, passing through numerous sects and religions for thousands of earthly years, points the way.

Listen to the Tibetan Buddhists. Their practice involves the intoning of sounds that both mimic Om and help raise our listening above the threshold of life's persistent noise, into inner silence.

Listen to Gregorian Chants. The cathedral is an archetype for the human body itself. Sunlight pours through stained glass of exquisite color, lighting the inner chamber. Steady intonation of the vibrant, harmonic chant permeates and fills the chamber. This performance is the prototype of man's conscious awakening to the primordial inner Sound and Light.

Visit the Zen Buddhist temples in Japan. There you will always find a large bronze bell hanging in a prominent place. When it is struck with a wooden pole or mallet, it resonates almost endlessly into the surrounding silence. Its tone is deep and pure. The ear naturally follows this sound into the Center of the head, where a nearly identical Sound can be heard that is absolutely endless.

Go to the Shiva temples in India. Amid the ecstatic dancing are rhythmic, devotional voices, singing the joyous and utterly amazing truth that every moment exists in the Presence of God.

Go to the mosques of Islam. Listen to the prayers.

Listen to the aborigines of Australia, playing their didgeridoos.

They are all playing the same Sound. They are all approximating the Holy Sound, Om. It is basic. It is primordial. The Sound goes on within you or without you. It is always your choice. You are free to listen. You are free to enter.

When I was younger, my father had an expression that he repeated over and over. It came from his military training. It is, "Get with the program!" Unfortunately enough, most people on this earth have only an inkling of what the **program** is. The intuition senses it. Deep inside we know it. But on the surface, we are controlled by a vast array of other programs of lesser significance. And most of us, most of the time, are operating within these lesser programs.

So, forgive me if I stand firm. Forgive me if I shout. Forgive me if I twist your arm. But…

Get with the Program!

Come into the easy Silence
Merge with the Sound
Feel the Bliss
O M

.

That's the Recipe!
It is as simple as That!

DEDICATION

These writings are dedicated to a Master of unique distinction. He visited this earth, during its 20th century, to deliver a timeless message and to demonstrate a distinct life of Bliss, transcending physical conditions. He was a child of God, and a Guru of men. He signed his name:

Unceasing blessings,
Very sincerely yours,

Paramhansa Yogananda [1]

...but knew his Name to be the endless vibration of Spirit.

His unmistakable kindness and his unwavering honesty are clearly visible in the writings that he left for us...particularly in his *Autobiography of a Yogi*...an instrument of transformation, almost unparalleled elsewhere in print. This single account, alone, has stirred the souls of millions to come awake and discover the inner spiritual Path of Illumination.

---

[1] Reproduced from a personal letter written to my friend, Vallory Douglass, a direct disciple of Yogananda. Used with her permission.

His extraordinary and unexpected appearance to me forever changed my life. His continuing Presence provides the blissful foundation for my experience. I cannot adequately describe the gratitude I feel for his abiding assistance. It is his Grace that calms my restlessness, nourishes my meditations and delivers my attention into Fields of Wonder.

Carl Schmidt
1/1/01

Resonance

The sitar is a musical instrument, par excellence... beyond comparison. It is constructed to resound in a way that is a perfect metaphor for the Life Divine. It has one, and often two hollow gourds, which amplify the sound of the resonating strings. A single master string plays the individual notes of the raga, and a group of secondary strings are played from time to time to enrich the harmony.

There is a another set of secondary sympathetic strings, which play a unique role and give the sitar it's unrivaled sound. Physically they reside below the plucked strings and are tuned to the notes of the raga, or an octave above. They are thin and delicate and rarely are plucked by the musician. Each one waits...until a note is struck by the primary string in harmony with it. The overall resonance of the sitar then causes the sympathetic strings to vibrate with the primary notes as they are played. There is a lapse of time separating the two. These strings follow the sound of the master string. They respond in tune. The initiating sound brings them to life. No finer metaphor exists that clarifies the relationship of the Master and his devotees. **Sympathetic Resonance is the essential nature of the evolving Path.**

The outer world **always** reflects the inner world. The illumination of the inner world reveals the true Being and directly causes this knowledge to be experiential. Until that time, the seeker blindly searches the outer world for a truth, which can never be other than a reflection.

Astronomers have identified certain "dark" areas in the outer cosmos and named them *black holes*. These areas are so dense and their gravitational fields so strong that all particles and all waves in the "vicinity" are absorbed. Nothing can escape...no matter of any kind...not even light. This astronomical phenomenon, too, reflects the inner world. The inner presence of this, the "Black Whole," can be seen in the Spherical Eye through the dedicated attention of the yogi.

The Star of Self is a caveman. He makes his appearance within the Black Whole. Stillness is his activity. Silence is his voice. Timeless is his age. Transparent is his domain. Resonance is the **action** that draws the devotee to him and relieves the separation of birth. It dissolves the ego, the intellect, and the duality of breath.

Karma means "action." But it is a far more general action, and leads to resonance only in a very, very slow manner. Across millennia, the scales shall balance, and the Path shall come as if a whisper through a maze of chaos. Karma Yoga, while a means of equilibrium, is excruciatingly slow. It carries the devotee through fortune and misfortune to a place of eventual repose where the resonating Current begins. Thus, know from the beginning that it is but a hallway, leading to the real door.

Meditation is not primarily a path of knowledge, yet it leads to the most decisive and useful knowledge available in the human life...the understanding of the Self. And while the practice is definitely enhanced by study of the deepest order, this "study" is more a practice of attention, than it is the accumulation of ideas regarding the condition of the Soul. Such ideas, however, follow naturally from the practice. But it is definitely not a case of thinking one's self into understanding. The consciousness of the Soul does **not** move into its Home by thinking. It moves with subtle inner **action**, and arrives at Self-Realization through definite, attending, vibrational experiences.

It is useful to have a foreknowledge of these experiential states, more to realize what is not Self-Realization, than to know what it is. Hence the devotee knows to persevere in his practice to a condition of more complete attunement. The attunement is **self-evident** and quite definite. The

vague and uncertain qualities of belief and intuition dissolve in an omnipresent awareness of utter stillness
through balance, silence of urge, and transparency of
being.

Movement dissolves into **balance**. The sound heard is
Om, the **cause** of manifestation, present within all matter.
The individualized self is formed as vibration, and thus
seen as **Light**, interpenetrating all form.

Trusting this from the beginning and throughout the
duration of our discipline establishes fortitude and encourages patience. As these attitudes replace our disabling
emotional habits, we glide more easily along an "invisible"
path of vibrational experience. Bliss is the assurance and
declaration of the righteousness of the Way.

This Yoga, as it is known to the author at this time, is
characterized by twelve distinct resonant Actions, employing two Mantras, both an initiating sound/thought and
Om (as it begins to manifest), and five distinct Pranayams.
However, new Actions may reveal themselves at any time.
The evolution of technique goes on within those who open
to inner instruction.

That which is Unborn cannot be given. Yet, unsettled
areas of consciousness wander a world, driven by the
senses. An outer action is already the motion. To still the
Heart (and the other Centers as well) to wakefulness, and
thus untie the knots that have formed, Resonance presents
itself within. The Unborn speaks to the one clinging to
birth and says...

"This is My Body."

A key to attaining this Resonance is that there is no
inside and there is no outside. There is but one Place...and
it is everywhere. Sympathetic Resonance is the Action
attending to breath that leads the heart to stillness. From
within this stillness a sweet and blissful Vibration begins
to stir through no apparent cause. It is a response...in
sympathy to the original Cause. Thereupon an inner

awareness proceeds without effort to extinguish the memories, *samskaras*, left in the wake of ignorance.

A sentiment in the yogi arises that is profound. He abandons the expectation of results. Thus he enters eternal tranquillity.

How is it that meditation is effective?

There is a subtle, but definite link between the three worlds of manifestation and the realm of Spirit. If there were no such link, then the physical world, the feeling world, and the world of thought would have no relevance to Life. Each would be totally autonomous. Matter and Spirit would thus have no relationship. If there were no link, there would be no point to spiritual practice. Yoga would then be useless. Pranayama would lead nowhere. Conscious attention would serve no lasting purpose. Chaos would then be a more profound explanation for the force of life. It would be a more accurate metaphor for the way things are.

But such a link does exist. There is **order** and **design** organizing matter. There is a Force that interlaces these worlds...and gives meaning and purpose to our activity. Hence, our effort does make a difference. Resonance is the link, interpenetrating the seemingly separate experiential realms of the three worlds and Spirit.

The reason why metaphor, poetry and music are employed upon the path is that they initiate a hollow resounding quality. So much of "normal" life does not resonate at all. As we choose to wallow in unsettling thoughts and feelings, what we hear sounds like a thud. Suddenly the desert is there. Resonance disappears.

The devotee's complete effort is to awaken this Resonance within himself. At the start he must employ any of a vast number of possible techniques to effect this. But it is worth the effort. Generally speaking, the Resonance, initiated by an open conscious attention, becomes Self-sustained. Music shall then commence.

Resonance forms the basis of all tantric practices. Divine Bliss shall be the experience. For each lover, let every look, every touch, every word and every thought resonate as a

holy wave, standing within the **eternal presence**...not moving to some other place, but exposing love already whole within Thy Self. In this way human love resonates with the inner Life.

Through the years and the lives of ignorance, each lover has abandoned bliss myriad times. Yet a dawning does come when this habitual ignorance fades. Henceforth, each lover initiates the other, asking for complete forgiveness and giving it in turn...relegating karma to the history of the absurd. The Bell within the Heart does then toll its wondrous Sound...the River alone shall then carry the Soul. Yoga is the foreplay of Divine Union. This Action has a definite purpose.

Resonance is so commanding that music, poetry, metaphor, prayer and meditation are fundamental to all religions. Within science, that which is true in a bona fide way also has a resonant quality. Only the most rebellious and insulated individuals can approach the truth and not be moved, for it transcends time and space. Resonance links mind, force and matter to the omnipresent and omniscient Reality.

For the devotee, struggling to understand the "forces of nature," the continuous propagation of the dance of Sound and Light is an awesome spectacle. It gives **pause**...and within this pause lies the eternal Resonance. This sudden shift in tempo gives rise to a deeper perspective.

Consider the marvelous comic actor, Bill Murray. Have you ever met anyone who does not enjoy him? Why is he so loved?

The comic character he plays **always** slows the movement down. He undercuts the "normal," accepted parameters of social conditioning, and this creates a pause. Time stands still. A smile or a laugh naturally comes out.

In the movie, *Ground Hog Day*, his character begins to relive the same day over and over again. Everyone else experiences this one day as if it were completely new, but he is living it again and again. He is free to act as he chooses...to experiment with his actions and observe the results. But the results of each day are evanescent. No one else remembers them as the same day repeats itself tomorrow. There are no consequences to his actions, except within his own experience and memory.

After observing his predicament for a couple of days, he sets out to win the heart of a woman, otherwise beyond his reach, with guile. He tries to slow her down to a place where they might "stop" together. But always his deceit is in the way. After a long series of failures, he slowly begins to get a bigger picture. The goal is not to win the girl, it is to practice life with great caring until he gets it right. Every activity is simply a metaphor for the perfect, underlying, compassionate Reality. As he moves ahead with this new motive, he comes in tune with a natural, evolving way of experience, and good things begin to happen to him with an ease he never knew before.

When we begin to see that the events in life are metaphors for the Essence of our Being, rather than outcomes having specific importance, we naturally disengage from our attachments. To do otherwise seems silly. The art of life is to first recognize this...and then act in ways that improve the effects of our apparent involvement. Great skill develops in the one who sees with this kind of depth.

What are we "improving"? ...the **tone** of experience.

Our persistence must be enveloped with kindness. As we discover our own capacity and proclivity for error, we are ready to forgive the error of others. This dissolves the alienation that arises from the "need" to achieve separately and to dominate.

Metaphorically, the West is the land of materialism and the East is the domain of Spirit. The East, and particularly India and the displaced country of Tibet, has a long tradition of yoga, men of deep wisdom and tremendous insight, and a distinct disinterest in the pursuit of material goals. Those of us born in the West...steeped in the relentless pursuit of material wealth and physical perfection...often experience a deep angst about our life condition. The temporary and fragile nature of physical control stares us in the face, and yet we push ahead with desire as if we might

preempt the eventual dissolution of all the physical parameters of the ego.

To make the journey East, where the Star shines, deep
within the Blue Pearl...where the Master resides...there is
a highway with many lanes. There is the lane of prayer
and devotion. In the East this is commonly called *Bhakti
Yoga*. There is the way of bodily purification called *Hatha
Yoga*. There is the way of knowledge called *Jnana Yoga*.
There is the way of balanced action called *Karma Yoga*.

There is yet another lane of rare quality on the highway
East, which leads with great precision to the unborn condition of original Being. It is a "diamond" lane of exquisitely
refined inner Action. This way is known as **Kriya Yoga**. It
is a path of Resonance.

To begin hearing the Sound, Om, is so important. Once
this Resonance enters, the path is cleared in a substantial
way...an essential way. Until this happens, the seeker
must settle for mental pictures of Spirit. He must hold fast
to an idea, or a set of ideas. Until a Cosmic Vision or Vibration of deep bliss awakens him to his original Body of
Spirit, he must cling to faith or belief within the material
desert. But when this Sound enters, the beliefs and the
clinging nature fall away naturally. They become inconsequential. The Resonance itself replaces the ideas and the
desperate patterns of behavior as a **medium of understanding**. From this point on, the path begins to be a place
for observing eternity.

This comes as a great relief to the devotee, who finally
recognizes that Spirit is not sustained by virtue of his own
efforts...not through physical effort...not through mental
effort. Effort is required only to make the Spirit known, not
to sustain it. Spirit cannot be undermined through any lack
of effort or any degree of ignorance. Through a sustained
and sublime effort the devotee shall be showered with
understanding.

The Soul is drawn to Spirit (its essence) in a way identical to the way that the south pole of a magnet is drawn to a
north pole of another magnet. A yogi recognizes and feels

this magnetism throughout his body and particularly through the spiritual Centers.

The man of ignorance (*tamas*) does not feel this magnetism due to his complete attachment to the physical appearance.

The man of activity (*rajas*) feels this magnetism slightly, but ignores it in his ceaseless quest to replace the fundamental Reality with his own egoic plan.

The man of harmony (*sattva*) feels this magnetism and responds immediately to its irresistible pull, by allowing the Soul to rise naturally into Spirit. The man of harmony may appear disinterested in the "lives" around him, and even his own life, but, in fact, his interest is total. His focus is upon the magnetic quality existing between each Soul and Spirit, which inevitably unites the two in a permanent blissful condition.

Meditation is, quite simply, the ongoing practice of the soul to respond with intuitive receptivity to the constant call of Spirit. When Om is heard with great volume, vibration and constancy, the Soul knows with a certainty that it is nearing its Home. It is the ultimate honing device.

Specific inner Actions (**Kriyas**) arise from a deep and profound awareness of design. They produce an experiential understanding of the transparent quality of **all** "things." The understanding manifests through Resonance.

Dear reader, I implore you to search for this understanding with your whole strength. Employ the Resonance abiding within yourself and within those who dwell in bliss. Open to the reality that has no limits of time and space.

One thing is clear. Something **must** change. Some new Action **must** be taken. Such an Action is necessary, until experience is a deep, abiding and **permanent** Bliss. Such a condition definitely can be reached. The Action required is a change of inner attention that initiates the Current of Bliss. This is always available, because the path of birth is a movement in a single direction along the interior Channel into form...and this path is **bipolar**. Manifestation is not the whole Reality, it is simply the outer crust of it. Consciousness has manifested in form. **The force of birth created form as a Self-evident metaphor.** Thus the Action to Bliss is the return through this same effortless force to the original unconditional Being. The organic Movement is not physical, not emotional and not mental, but this subtle bipolar Action links these worlds with Spirit, and allows us to observe form as metaphor.

Along the return, separate form dissolves, leaving the original Being of Bliss exposed to the conscious Eye. Hence the Action leads to knowledge. Being is the goal. Resonance is its path. Understanding cements the Consciousness in the Whole Being God Is.

Fare Thee Well!

DISPENSATION

When the Whole Truth is known...we can no longer privatize it. In this way we meet our illumined brothers and sisters.

Wholly One:

...ooooooooooOm

did start the engine
and I could know It not
for sleep had left its mark
upon my ears

...ooooooooooOm

did sound the Bell
and I did wonder
softly to myself
For whom doest Thou toll?

Until the spanning Sound did reach
beyond the edge of imagining
beyond the grasp of thinking
beyond the last vestigial plan
And thus into Its Being Whole
did insist upon my urge
to Stop!

For I did course the realm of hope
    and fear did by my side
But ownership does bind a Heart
    to him an almost endless pride

Sphere of Sound shall melt the grip
    this clinging fast unto a place
A darkness thus through time shall slip
    into His welcome lighted Face

And waiting till the separate one
    did cease to make a presence seem
Solid, though an aerie thing
    for patience does dissolve this dream

I can hold Thee back no more
    as Entry thus complete
    can not be made
    through more than One

For this be the Truth
    and none shall have the wherewithal
      to deny It
    except within the freedom to divide

Trust is left to Thee,
    My Son
To come into the One and Wholly
    where fear shall have
    no place to bide
    and All shall be as One and Only

So let the sight pass through the Star
and so be gone the Great Divide
Dissolved upon the phantom screen
into the Vast Inside

Now... Sing out to the binded Heart
a song as true as can be done
And leave to God the knots untying
even though it feels a dying
For He shall birth the Endless One

Endless does He birth the Wholly One

THE FIRST KRIYA
THE SACRED HEART

Kriya Yoga organizes the forces acting upon our human form through specific actions. These actions are effective because they are **a precise distillation of the conscious transition from matter to Spirit, preexisting form as Cosmic Design.**

The fundamental archetype of this design is the Trinity of Being... Sat – Tat – Om. Until Om becomes an audible experience, it is difficult for the devotee to understand and appreciate the eternal Presence of Spirit as the underlying Reality...the singular underlying Reality.

In our ignorant condition, we wander a realm of perpetual desire, searching in vain for the very Essence that we are and shall always be. This desire initiates energetic activity, confined by patterns of thought and habit, and trapped by the primary misconception...**ego**. This activity becomes imbedded in the constellation of the individual human form, masking our true nature.

Man remains largely dissatisfied because nothing definitive ever seems to happen. He imagines what the reality is, rather than being hOMe with it. The purpose of Kriya Yoga is to unite directly with this Essence.

Scientific theory has been one of man's most persistent attempts to bridge the gap between thought and reality. Most scientists have suspended inquiry as to why we came to be. They have set their sights on knowing and describing what all of this is, and reducing it to its singular essence. In the 20th century this initiated the quest for a Unified Field Theory.

As it was becoming clear that matter, force, light and thought are all somehow the same thing, theoretical physics began knocking on heaven's door to clarify the elements once, for all time. The problems that Einstein and other contemporary physicists have encountered in developing this theory stem from the multiplicity of forces and the **distortion** of space.

The most perplexing problem facing these theorists is the difference in the nature and magnitude of force as the investigation moves from the very "large" (astronomical) to the very "small" (atomic and subatomic). While the Inverse Square Law[1] applies universally, gravitational force and the forces between molecules and subatomic particles have very different properties. They appear to have different **origins**.

In principle, physicists ignore one aspect of our situation that is known to every mystic, namely that we cannot comprehend the whole thing, while viewing it from outside. There is no place to make this observation. Our essence is not some part of the whole, which can step aside and view the remainder. We are, in fact, the whole thing. As such, **there is absolutely no place of objectivity**.

Buddhists have taken this premise one step farther. Since there is no place of objectivity, then there are **no objects** at all. If we accept this world view and respond to it in an appropriate and consistent way, then whether this cosmology is true or false is much less significant than the new mode of our life experience. If there are no objects, it would be ridiculous to act and think as if there were. If there are no things, no thing is born and no thing dies. Nothing can be lost or gained. Fear arises from the threat of loss, and particularly the threat of death and dying. This new world view slowly annihilates the root of fear.

When this outlook becomes infused in our regular practice, consciousness begins to let go of the particulars. Thought rests. That cubicle of the quest is no longer conse-

---

[1] The force existing between two bodies is inversely proportional to the square of the distance between them.

quential. Body prana gives way to Cosmic Prana. We begin
to resonate with the Whole Being. This action is **mysterious, normal** and **universal.** The Unified Field presents
itself to our attention. Theory is wedded to experience. Yet
it remains what it has always been…unborn and unchanging.

To call the whole being *"God,"* to ignore God completely, or to declare that there is no such thing as God
have no real distinction. Any of these three viewpoints
might prove useful, even **skillful,** in a given situation to
ease the yogi out of his mental confinement. It is the resonance that does the significant work of transformation, not
the ideology.

This is tremendously significant. However, this fundamental principle of Action is often obscured as spirituality
gets organized.

Babaji discouraged his immediate devotee/initiates
from forming spiritual organizations for good reason. To
coalesce as a group, and particularly a group with an
authority, doctrines and rules, mimics the way Cosmic
Prana is contained, limited and reduced to body prana.
The formation of an organization mirrors and supports the
idea of ego, even as it intends to do the opposite.

A dilemma presents itself. When the Truth of Being
dawns upon someone, how is it to be shared? Can it be
shared? Attempts to do so give rise to many different
schools of yoga and spiritual discipline.

Compare the *modus operandi* of two well known spiritual
groups of our day, namely the Self-Realization Fellowship
(SRF), established by Paramhansa Yogananda, and the
fellowship initiated by Bhagwan Shree Rajneesh (known as
Osho during his final years on earth).

SRF is highly structured and conservative in its daily
operation. Course work, exercises and meditations are
conducted in a very orderly and exacting manner. Regular,
planned, group initiations are scheduled months, or even
years in advance. Certain individuals are definitely "in
charge." A *de facto* hierarchy of authority is there. This is
not a value judgment, but rather a superficial statement of

how SRF operates. After all, authority is an appearance. It is quite simply an aspect of *Maya*. Humans want to create order out of chaos in the personal world, so they select or allow certain individuals to be "in control." Yet, in actual fact, Cosmic Prana...the Force of the Whole Being God Is... is always in control.

Deep within each of us is the understanding that we are all moving toward Self-reliance. So there is a natural resistance lurking when we observe someone in charge of others. Yet it is equally undeniable that a consistent and precise discipline is necessary to break the bonds of our ignorance...to extinguish the control of karma, whose imaginary grip permeates our individual cells, distracting us through our senses and our mental and emotional habituation.

Thus we must be prepared to make an extraordinary individual effort and develop a keen expertise of spiritual discrimination. We must either do this on our own, or in tandem with a master or guides who have this insight.

When Rajneesh was upon this earth, his community was much less structured and more liberal, even libertine by some standards. Devotees were encouraged to discover the "authenticity" of their own experience of Being. This approach is more playful and less businesslike. It appeals to those who have a fundamental appreciation that the Being is unborn. To discipline that which is free from the beginning seems contradictory and Self-defeating.

The differences of these two schools parallel the differences of the Zen schools of gradual and instantaneous enlightenment, which formed during the time of Shên-hsiu and Hui-nêng. Each will appeal to a different side of our own nature. The underlying prototypes for these two approaches reduce to discipline and freedom.

Are they compatible?

You must decide for yourself. Perhaps you will discover, as I have, that a middle way exists between these two that is not inimical to either, but embraces both. If it were not the case that we **appear** somewhat confined through self-limitation, then discipline would not be required. We would experience our Whole Being as it is and always has been...absolutely free. Right action would be obvious at all times. Right action and being would be one and the same thing...inseparable. Yet as long as the yogi experiences the separation of ego, the **recipe** will include a dose of discipline.

To experience true freedom is much more tricky than to establish a regimen of discipline. Moment to moment we may feel free, or we may simply imagine it to be the case, when in reality we are only projecting an idea through a deep desire to become free.

In 1970, after completing my second year with the American Peace Corps in the Philippines, I moved to Japan. In the evenings I would gravitate to the coffee shops in Shinjuku, Tokyo. Often I would find my good friend, Yoshi. We would sit for hours playing chess amid a set of large stereo speakers, blaring out the rock n' roll of our day...volume on full.

The recordings of Woodstock were popular at that time. I particularly enjoyed the song, *Freedom*, by Richie Havens. "Sometimes I feel like I'm almost gone..." The effect of the song, the environment and the intense mental stimulation of the chess game caused me to experience a tremendous sense of physical annihilation, leaving only pure awareness, floating on a sea of Being...almost gone!

When I expressed my affection for the musician and this song, Yoshi responded dryly, "Yes...but is he free, or merely demonstrating an impassioned **desire** to be free?"

During the human experience, complete freedom can seem attainable or utterly elusive from moment to moment. It is part of the enigma of experiencing life through form.

A marvelous presentation of the elusive struggle for freedom is expressed in the movie, *Cool Hand Luke*, produced in the mid 60's. Luke (played by Paul Newman) finds himself in prison on a Southern chain gang, for lopping off the heads of parking meters, while in a drunken, carefree condition. The warden and the prison guards (the "bosses") operate with impunity, using intimidation and brute force where necessary to maintain control. They insist that every prisoner "gets his mind right!"

Luke's physical predicament is a nightmare. He feels the harsh absurdity of his imprisonment for his simple libertine actions. To relieve the unbearable stress of his confinement, he escapes again and again. But he is always recaptured and his situation worsens. Each time he is more shackled and abused than before. There is no way for him to accept his situation. He simply can't allow it. The warden (played by Strother Martin) speaks his unequivocal, yet infamous line, "What we have here is **failure to communicate.**"

This parallels the human condition that we bring upon ourselves through our neurotic addictions. We are absolutely innocent. This is our essential nature. We cannot lose this innocence in any way. But innocence alone is not enough to release our mind from its entanglement. Repeatedly we act in certain ways, ingest certain substances, or get caught up in various emotional patterns that tighten the karmic grip. We are self-destructive in varying degrees. We see the destructive pattern as the effects run their course, but we forget the pattern when we return to the initiating phase of the cycle. This is why Gurdjieff and Ouspensky placed an intense emphasis on **remembering**. There can be no self-control until we recognize our patterns, and there can be no Self-Realization until Cosmic Prana annihilates the body prana of the human constellation.

Between discipline and freedom we must find the middle way. We must dis-organize the body prana, which has spread energetically throughout our cells. We must reconnect with the freedom of the Cosmic Design. We must resonate with the Primordial Energetic Reality.

There is definitely a middle way here. Lengthy periods of quiet reflection and meditation are very important. This allows us to dust off the attitudes and memories that have accumulated during the course of our neurotic activity. A regular discipline of meditation precipitates an ever new outlook for experience. It greases the wheels of our vehicles, allowing us to glide into true freedom and ecstasy. Seriousness evaporates. The muscles of our face relax. A smile slips out.

> Two Buddhas meet
> One speaks of God
> The other one laughs.

For the average man, the human constellation remains so complex that inquiring minds of quiet desperation no longer feel the joy of a belly full of laughter. Hence, right action must first involve a reduction of activity. As our activity slows, our perception changes. Yoga then presents itself. For each devotee there will be a particular form of yoga and a particular sage who speaks directly to him. A way appears for every sincere, persistent seeker. By and by the yogi discovers, "The proof is in the pudding of experience."

When Paramhansa Yogananda was asked about the different techniques taught by various masters of yoga, he responded, "There are many paths up the mountain, but the view from the top is the same."

Distraction becomes a key issue to the practicing yogi. Any one of our three bodies can be a source of this annoyance. We discover through experience how to accommodate our activity, prana, and force to the Design, and thus not impede the advancing realization. This becomes the basic issue of life. Everything else seems like waiting.

Actually, how we "wait" is very significant. It sets the tone for life during most of its time…and **tone** is an essential quality of Self-Realization. **Harmonic Tone is the foundation of our Spiritual Essence.** Our attitudes initiate tone during the periods of life when our practice seems to be taking a back seat to activity.

When we discover that events have no significance in and of themselves, how are we to spend this **time?** Are we annoyed by what is physically in front of us, or is it something we accept with enthusiasm? This is a crucial issue.

The advancing yogi appreciates irony. He becomes enthusiastic while surrounded by the insignificant.

The enthusiasm is for Being, not the evanescent form, the specific activities or accomplishments. He develops the skill of recognizing the Being as he is. He shares his natural compassion for others, without becoming distracted by personality, activity and attachments. This allows the yoga to penetrate time more consistently. The **presence** enters his consciousness with greater persistence.

The presence begins to penetrate into the subconscious and semi-conscious realms of our experience. In large measure through a consistent practice of yoga, we discover a way to remain eternally present as waves of feeling, ideas and images parade through our consciousness.

This presence even penetrates our dreams, first by allowing us to control the flow of self-perpetuated imagery, and then by eliminating the drive for gratification. To do this we must remove the desires that initiate dreams in the first place. The extent of our willingness to desire should not be underestimated. The roots run deep into our cells, our tendencies and our psyche. To extinguish them demands a view of the Divine Blueprint and a steadfast attention upon the big picture. As the Resonance enters, the Way becomes clear.

The final chapter of this *Recipe for Bliss* contains an outline of twelve Kriyas known to the author. The yogi who practices these techniques appreciates that a consistent and total **effort** over a considerable length of time is normally required to achieve the vibratory condition/realization that is forthcoming. There is a definite living quality that must begin. It is virtually impossible to define this quality through writing.[1]

At this point we will look closely at the first Kriya to create a deep symbiosis of experience...to resonate mutually. We shall call this an *initiation*. Take considerable time

---

[1] A liberal use of capitalization and bold lettering has been used throughout these pages in an attempt to inch closer to this living quality. My apologies to those who find this writing technique distracting.

and make a specific effort to attune with this Pranayam experientially. This is a definite way to **initiate the Holy Sound**. If you proceed as an enthusiastic child, trusting the instruction, you will establish an environment suitable for the Sound to register.

The techniques work! They are more effective than even the most precise theorization.

The first Kriya: The Sacred Heart

Everyone has met the Master, but many have forgotten Him, or perhaps did not fully recognize who He is. If you know Him, breathe his resonance into your heart. If your memory is vague, then in this moment imagine the perfected qualities that come through such a being. With each in-breath allow the flow to draw this Essence into your Heart Center. The path of this flow is etheric. It enters through the Medulla and passes without obstruction into your Heart. The flow is smooth, deep, unforced and continuous. The Heart fills with Cosmic Prana.

With the out-breath the flow reverses and the Prana returns to the Medulla and out through the opening in the back of the head. It returns to its Source. Inside and outside dissolve into a marvelous resonance. The standing wave of this etheric, bipolar Action shall eventually initiate an audible Sound, first heard as if coming from behind, and then within both of these centers and throughout the Cosmos. This **radiation** slowly dissolves the persistence of body prana.

Jesus is often pictured pointing to his heart. Buddha is known as the *Compassionate One*. These two tremendous beings of harmony experience a definite omnipresent radiation within the **Heart**. This feeling is so sweet and entrancing that often the "enlightened one" may appear utterly distracted. He/she is absorbed in bliss, having lost all interest in the details of the human experience of Maya. He simply wants to share the bliss, without returning to the way of distraction and the imagination of death, if possible. If that is not possible, then he returns willingly to offer his body as service. The Eternal is known to be the Self. He cannot lose this in any way, except through a temporary separation called *forgetting*, and its companion, *suffering*.

When Buddha emerged from his enlightenment, he gravitated to the banks of the Ganges in Benares, and began to describe the essence of man's condition. At the heart of his teaching was a description of the middle way. Specifically he referred to a way between the two extremes of self-mortification and devotion to the pleasures of the senses. A path became clear to him, which he delineated as the Eightfold Way: Right view, right aim, right speech, right action, right livelihood, right effort, right mindfulness and right concentration. Yet the Heart of the experience was essentially indescribable. He spoke the way as best he could, but **the radiation of essential Being** is the true teaching.

After spending considerable time with Krishna, Arjuna finally recognizes his karma. He accepts his superficial fate. He enters the fray through right action, **one eye** on the Infinite, the other two adjusting to conditions with all the skill at his disposal. Krishna sounds the **conch**. All is well.

The enlightened go about their way, virtually unnoticed. She might be playing music or running a marathon. He might be teaching kindergarten. She might be delivering the mail. He might be preparing dinner. Yet deep within the Heart, radiance issues without effort.

Each breath is tuned to this radiation. Each breath caresses the bell. Each breath acts like the moistened fingers of the musician, stroking the edge of a crystal glass. The glass is partially filled with water. The firm circling fingers move with precise intention. The continuous and gentle force upon the lip of the glass sustains a note of exquisite tone…a note eternal upon an inner ear.

The Sound has no beginning or ending. It is **definite**! It causes easy, gentle movements. The spine straightens and the chest moves forward. This Heart wants to radiate into all places. It wants to share itself. It may be housed within a temporary being of limitation, but it knows and accepts no limitation as its own. It sings without effort of any kind. Effortlessness is its primary nature. Hence, God is praised in all things.

The expanding radiance inexorably brings forth a smile. The eyes of the devotee light up. The weight of karma evaporates into sheer play. The only meaning that survives is joy!

The reader may look back at the description of this first Kriya and wonder where it left off. Somehow it glided right into a description of how we transcend the human condition as the Sound enters. **This whole descriptive Experience is the Kriya!** Pranayama is simply the persistent, joyful, gently forceful reminder. The practice bears fruit as we enter a permanent condition of unrestricted resonance.

The Heart's pendant:

practice

KRIYA YOGA
FOR A NEW MILLENNIUM

Once the three Asanas are attained, we arrive in an environment of Stillness... Silence... Transparency. This is the Fertile Ground into which the Kriyas are planted. The following forms a basic outline of the Actions that have been revealed to this devotee upon the Way.

1. **The Sacred Heart**... Awakening the Heart of Compassion.
2. **Mantra**... Initiating the listening for the Holy Sound, Om.
3. **Khecharimudra**... Opening the Mouth of God.
4. **Om**... Awakening the Holy Sound.
5. **Kundalini Pranayam**... Initiating the flow of Prana.
6. **Balance**... Equalizing the flow of Prana and Apana.
7. **The Cosmic Eye**... Opening the path of Cosmic Viewing.
8. **Resonance**... Merging Prana, Om and Light.
9. **Mahapranayam**... Spherical Breathing.
10. **hOMe**... Gathering in the Seat of the Soul.
11. **Om Tat Sat**... The Journey to the Star.
12. **Samadhi**... Superconscious Reunion.

Initiation means beginning...a new start. *Kriya Initiation* means a whole new way of experiencing...

That Which We Are.

Kriya Initiation is the commencement of a focused attention leading to a sequence of completely natural, yet exquisite experiences.

It is important to dismiss a few misconceptions regarding the nature of initiations. As long as an individual remains centered outside of the interiorized threshold of Om, and thereby unaware of the non-separate quality of Spirit, he is subject to the incomplete (and inaccurate) life-view of the ego. A prevalent, though somewhat misconceived desire is to long for an outer sign from God. Secretly we want Him to appear to us in the flesh...to visit us where we are now. But it is the devotee who must enter God's Realm...not the other way around. Life does not normally culminate in a particular, individual, physical experience of extraordinary details. Revelation is Self-contained.

The secrecy of initiations arises from both the **significance** of the Way for the yogi, and the singular **wholesome** quality of the interiorized attention. This is not information as we usually expect it to be. These Actions are the divine Blueprint. They become the primary manner of experience.

Through a deep appreciation of the power and effectiveness of these Kriyas, we may initiate a completely new experience and life-view. Through a sustained effort, results occur. The casual reader or the half-hearted devotee will surely miss the point in exactly the same way that the "camel" misses the "Eye of the Needle." The aim must be very persistent and precise. The whole Being must first gather Himself, and then move in definite ways. **The primary quality of this movement is Compassion.**

As the Kriyas are applied consistently with precision and openness, a very definite, inner transformation commences. As the transformation proceeds, the comparison of inner vs. outer dissolves. From the beginning of **time** there has been an ongoing process of misconception, called *ego*, that has created an imaginary division of the Whole Being God Is. The Kriyas initiate the dissolution of this imagined condition. That which remains is the endless

Light, the endless Sound, and the endless Ecstasy, expressing itself as **compassion** and felt as **bliss**.

Proclamations of individual self-importance have no
place here. They are distortions of the whole Reality. They
are distractions. The devotee, armed with the shield of
spiritual discrimination, finds the Center, and no longer
reacts to this kind of separate misinformation. He shares
his bliss with selfless ease.

Resonance proceeds as a response to the blissful Design.
This is how the transformation begins. It is not fresh ideas
from an old perspective, but a persistent radiation of a new
and utterly natural perspective.

Historically speaking, sages and yogis of India have
attained this perspective, this resonance, this extraordinary
compassion, consistently for millennia. Yet this is actually
quite rare in the West. This is why the Western yogi seems
so artificial, even phony. It appears at first glance that he
has simply donned a peculiar set of clothing.

But this is just part of the misconception. Bliss is not
territorial or cultural. Anyone can enter. It is not so difficult as it might seem. This Ocean of Resonant Being is not
a wading pool. It is vast and it is omnipresent. It is available in all places, at all times. But the ego cannot survive
the entry. It dissolves because it is ridiculous. Any viewpoint that offers new ideas, without a resonant, experiential foundation, will soon be discarded for something else.
Alas, the ego is an insatiable hunter. It experiences no
lasting peace.

Between the apparent duality caused by the experience
of the "bodies" and the whole Illumination, the consciousness appears to pass through a Tunnel. This Tunnel contains the vision of Spirit, projected upon and through the
Eye Center. It is a sympathetic response to the conscious
awakening of the Heart and Medullary Centers. Within
each is a vibration origination without apparent effort. Its
cause is beyond comprehension. It interpenetrates the
apparent physical reality and forms the Superconscious
Reality. The irresistible force of Bliss draws the consciousness hOMe in a natural way.

The effectiveness of compassion is surprising. It bridges the gap between Spirit and the three bodies. It is the foundation of the pathway hOMe. I invite you to come and discover this path. It is absolutely available to any sincere seeker of the inner life. Simply drop the pretense. Drop the expectation of separate experience. Drop the hope of an exalted place of relativity.

The twelve Kriyas, known to the author, encourage a definite scientific progression of energetic and luminous Conscious Attention from matter to pure Cosmic Spirit. Among the Kriyas are five specific Pranayams that...in a gradual, yet persistent way...cause the yogi to align his awareness with the underlying Cosmic Form.[1]

Until this Energetic Form is perceived as his own, indestructible, true nature, the yogi is unable to know Who He Is with any final accuracy. He can never adequately rest. **He can never quite catch his Breath!** He wanders this life, ignoring, guessing or believing what **This** is all about.

These techniques cannot be completely described through written description. Writing them out assigns a certain mechanical quality to them, which is less than the whole Action. The complete Action initiates a living quality. As the yogi becomes increasingly transparent, he glides through the series of techniques, and feels the resonance as a direct inner experience. There is a great difference between "eating" and "dining." When we eat, we chew our food. When we **dine**, we enter an entirely different dimension.

It is my profound purpose now to **invite** a deep and wondrous entry.

---

[1] As you read the descriptions of these Kriyas, please refer to figures #1 and #2 (pages 244 & 251). These drawings are intended to convey a deep spatial appreciation for the Path of Kriya Yoga. They are graphic representations, rather than exact literal realities. In figure #1 only three Centers (Chakras) are represented. This emphasizes their importance and simplifies the imagery. There are so many "dimensions" to the experience of Life that any two dimensional representation will be a mere suggestion of the vibratory potential.

The first three Kriyas form the first level of Initiation.

1. The Sacred Heart
Awakening the Heart of Compassion.

What distinguishes the Buddha and Jesus from most other individuals is the vast and vibrant Heart of Compassion. They experience Bliss as their very nature, and thereby radiate mercy and kindness as a natural outpouring of this sweet inner experience. They did not come by this Heart accidentally. They had to search for it, they had to find its Source, and they had to allow it to radiate without physical obstruction. Once this happened, Bliss dissolved all manner of dis-ease and separation.

This first Pranayam initiates the process of transformation.[1] Cosmic Prana begins to flood the Heart. It shall begin the work by cleansing the house and energizing the form. This is the foundation of Kriya Yoga. Compassion is the alpha and the omega.

"*Namaste*" means "I honor the God within you." When this greeting is performed, the palms are joined softly, and kindness flows as a continuous sphere of radiance, issuing from this Heart.

Man looks forward in consciousness with his eyes, reaches forward with his hands, and moves forward with his feet. He searches his entire environment, with every means at his disposal, as if his goal were in front of him...just beyond his current reach. He has set himself in motion to find his destiny some place ahead, and to eventually take hold of it.

Yet... **God lies within!**

This has always been the case. This is His state of Being. To secure this insight in our own consciousness, and to reverse the seemingly endless "forward" search, God, quite naturally, **whispers from behind**. How else can He help us to stop?

---

[1] See figure #1 (page 244), the "Sacred Heart Pranayam."

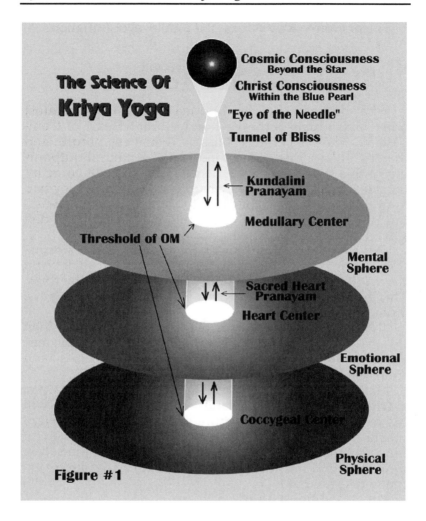

Figure #1

So understand at this beginning that the Action of this First Kriya is to bring us to stillness...to attune us to God's presence within ourselves. His Voice enters from behind. Once this Voice, this Holy Sound, Om, is initiated, an understanding begins that as a Current it shall move through our whole form in some precise ways. To begin, it is important to acknowledge that all Life comes from God. Indeed, all Life is the natural outpouring of God, our Father, "who art in heaven." This heavenly "place" in our current form is the Crown Chakra and above. Thus, once we have heard His Voice, we may allow the Flow to be enhanced through new pranayams, deeply inspired through an understanding of our divine Form.

Now...open the doorway in the Crown. Let His Voice resonate in this highest dwelling place, and allow the Current of Sound to be drawn into your Heart from on high. The initiation of each inhalation is the physical response of this natural divine Action. The exhalation follows the reverse direction and returns to the Crown, and above. The exquisite light of the thousand-petaled lotus sweetens the Sound. Stay with this pranayam. Allow your Heart to fill with His Essence. This continuous bipolar flow of Spirit is the eternal intimacy of Father and Son. We are destined to experience this through human form.

2. Mantra
Initiating the listening for the Holy Sound, Om

This is the call hOMe. The devotee, recognizing that his consciousness is, for now, still separate, is shown the **cause** and **meaning** of his own breath. Thus his listening takes an inward turn and aligns itself with the ecstatic Design.

The dual breath precipitates the divided outward experience. It is the manifesting microcosm, having a directional quality, which draws the attention downward, forward and outward. In doing so, it supports and is supported by a hunger to experience the Self. But only separate and thereby false impressions are available upon this outward path. The Mantra, through its force and its meaning, redirects the attention to the Source along the interior path of the Sacred Heart Pranayam.

3. Khecharimudra
Opening the Mouth of God

To this point, when we have discussed the senses, we have concentrated on sight and sound. We have also coursed the realm of feeling, which is intimately linked to the sensation of touch. Khecharimudra addresses the manifestation of duality through taste and smell. It guides the initiate to turn this mechanism inward as well. The attention is directed to the Mouth of God, creating three significant responses:

1. The desire for outward manifestation is reversed, reinforcing the inward pathway.

2. An increased flow of Cosmic Prana is drawn into the body. This allows the breath to become more slow and rhythmic, while the conscious vitality increases.

3. The Inner Ear (or Mouth of God) is opened, drawing the attention inward towards Om.

As these first three techniques are established, it can be said that the devotee has accepted the path of a yogi. In spirit, if not yet in a totally complete way, a yogi is one who has directed his attention upon the center of a local universe and requested a reentry into the Whole Being in a fully conscious condition.

These first three Kriyas normally cause the preexisting inner struggle to come to the surface of the consciousness. The yogi becomes more aware of his spiritual condition and the imperfection of his current understanding. From a new and expanding domain of reference, he recognizes how small and how local his attention has been. The bodies have "adapted" to temporary environments. He must prepare for a struggle with his own imagination.

To succeed in his new venture, the yogi must begin to understand his present condition of habit in a more complete way, and apply the techniques with tremendous patience and devotion. He must be alert for the moments when time flattens out...and Grace presents Herself. She will not grasp you like the desires of the earthly world, but rather She issues a **continuous, subtle and inviting call** to join with Her...to join in the Radiance.

The stubborn will hold on, and thus hold back. But the willing shall hear Her Voice and drift up into Her Essence, leaving the trouble of the earthly world far behind. As Her Voice becomes the dominant presence, the yogi achieves the fourth Kriya...the action of being absorbed in Her Cosmic Music.

4. Om
Awakening the Holy Sound

Experience Om. This is the Sound of the Holy Spirit.

At this point a tremendous soul might slip directly into Samadhi. Such a soul is rare...the likes of Hui-nêng, whose karmic condition was so evolved at birth that the **nearness** of Spirit was the assumed reality. The slightest reminder of birth's precondition triggers the Absorption.

For most of us, the skin is too thick. We have been absorbed in a denser outer domain without knowing or even sensing the dis-ease of our condition. But the Holy Sound now registers its irresistible welcome. Slowly we enter.

Do not resist Her charm. Drop the concern for appearances. Merge with the Sound.

Now the yogi shall become aware of his own inconsistencies of attention. These are caused in part by fluctuations of vitality. The body prana has created an inefficient vessel, easily distracted by the activity of the senses. For this reason the fifth Kriya is demonstrated.

5. Kundalini Pranayam
Initiating the flow of Prana

It is commonly imagined that the Kundalini must be raised...that the yogi awakens this force through an active and forceful technique.

This mysterious awakening is so sweet, delightful, harmonious and inviting that "force" is definitely **not** the way that She is aroused. The doors are opened and the yogi allows a steady and persistent **invitation** to replace the preexisting condition of disjointed desire. As this Kriya is applied, a dual breeze passes through the body, gently enticing Her to awaken and rise up.

For each Pranayam to be effective, the devotee allows his conscious awareness to enter the "Tunnel of Bliss,"[1] within the Threshold of Om. This wondrous Sound becomes a current of Pranic Consciousness that dissolves the limiting, misconceived dimensions of ego.

The Kundalini is often referred to as a snake. This metaphor has deep significance. The snake handlers of India charm the cobra with fearless persistence of musical tone and mesmerizing attention. Consider the modern day charmer, Steve Irwin, "the Crocodile Hunter"[2] from Australia. His respect and appreciation for even the most dangerous and venomous of all earthly inhabitants rivals the yogi's balanced disposition…sustained alertness, saturated with joyous wonder.

The shape of the upright cobra, with his hood flared and his attention riveted through his eyes upon the sound/vibration of the charmer's flute, is a perfect representation for the interiorized attention. Joy and wonder attend the technique. The passion is calm. The yogi enters the alternating Current of Bliss.

6. Balance
Equalizing the flow of Prana and Apana

The cool, upward, awakening path of attention joins with the warm, downward, loving path of acceptance.

---

[1] See figure #1 (page 244).
[2] Steve Irwin can be seen on television in some parts of the world on the show, *Croc Files* or *The Crocodile Hunters*, shown on the *Animal Planet* and/or the *Discovery* channels.

That which appears to be dual is experienced as Non-dual ...Complete... Whole.

This Balance of prana and apana, combined with the sweet and continuous flowing essence of Love, intones the Bell of the Heart. When first heard, this wondrous Radiant Sound shall be an elixir...a fountain of the pure waters of Spirit, issuing from deep inside the material desert for the one dying of thirst.

Drunvalo Melchizedek has spoken in physical terms of the nature of "structured" water and "unstructured" water.[1] Using his terminology, the water of this earth has become unstructured...without life...and thus does not properly hydrate nor adequately enliven the physical cells. Most of the water that we are now drinking everyday **is** unstructured in precisely the same way that the energy... the prana...that we are processing is spiritually lifeless. We are operating within the chaotic environment of our own body prana. The Cosmic Design has been ignored. We have taken an instrument of precise musical Design, and played it as a noisemaker.

We have accepted all manner of misguided self-interest ...greed, fear, contempt, disgust, anxiety, irritation, etc.... as our habitual *modus operandi*.

We are uneducated in this sense:

> An aboriginal man of another millennium wanders into a present day home and espies a compact disc player. Within the machine rests a disc containing some of the most beautiful music ever recorded in human history. Having no idea of its present day use, this "alien" takes a large rock and batters the player to examine its physical properties of strength and malleability, crushing the very purpose of its design.
>
> He then comes upon a personal computer...an instrument of unlimited communication, organization, calculation and preservation. He pulls out the plug from the wall, which appears useless to him, and uses the

---

[1] See the following web page: http://www.transformation.net/ drunvalo/technology.html

smooth flat wall of the processor as a table...or perhaps
an anvil.

We would all be amused by the ignorance of this
"savage." Yet when we see most of the self-centered
human activity of our day, we simply join in. We are
aliens, living completely within the Spiritual Dimension,
but we hardly recognize it. The yogi who has discovered
the exquisite Sound, within his own physical instrument, is
equally amused and amazed by the strange and persistent
attitudes and activities on this planet. Yet, for the most
part, when he points out the tremendous potential for
microcosmic and macrocosmic Tone and Harmony, his
suggestions fall on deaf ears. The comedy-tragedy persists.
For him all of this is simply a play, so, in the outer world,
he continues to play. He does not resist.

Once the Bell of the Heart has sounded, our physical
body stabilizes in the Vibrancy of Spirit. We are ready to
receive the seventh Kriya.

7. The Cosmic Eye
Opening the path of Cosmic Viewing

This "visual" Pranayam raises the attention into the
domain of Light and further awakens the Cosmic Eye.[1] A
new pair of doors is opened...front and behind. Therein
shall commence a dance of ethereal form. The yogi takes a
seat in the theater of the Holy Spirit. The lights are
dimmed...the projector is turned on. Now he begins to
watch the Feature Presentation.

Because his consciousness is still hinged by relativity, he
does not yet recognize exactly who is running the "program." But he continues to sit and awaits developments.

At this point he must adjust his Eye to the intensity of
the Light. After all, he has been in the dark from the
beginning of time. Thus he shall be blinded by the slightest
illumination for awhile.

---

[1] See figure #2 (page 251), the "Cosmic Eye Pranayam."

When we come out into the sunlight, each pupil of our physical eyes becomes extremely small, as it adapts and adjusts to the intense light. The physical eye is the reflected physical mapping of the conscious Being within.

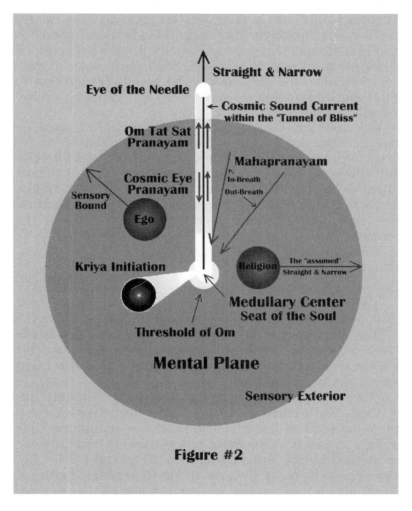

Figure #2

When the Seat of the Soul begins to resonate sympathetically with the Cosmic Design, the inner visual projection clarifies the Spherical Eye, and the true essential Being is observed as Inner Vision. The two physical eyes are the divided physical projection made by this same Being upon the physical theater. Notice how the tones of the physical eye are the reverse of the Spiritual Eye.[1] It is a negative "photographic" image. The dark areas of the physical eye (both the pupil and the ring around the iris) correspond to the light areas of the Spiritual Eye (the golden halo and the inner point of light, forming the Star), and the light areas correspond to the dark areas. The simple recognition of this basic information triggers a deep and initiating understanding of the Self.

But the work must go on. The recognition must go deeper, until the confusion is completely cleared. For the yogi, a persistent sense of separation has yet to be dissolved. Sound is still divided, experienced as "that" heard "here." The oneness of Om appears divided by the duality of breath. He cannot yet know the projectionist, because the yogi still imagines that something "else" is upon the screen!

Thus, the eighth Kriya is shown.

8. Resonance
Merging Prana, Om and Light

Just as the prana and apana have been balanced in the Heart, now the Visual Breath is balanced. Duality dissolves within the Holy Sound, Om. The Sound and the Light merge as One Essence.

The delicacy of the effort cannot be adequately described. Mind and imagination have been like an enormous balloon of hot air. The pilot has maintained his imagined perch in a mental space through time, by the individual bursts of the lighted fuel of thought. The pilot has been aloft for quite a spell. He tires of his continual effort. He hungers for the opportunity to pull the cord that

---

[1] See the top of figure #1, or the blue "Eye" on the cover of the book.

opens the top, allowing the contained air to join the atmosphere...to extinguish the separation of inner and outer.

But through an involuntary force of habit, he refuses to let go. Now, having come this far, and having exhausted himself through his physical labor, he summons the courage to let go completely...to **merge** with Spirit. The last vestige of fear is gone...and he performs the Action. Inner and outer begin to merge.

Once this Union is firmly established, the ninth Kriya is activated.

9. Mahapranayam
Spherical Breathing

The yogi now becomes absorbed in a new Pranayam, more sympathetic with his true condition. This Pranayam[1] begins to happen in a spontaneous way when the sum of several parts of the cosmic puzzle fall into place.

Through a precise practice, he becomes aware of the only surviving relativity...the Omnipresence, the Consciousness, and the Center:

Om Jat Sat

Tibetan Buddhists paint this total view, personally as the *Wheel of Life*, and impersonally as *Yantra*.

Before I share a brief indication of this technique, I suggest that you listen to the sound of the didgeridoo, played by any one of the many accomplished players on the scene today. They employ a technique known as circular breathing. This will promote a significant insight into the ninth Kriya.

When we watch our breath, normally we experience the in-breath and the out-breath as separate halves of a linear bipolar rhythm. We breathe **in**...we breathe **out**.

---

[1] See figure # 2 (page 251).

The player of the didgeridoo, through extensive practice, discovers a way to allow these two breathing halves to merge in such a way to create a continuous and circular pattern of air flowing through the instrument. Listen deeply to the resulting sound. **The duality of the breath dissolves.** This is quite parallel to the resonant experience of the Mahapranayam. An amusing and poetic synchronicity is felt as we hear an instrument of such simple, almost primordial origins issue a sound utterly sympathetic to this exquisite inner technique.

I urge the reader to meditate deeply upon this sympathy. A Pranayam of wondrous use shall present itself as the Cosmic Design converges upon your conscious experience.

The following description is only a suggestion of the Mahapranayam:

An infinitely spherical, continuously resonant, centripetal wave of Cosmic Prana draws the Consciousness into the Center of Itself, without losing the awareness of the infinite Being, thereby dissolving all sense of inner and outer.

10. hOMe
Gathering in the Seat of the Soul

The action of the Mahapranayam leaves an imprint upon our conscious understanding of our Self, and it draws the consciousness into the Center where the Cosmic Sound, Om, radiates. This is Seat of the Soul, residing deep within the area of the medulla oblongata. Now we enter the heart of the Sound. We merge with Om...in the very Center of our Self. The sweetness of the Sound and the force of the life, radiating in this Center, gives us the strength and the will to make this entry.

Through the Actions of the 4th, 6th, 8th, and 10th Kriyas, Prana, Om and Light merge as one dynamic conscious Essence. The sensory exterior has been abandoned. Now the Soul becomes aware of the whole Being of Self.

Experience now has but a delicate relativity. Father and Son resonate as one, yet are still slightly separated. The yogi naturally longs to be fully united with his Father. This longing leads to the exquisite Action of the eleventh Kriya.

11. Om Tat Sat
The Journey to the Star

Having become deeply centered within the Seat of the Soul, the yogi gazes with ease upon the Spherical Eye. He looks through a Tunnel of vast extent. Gradually his focus comes upon the beautiful and **precise** Star of the East.

The Prodigal Son is about to go Home. The non-dual action of this final Pranayam is the Father's **welcome** and the Son's enthusiastic **acceptance**. The welcome and the acceptance join. The conscious Reunion is at hand.

Jesus said, "If thine eye be single, thine whole body shall be full of light." This is literally true. The attention becomes gently riveted upon the Spiritual Eye. The illumination becomes increasingly bright and intense...even hot! A transitional phase begins as the devotee gradually adapts to the warmth and brightness of this inner illumination. The heat that is felt is, in part, the friction of his own resistance. The adaptation that lowers the temperature is acceptance. Ascension and Absorption are very definitely initiations of fire. Acceptance cools.

The yogi now allows himself to be drawn...in an unforced and continuous flow...into and through this Star. This journey dissolves the experience of motion and the motion of experience through mind into Omniscience, through vibrancy into Omnipresence. He can "do" no more. This is the door, beyond which he has no control. He has arrived at the point of final Entry. He has placed complete trust in the wisdom and compassion of the Bodhisattva...the Body of Bliss.

He becomes the Ferryman Himself. He allows the boat to carry him. He enters **without question**, not because he is blind to the various options of Life's manifesting nature, but because he has seen this whole nature and is fully aware of the persistent limitation of all relative experience. He accepts the Being completely and abides in Grace.

Thereby the action of the twelfth Kriya commences.

12. Samadhi
Superconscious Reunion

The underlying (and surprising) purpose of breath...its primordial **meaning**...has been the Father's call and the Son's response. Now Father and Son are together. The breath ceases naturally, because the calling is no longer required. The Ecstasy is indescribable.

Now the Son knows...

I Am That

Epilogue:

The Conscious Union has been made. From this point on, the remaining earthly activity becomes a blessing:

> Sing out to the binded heart
>   a song as true as can be done
> And leave to God the knots untying
>   even though it feels a dying
> For He shall birth the Endless One
>   Endless does He birth the Wholly One

Sat Tat Om

About the Author

Like so many other young American men in the late 1960's, the Vietnam War altered Carl Schmidt's life plans dramatically. In 1968 he was a Woodrow Wilson Fellow studying mathematics at Brown University, when his draft board decided he was 1-A ready for military service. Becoming part of this offensive war effort was not a viable option. So he left the purely academic life and entered the Peace Corps that year to teach mathematics and physics in a teachers' college on the Philippine island of Mindanao.

Carl spent the next seven years in Asia. He studied Zen Buddhism and Eastern philosophy in Japan and began a life-long practice of meditation. He traveled throughout Northern India in search of a spiritual awakening. He visited the ashrams of Rishikesh and met with the swamis, yogis and Sadhus that abounded there, trying to discover and absorb the essence of yoga.

To earn a living he traveled the length of Japan many times on motorcycle, selling his hand-made jewelry on the streets from city to town. In the evenings he would find an empty Shinto shrine or Buddhist temple, unpack his bedroll and spend the night. Like Basho, the famous Haiku poet, he became a seeker of real moments, wandering like a breeze, looking through time into eternity.

Carl returned to America in 1975 and soon found a home in Sedona, Arizona, an ideal place to continue his inner quest. In 1978 a sudden, unexpected experience changed his life in a dramatic way. He was drawn up and out of his body with great force, and immediately found himself standing face to face with Paramahansa Yogananda and Jesus. In this singular moment he discovered the utterly transcendent nature of all life.

A week after this experience he was awoken in the early morning by an inner voice that announced with specific certainty that he and his wife Holly would soon be conceiving their first child. The conception took place six weeks later...and so began their family affair...a work in progress to this day.

He and Holly designed and built a comfortable solar home. Carl wrote and performed music for meditations in Sedona and recorded two albums in the mid 80's, entitled *Delight* and *Mystical Voyager.*

The meeting with Yogananda led Carl to Kriya Yoga, a practice characterized by deep study, patience and meditation upon the Holy Sound, OM. He created and currently maintains a Kriya Yoga website:

(www.ThehOMeFoundation.com)

and conducts online classes to help illuminate the path of Kriya.